Identity and Transformation in the Plays of Alexis Piron

LEGENDA

LEGENDA, founded in 1995 by the European Humanities Research Centre of the University of Oxford, is now a joint imprint of the Modern Humanities Research Association and Routledge. Titles range from medieval texts to contemporary cinema and form a widely comparative view of the modern humanities, including works on Arabic, Catalan, English, French, German, Greek, Italian, Portuguese, Russian, Spanish, and Yiddish literature. An Editorial Board of distinguished academic specialists works in collaboration with leading scholarly bodies such as the Society for French Studies and the British Comparative Literature Association.

MHRA

The Modern Humanities Research Association (MHRA) encourages and promotes advanced study and research in the field of the modern humanities, especially modern European languages and literature, including English, and also cinema. It also aims to break down the barriers between scholars working in different disciplines and to maintain the unity of humanistic scholarship in the face of increasing specialization. The Association fulfils this purpose primarily through the publication of journals, bibliographies, monographs and other aids to research.

Routledge
Taylor & Francis Group
LONDON AND NEW YORK

Routledge is a global publisher of academic books, journals and online resources in the humanities and social sciences. Founded in 1836, it has published many of the greatest thinkers and scholars of the last hundred years, including Adorno, Einstein, Russell, Popper, Wittgenstein, Jung, Bohm, Hayek, McLuhan, Marcuse and Sartre. Today Routledge is one of the world's leading academic publishers in the Humanities and Social Sciences. It publishes thousands of books and journals each year, serving scholars, instructors, and professional communities worldwide.

www.routledge.com

Identity and Transformation in the Plays of Alexis Piron

❖

Derek Connon

Routledge
Taylor & Francis Group
LONDON AND NEW YORK
2007

First published 2007 by Modern Humanities Research Association and Routledge

2 Park Square, Milton Park, Abingdon, Oxfordshire OX14 4RN
52 Vanderbilt Avenue, New York, NY 10017

Routledge is an imprint of the Taylor & Francis Group, an informa business

First issued in paperback 2020

ISBN 978-1-904350-69-9 (hbk)
ISBN 978-0-367-60409-7 (pbk)

CONTENTS

For Ceri

ACKNOWLEDGEMENTS

❖

Thanks to the University of Wales Swansea for a sabbatical that helped in the completion of this study and for a contribution to the publishing costs of this volume; to my colleagues in French for taking on the extra work created by my absence; to Peter Lang and the editors of the *Modern Language Review* for permission to reprint the material detailed below; to Malcolm Cook, Nicholas Cronk, John Dunkley, Andrew Rothwell, Richard Waller, and the late Barry Russell for supporting my researches into Piron in a variety of ways; to Malcolm Cook again for providing the cover illustration; to Guy Snaith for advice on *Le Comte d'Essex* and to Pius ten Hacken for help with the Dutch language; to Ritchie Robertson, Graham Nelson and Polly Fallows of Legenda; to Michael Cardy, who read the first draft, for his help, advice, and enthusiasm for Piron; to Carolyn and Benjamin for their support (and for letting me use the computer).

ABBREVIATIONS

A	*Atis*
AD	*Arlequin-Deucalion*
AdO	*L'Âne d'or d'Apulée*
AdT	*L'Antre de Trophonius*
AM	*L'Amant mystérieux*
Cal	*Callisthène*
Cap	*Le Caprice*
CdT	*Les Courses de Tempé*
CEM	*Crédit est mort*
Chim	*Les Chimères*
Clap	*Le Claperman*
CN	*Colombine-Nitétis*
E	*L'Endriague*
EdA	*L'Enrôlement d'Arlequin*
EdJ	*Les Enfants de la Joie*
ÉdP	*L'École des pères*
FA	*La Fausse Alarme*
FC	*Fernand Cortès*
FV	*Le Fâcheux Veuvage*
GW	*Gustave Wasa*
HM	*Les Huit Mariannes*
M	*La Métromanie*
MdM	*Le Mariage de Momus; ou, la Gigantomachie*
P	*Philomèle*
R	*La Rose*
RdD	*La Robe de dissension; ou, le Faux Prodige*
T	*Tirésias*

G	Francisco López de Gómara, *Histoire generalle des Indes Occidentales*, trans. by Martin Fumée, 5th edn (Paris: Michel Sonnius, 1584; repr. 1605)
P	[Parfaict *frères*], *Mémoires pour servir à l'histoire des spectacles de la foire, par un acteur forain*, 2 vols (Paris: Briasson, 1743)
V	René Aubert de Vertot d'Aubœuf, *Histoire des révolutions de Suède*, 2 vols (Paris: Ménard et Desenne, 1819)

INTRODUCTION

It may well be that Piron is still best known to the general public, if he is known at all, as one of the most significant enemies of Voltaire; that people will be aware of the existence of the *Ode à Priape* (although how many will have read it?) and the scandal surrounding it, which dogged its author for the rest of his life;[1] even that the text of his that most people will have read in its entirety will be no more than the two-line epitaph he wrote for himself (and which will no doubt be quoted at some point in this study). Nevertheless, the work that has kept him alive as an author for successive generations, even if it has disappeared from the stage, is one of his plays, his greatest comedy for the Théâtre Français, *La Métromanie*. In the characteristic French periphrasis that strips the author of his personal individuality and identifies him simply as the vessel through which a work has passed, while more famous authors may be identified by any number of their works, Piron has always been, for those who want to praise him at least, 'l'auteur de *La Métromanie*'.[2] It is true that it perhaps owes some of its celebrity to the fact that it is one of the works that arose from Piron's rivalry with Voltaire, but the absence of any direct reference to that author means that it would soon have lost its appeal if that were the only reason for reading it. Not only do its themes and the way they are handled make it one of the most original comedies of the period, it is also full of examples of Piron's celebrated wit, and these are surely the real reasons for its durability.

Piron was one of the few authors of the time to write so widely for the theatrical troupes of his age. He never indulged in the relatively specialist work of writing opera libretti (although he did parody them), but he wrote for the three other main theatres, the official Théâtres Français and Italien and the unofficial Fair theatres,[3] and in recent years, another work has re-emerged to rival the celebrity of *La Métromanie*, that is *Arlequin-Deucalion*, the monologue that he wrote to be performed by the Fair actor Francisque and his troupe. Piron's involvement in the Fairs had never been forgotten, but it is the increased interest in the Fair theatres themselves in recent years that has brought *Arlequin-Deucalion* back to the fore. Dominique Lurcel's 1983 anthology of plays from the Fair repertoire[4] even reintroduced us to two of the works he wrote in the form more usual at the Fairs, *opéra-comique*. The almost anarchic spirit of invention found in these plays cannot fail to appeal, and those who know them invariably respond to them with enthusiasm.

Nevertheless, most of his works remain hard to come by in modern editions. *La Métromanie* has generally been available, and the modern editions of *Arlequin-Deucalion* are detailed in the chapter devoted to that work. In addition, the Bibliothèque Nationale includes on its Gallica website, alongside *La Métromanie* and *Arlequin-Deucalion*, three plays that are not otherwise currently readily available in print, the other full-length *grande comédie L'École des pères*, and two of the tragedies, *Callisthène* and *Gustave Wasa*, but the failure to observe proper conventions with regard to the layout of verse drama makes these texts difficult to read properly. The only modern source for the rest of the plays is the complete edition by Pierre Dufay, published in ten volumes between 1928 and 1931, but, despite its undoubted qualities, not only is this now showing its age, it is also perhaps even more difficult to come by than the eighteenth-century editions of Piron's works. Hence, the difficulty of obtaining copies of many of the texts has proved an obstacle to increased familiarity with much of the dramatic output we are concerned with here and with his poetry too.

The issue of topicality is also a potential problem with regard to many of Piron's works. It is even a feature of *La Métromanie*, which has its roots in a satirical response to a contemporary event, but, by universalizing its subject, that particular work transcends topicality. In other cases — both his satirical verse and much of his writing for the Fairs — topicality was the point, and so there is no attempt to universalize the specific objects of satire. The acting conditions at the Fairs, which led to the development of *opéra-comique* and the use of monologue in *Arlequin-Deucalion*, arising as they did from an attempt to defy the law, are also impossible to reproduce in the modern theatre. Modern productions of *opéra-comique* also suffer from the fact that most of the tunes that would have been so familiar to the original audiences have now been forgotten, so that a particular dimension of the original performances has been lost to us; any attempt to replace them by tunes that are familiar to a modern audience would risk being merely uncomfortably anachronistic, but is in any case largely impossible both because of the complex rhythmic structure of the *couplets* resulting from their being written to fit the original tunes and because of the frequent use of refrains retained from the original words, something of which Piron was particularly fond. And yet, even if this means that a work like *Arlequin-Deucalion*, one of the most topical of all his pieces for the Fairs, is unlikely to work on the modern stage, it has not prevented the increasing popularity of that work on the page, and neither has the issue of the tunes stood in the way of a growing interest in *opéra-comique* in general. For readers, the wit of Piron and, indeed, of the other authors for the Fairs transcends these limitations.

The reason for the relative lack of attention paid to Piron's tragedies is easier to explain, for they share with other eighteenth-century tragedy the failure both to sustain the subtle psychology or sense of universality and inevitability found in the great classics of the previous century, and to find anything else that will successfully replace it. Hence action replaces psychology, the particular takes over from the universal, and instead of inevitability we have coincidence. Nonetheless, even in these works, Piron is never less than interesting and inventive, and both his choice of sources and his handling of them give a particular slant on the author's working methods. We may be led to wonder whether he always avoided the pitfalls he identified in the works of those authors he parodied for the Fairs and the Théâtre Italien, but, even there, he usually shows some originality in his handling of the clichés.

Pascale Verèb, in her important study *Alexis Piron, poète (1689–1773); ou, la difficile condition d'auteur sous Louis XV*,[5] does not neglect the dramatic works, but, as her title indicates, her main centres of interest are Piron's life and his poetic writings. The invention, variety, and depth of interest of his writing for the theatre have led me to concentrate exclusively on that aspect of his literary creation, paying special attention to issues of identity and how it can be concealed and transformed, a particular focus of interest for Piron. This is a study which can profitably extend beyond the characters, leading to an examination of the plays too, and of how they transform their source material to serve the author's dramatic ends.

La Métromanie is an obvious place for any study of Piron's plays to begin, not only because it is the most familiar of them, but also because it is one of the richest, showing us a great deal about his preoccupations and working methods. And its celebrity is justified, so that the sustained originality of its invention makes it a good starting point not only for the critic, but also for any reader who is new to Piron's work. The subsequent chapters concentrate on those other works that most lend themselves to in-depth study, beginning with his other *grande comédie*, *L'École des pères*, before moving on to the tragedies, again beginning with the most successful, *Gustave Wasa*. A chapter on the two shorter plays first performed at the Théâtre Français as a double bill, the comedy *L'Amant mystérieux* and the pastorale *Les Courses de Tempé*, completes the study of the plays written for that theatre.[6] I begin my study of the earlier plays for the Fairs and the Italians with chapters on the two works not written in *opéra-comique* form, *Arlequin-Deucalion*, the monologue for the Fairs, and the comedy for the Italians *Les Enfants de la Joie*, and devote a separate chapter to the parodies, before concluding with the rest of the *opéras-comiques*. That there is an element of reverse chronology in this is not entirely accidental,[7] for it is perhaps easier to see how the *opéras-comiques* prefigure the preoccupations of the later plays and therefore reflect Piron's own creative spirit as well as that of the form in general when they are studied after those later works.

Any work on Piron to be written since the appearance of Pascale Verèb's *Alexis Piron, poète* must acknowledge a debt: her study is particularly valuable for her bibliographical research and the information she gives about first performances of the works for the Fairs and the Italians. The edition of Piron's complete works compiled by Rigoley de Juvigny and first published in 1776 has significant claims to be regarded as definitive, but I have followed Verèb in preferring Dufay's collection as the source of quotations, for Rigoley fails to give the full texts of the important and often lengthy prefaces Piron wrote for the *Œuvres* of 1758. Act and scene references are sufficient to identify quotations in the plays themselves, particularly in view of the fact that many readers may be using Rigoley or, where they exist, alternative editions, but I have added page references for the lengthy prefaces. The time is ripe for a new critical edition of these works, both to make them more readily available and to bring to them the benefits of modern scholarship.

Notes to the Introduction

1. In his introduction to a collection of 1866, Sainte-Beuve went as far as to say: 'Pour bien des gens, Piron est resté l'auteur de l'*Ode à Priape*, rien de plus' (*Œuvres choisies de Piron*, ed. by Jules

Troubat (Paris: Garnier, [1866]), p. 13, n. 1). It was the ultimate cause of his failure to become a member of the Académie Française, and, in the preface to *La Métromanie*, he laments, without actually naming the work, that such a youthful indiscretion should have dogged him for the rest of his life.

2. His detractors, of course, are more likely to use the formula quoted by Sainte-Beuve referred to in my previous note.
3. Louis Fuzelier, of course, outdid him by writing for the Opéra as well as the other three theatres, and, while Piron began by working for the Fairs and the Italians before moving to the more respectable and respected world of the Théâtre Français, the career of Lesage, who began with the French actors before giving up on them to make a living with the Fairs, describes a more or less opposite trajectory. Lesage is not the only author to have written for two troupes, but to write for three was less common.
4. *Le Théâtre de la foire au XVIIIe siècle* ([Paris]: Union Générale d'Éditions, 1983).
5. Studies on Voltaire and the Eighteenth Century, 349 (Oxford: Voltaire Foundation, 1997).
6. There is one exception. I have not made any individual study of Piron's other short pastorale, *La Fausse Alarme*, since it would largely involve the repetition of points made elsewhere. Issues of interest relating to that work are, however, raised where relevant.
7. Although it is *Fernand Cortès* and not *La Métromanie* that was Piron's last play.

CHAPTER 1

A Comic Masterpiece

La Métromanie

The fact that *La Métromanie* (1738)[1] is undoubtedly Piron's most famous play would, in itself, make it a fitting starting point for this study, but there is a further justification: it is a play that has its roots in a real-life incident, a hoax involving an assumed identity, something which clearly relates very closely to our central theme. The story is not unfamiliar, but it is still worth retelling, for it adds a topical dimension to the play, making it clear that it is the most major work to result from Piron's Voltaire-baiting. The poetess Antoinette Malcrais de La Vigne began publishing her verse in the *Mercure de France* in 1729. Her admirers included a number of the most influential authors of the time, among them Destouches, Fontenelle, La Motte, and, of course, Voltaire. In 1732 Voltaire even resorted to the *Mercure* himself to address to her his own verse tribute in which he undertakes to describe himself to her. Although Voltaire would later edit out the direct praise of the poetess, the original version of his *épître* begins as follows:

Toi, dont la voix brillante a volé sur nos rives,
Toi, qui tiens dans Paris nos Muses attentives,
Qui sais si bien associer,
Et la science et l'art de plaire,
Et les talents de Deshoulière,
Et les études de Dacier.

J'ose envoyer aux pieds de ta Muse divine,
Quelques faibles écrits, enfants de mon repos;
Charles fut seulement l'objet de mes travaux.
Henri Quatre fut mon héros,
Et tu seras mon héroïne.[2]

He continues by suggesting that, at the age of thirty-six, he is too old for love and has taken refuge in the arts instead, but that her verse could tempt him to fall in love again:

Je fais ce que je puis, hélas! pour être sage,
Pour amuser ma liberté;
Mais si quelque jeune beauté
Empruntant ta vivacité,
Me parlait ton charmant langage,
Je rentrerais bientôt dans ma captivité.[3]

It subsequently transpired that 'la muse bretonne', as she had become known, was the creation of Paul Desforges-Maillard, who had used the deception to gain a degree of celebrity that had been denied him as a mere male poet.

Voltaire chose to take the trick in good part, and in February 1735 wrote to Desforges-Maillard assuring him of his continued admiration, and inviting him to send him any new verses he might write:

> Votre changement de sexe, monsieur, n'a rien altéré de mon estime pour vous. La plaisanterie que vous avez faite, est un des bons tours, dont on se soit avisé; & cela seul serait auprès de moi un grand mérite. Mais vous en avez d'autres, que celui d'attraper le monde. Vous avez celui de plaire soit en homme, soit en femme. Vous êtes actuellement sur les bords du Lignon, & de nymphe de la mer, vous voilà devenu berger d'Astrée. Si ce pays là vous inspire quelques vers, je vous prie de m'en faire part.[4]

Desforges-Maillard clearly followed up the invitation, for letters offering material assistance and praising his poetic abilities followed in March and June.[5] Of course, to have offered anything other than praise would have been tantamount to an admission by Voltaire that his æsthetic sense had been distorted by romance, but his true feelings are perhaps more accurately conveyed by the advice to Desforges-Maillard in the second of these two letters to make sure that he has a good day-job and to reserve poetic composition as an amusement for his spare time, feelings that are confirmed much later in verses included in a letter to the Marquise d'Antremont many years afterwards on 20 February 1768:

> Vous n'êtes point la Desforges-Maillard:
> De l'Hélicon ce triste hermaphrodite
> Passa pour femme, & ce fut son seul art;
> Dès qu'il fut homme il perdit son mérite.[6]

Desforges-Maillard's feelings about this advice may be deduced from the fact that at this point the correspondence dries up.

Voltaire showed rather less equanimity when, in early 1738, he learnt of Piron's dramatization of the incident. He wrote to Thieriot on 22 January: 'Qu'es ce qu'une métromanie du maniaque Pirron? On dit que L'aventure de ce Maillart déguisé en la Vigne en fait le nœud. J'ay peur que cela ne soit point plaisant.'[7] Nevertheless, three days later he was putting a braver face on it:

> Je suis bien aise que Pirron gagne quelque chose à me tourner en ridicule. L'avanture de la Malcrais Maillard est assez plaisante. Elle prouve au moins que nous sommes très galants, car quand Maillard nous écrivoit, nous ne lisions pas ses vers, quand mademoiselle de la Vigne nous écrivit, nous luy fîmes des déclarations.[8]

Some two months later Voltaire actually saw the play, and, in another letter to Thieriot of 22 March, in the space of a single sentence goes from damning it with faint praise to damning it outright: 'J'ay vu la piromanie. Cela n'est pas sans esprit, ny sans baux vers, mais ce n'est un ouvrage estimable en aucun sens.'[9]

So how does he explain the play's success? His own role and that of a fellow author as objects of satire: 'Il ne doit son succez passager qu'a le Franc et à moy.'[10]

But even though Voltaire manages to turn the whole affair to his advantage here, the issue clearly continued to rankle with him, for he brings it up again after Piron's death in a letter written to the Abbé Duvernet in February 1776:

> Mes amis m'ont toujours assuré que dans la seule bonne pièce que nous ayons de lui [i.e. Piron], il m'avait fait jouer un rôle fort ridicule. J'aurais bien pu le lui rendre; j'étais aussi malin que lui, mais j'étais plus occupé.[11]

We may note the contradiction of his earlier judgement of the play's quality, even if it is couched in the form of a decidedly backhanded compliment (albeit one with which, until the rediscovery of *Arlequin-Deucalion*, posterity has tended to agree), as well as the pettiness of the assertion that he could have written a better play in reply if he had not been too busy. Nevertheless, the most important aspect of this remark is that Voltaire continues, as he has from the first, to see himself as the specific victim of Piron's satire, despite the fact that he was far from being the only significant author to fall for the hoax: Destouches in particular seems to have made himself look every bit as silly as Voltaire.[12] That phrase 'il m'avait fait jouer un rôle fort ridicule' even apparently suggests that the play not only dramatizes the incident in general terms, but actually puts Voltaire himself on stage. Given the nature of relations between Piron and Voltaire, his sensitivity is hardly surprising and seems likely to be justified, but it is, of course, also decidedly flattering to one's sense of importance — something of which Voltaire had no shortage — to be the object of the attention of others, even if that attention is mocking or critical. So is Voltaire's interpretation borne out by the text? Can he actually be identified with any of the characters in the play?

If we look at the relevant part of Piron's plot, the equivalences can be clearly established. Francaleu, the unsuccessful poet who finds fame by publishing in the *Mercure* as a Basse-Bretonne, Mlle Mériadec de Kersic, de Quimper — the addition of the qualification 'basse' heightens the comedy already inherent in the *alter ego*'s Breton origins, as does the use of characteristically Breton sounds in the name — is clearly the equivalent of Desforges-Maillard, while Damis, who responds to her and decides to marry her, represents all those writers who were taken in by him, and potentially Voltaire himself; Piron's own retelling of the story in the preface included in the *Œuvres* of 1758 suggests that the satire is aimed at a group rather than an individual:

> Elle [i.e. Malcrais de La Vigne] triompha au point que la galanterie bientôt mit pour elle en jeu la plume de plus d'un bel esprit qui vit encore; & qui, s'il écrivoit jamais son histoire amoureuse, nous souffleroit assurément cette anecdote. Ils rimèrent des fadeurs à *Mlle de Malcrais*. (*M*, préface, pp. 40–41, Piron's italics)

Yet Jacques Truchet points to an interesting aspect of the character of Damis: he is not the traditional poet of comedy, a purely ridiculous figure, but has more noble characteristics:

> Damis est enthousiaste, il est loyal, fier et modeste à la fois, élégant, honnête homme en tout point, brave de surcroît. Il est gai sans doute (ce qui manquera généralement à ses descendants du XIXe siècle), insouciant, mais il n'est ni

> libertin ni frivole; il possède un fond de gravité, et la poésie constitue pour lui une affaire très sérieuse, une mission [...] — une mission à laquelle il vaut la peine de se sacrifier totalement.[13]

Piron too describes him as 'bon, franc, généreux, brave & désintéressé' (*M*, préface, pp. 36–37) and 'leste, gai, doux, sociable & galant' (*M*, préface, p. 38), suggesting that he wished to counter the picture of the ridiculous poet popularized in literature:

> Voyant avec chagrin que dans tous les temps, & chez toutes les nations, les poëtes en général étoient livrés à la risée du public par les poëtes mêmes; & de plus les voyant taxés, par ce public, de bien des vices, qui sont, quoi qu'en puisse dire le beau monde, pires que des ridicules, j'avois pris à tâche de présenter sur la scène un poëte, qui, sans sortir de son caractère singulier, fût une fois fait de façon à nous relever d'un préjugé si peu favorable. (*M*, préface, pp. 37–38)

Perhaps Truchet exaggerates here — Piron himself points out that Damis certainly does have some ridiculous characteristics[14] — but this still remains a surprising portrait of Voltaire to come from the pen of Piron, and we might add that Damis's material circumstances do not match those of Voltaire at the time of the incident of the 'muse bretonne', for if Voltaire was already in his late thirties with an established reputation, Damis is a relative unknown awaiting the première of his first play, which flops.

So are there any resemblances between this character and Voltaire apart from his role in the 'muse bretonne' plot? Perhaps the most obvious lies in Damis's change of name to M. de L'Empirée. We may see this as having a purely literary source: it is as transparent a plot device as we find in the similar change of name of Arnolphe to M. de La Souche in *L'École des femmes*, a play to which we will have cause to return, and Damis's chosen pseudonym is both every bit as ridiculous as Arnolphe's and similar in form. We may remember, however, that Molière included in his play a sideswipe at one of his contemporaries whom he thought guilty of delusions of grandeur. The story with which Chrysalde ridicules Arnolphe's pretensions, in which a peasant called Gros-Pierre digs a muddy ditch around his little patch of land then calls himself M. de L'Isle, is clearly a direct reference to Thomas Corneille, who had redubbed himself Corneille de L'Isle.[15] Piron equally obviously has a contemporary target or targets in mind, for this is how he has Damis justify his new appellation:

> Oui; j'ai, depuis huit jours, imité mes confrères.
> Sous leur nom véritable, ils ne s'illustrent guère;
> Et, parmi ces Messieurs, c'est l'usage commun,
> De prendre un nom de terre, ou de s'en forger un. (*M*, I. vi)

Piron may have more than one individual in mind here, but surely the most obvious is François-Marie Arouet, whose pseudonym had by this stage acquired a *particule* to which he had no legitimate claims, so that he was by now generally known not just as Voltaire, but as de Voltaire. The fact that this *particule* did not necessarily originate with Voltaire himself would not, of course, have been a reason for Piron to refrain from satirizing it. Damis's choice of de L'Empirée simply adds to both the comedy and the satire by giving the sense of a ridiculously inflated ego, something of which Piron was not the only one to accuse Voltaire.

Other similarities are harder to pin down. We may point to Damis's supreme confidence in his own abilities: he has no doubt, for instance, that his play will win all four of the literary prizes he has entered it for (*M*, I. vi). This is certainly a quality Piron would criticize in Voltaire, and he makes it seem all the more misplaced when the play flops, but, no matter how malicious a satirist Piron is, such a failure is rather more difficult to link with an author as successful as Voltaire, and we will later see that this aspect of the character may have an alternative derivation. Perhaps too Damis's conceited willingness to assume that he is the Monsieur Cinq Étoiles addressed in Mlle Mériadec de Kersic's sonnet mocks Voltaire's gullibility in the Malcrais de La Vigne affair; it certainly anticipates the assumption of Voltaire and his circle that he is the specific object of satire in *La Métromanie.* Nevertheless, these aspects of the character are rather too generalized to be aimed unambiguously at any single individual.

Voltaire, however, is not the only candidate for the model for Damis. We have also seen that, despite his conviction that he is one of Piron's intended victims, he identifies another in Le Franc. Jean-Jacques Le Franc, later Marquis de Pompignan, was perhaps most famous as the author of the tragedy *Didon* (1734).[16] Although he would later become an enemy of Voltaire, at the time of the first performances of *La Métromanie*, Voltaire's feelings for him were more ambivalent, at times friendly, at times more strained; the final falling out with not only Voltaire, but the rest of the *philosophes* too would not come until his attack on the movement in his inaugural address to the Académie Française in 1760. At the time of *La Métromanie*, he was more likely to have been an object of admiration to the *philosophes*, since at the end of 1737 he had been exiled for six months for delivering an address entitled *Sur l'intérêt public*, calling into question the king's right to authority; indeed, this seems to have been a period when he was particularly close to Voltaire.[17] It is not clear why Voltaire implicates him as a fellow victim of Piron's satire in *La Métromanie*, for Le Franc appears to have had no particular role in the Malcrais de La Vigne affair, but it was an opinion he would repeat in more specific terms after battle-lines had been drawn, in a satirical reflection made in 1763 (the year in which Le Franc was made a Marquis) in the *Relation du voyage de M. le Marquis Lefranc de Pompignan depuis Pompignan jusqu'à Fontainebleau* — a text apparently narrated by Le Franc, but actually by Voltaire, in which he has his naive narrator discover a portrait of himself with the following inscription:

> Lefranc plane sur l'horizon:
> Le ciel en rit, l'enfer en pleure.
> L'Empyrée était le beau nom
> Que lui donna l'ami Piron;
> Et c'est à présent sa demeure.[18]

He also used the name M. de L'Empirée specifically to refer to Le Franc in a letter to d'Alembert in 1760.[19] Unfortunately Voltaire gives us no information about why he felt Le Franc was not just an object of satire in the play, but actually the specific model for Damis. He was, however, not the only one to think so: d'Argenson said similar things, as Pascale Verèb points out.[20] Certainly Le Franc had already been a butt of Piron's humour elsewhere: in 1734 he collaborated with Gallet and perhaps others[21] on a parody of his *Didon*, under the title *La Ramée et Dondon*, but the lack of any significant connection between him and the Malcrais de La Vigne affair makes it harder to see why he might be a target here. Like Damis, he was divided between literature and the law, but, unlike his alleged literary counterpart, he had a very successful legal career which lasted from 1730 to 1757, meaning that in 1736, the year in which *La Métromanie* was written even though it would not be performed until 1738, he in no way corresponded to the fictional character who has chosen literature in preference to the law from the outset; that detail refers much more obviously to Piron himself. On the other hand, like Damis he did suggest that it was literature that was more likely to commend him to posterity than the law.[22]

Another trait shared by Damis and Le Franc is the use of titles to which they are not entitled, for, although he did not officially become Marquis de Pompignan until 1763, Theodore Braun reports that he was calling himself Le Franc de Pompignan, or sometimes Le Franc de Caïx, and had also been using the title of *marquis* long before this. Perhaps he had already acquired the habit at the time of *La Métromanie*, making him rather than (or as well as) Voltaire the object of satire in relation to Damis's adoption of the name M. de L'Empirée, but the fact that Braun's earliest documentary evidence of the use of this title dates from as late as 1761 makes it far from certain, even doubtful, that he was using it early enough to be ridiculed by Piron in 1736; Braun also suggests that Le Franc's pretensions to the title had a degree of legitimacy, as is perhaps proved by the fact that it was eventually awarded to him.[23] On the other hand, Pascale Verèb points out that it is certainly Voltaire who is suggested as the object of this particular satirical attack by Piron's correspondence.[24]

Perhaps Voltaire simply saw a more general resemblance between Damis and Le Franc. Certainly he was a man of the world, who frequented various salons, and would therefore, like Damis, have been at home with different patrons, although his professional involvement in the law would have given him a degree of financial stability not shared by the fictional character. More than that it is not possible to say.

More obviously Voltairean traits are to be found in the character of Francaleu, the figure associated with Desforges-Maillard's role in the original hoax. This association means that Francaleu is even further than Damis from being a biographical portrait of Voltaire. Indeed, Piron makes him even less successful than the historical Desforges-Maillard, for he is such an incompetent amateur that he willingly accepts that the poetry he presents under his own identity is greeted by the open derision of his listeners:

> J'achève de brocher une pièce en six actes.[25]
> La rime & la raison n'y sont pas trop exactes;
> Mais j'en apprête mieux à rire à mes dépens. (*M*, I. iv)
>
> Ah! quelque humeur qu'il ait, il faudra bien qu'il rie;
> Et pour cela d'abord, je lis ma tragédie. (*M*, III. x)

Much as it might have amused Piron to give Voltairean characteristics to such a figure, this particular aspect of the character clearly has nothing to do with him. Another un-Voltairean trait is that he has begun to write verse only in his old age, a characteristic thought by Gustave Lanson to refer to Nivelle de La Chaussée,[26] showing that Voltaire is probably not the only victim of Piron's acid pen.

We see Voltaire in Francaleu most obviously in his habit of inflicting his writings on others, whether by repeated readings which, try as they might, they cannot escape, or by enforced participation in performances of his plays.[27] Of course, both public readings and amateur dramatics were regular entertainments in cultured circles of the period, but they do seem to have been a particular feature of life with Voltaire, and, if guests were occasionally given a change from Voltaire's own plays by being allowed to perform something by someone else, the same was not true of the public readings. Mme de Graffigny gives a vivid picture of life with Voltaire and Mme Du Châtelet in the letters written during a particularly unfortunate stay with them which began in December 1738, hence only shortly after the first performances of *La Métromanie* earlier that same year.[28] Her experience, at least as far as the readings and performances are concerned, cannot have been unique, and news of the activities at Cirey, where Voltaire had been living since the publication of the *Lettres philosophiques* in 1734, must surely have reached Piron's ears from other visitors before the composition of *La Métromanie.* As well as hearing readings of *Mérope* and *La Pucelle*, she found herself given homework, in the form of numerous books (not all by Voltaire) that she felt she must read in order to be able to discuss them. She clearly took much pleasure in most of this, particularly *Le Siècle de Louis XIV*, and so there was a clear difference between her experience and that of Francaleu's victims, but we can see how easily a satirist could put a different slant on Voltaire's behaviour. The amateur dramatics began as soon as the company was numerous enough to put a cast together, although the activity was at its height just before her departure, with the result that we find the most vivid descriptions in two letters written with her companion Desmarets just after they left Cirey, when they could speak freely.[29] Desmarets calculates that in the forty-eight-hour period immediately preceding their departure, he has been involved in rehearsing or performing forty-four acts of plays or operas. He also sheds interesting light on Voltaire's competence as an actor in the account of the performance of *Zaïre* given during this period, a performance in which Mme Du Châtelet played Zaïre and Voltaire Orosmane:

> Voltaire ne savoit pas son rôle, pas deux vers de suite, sans éxagerer. Me Du Chatelet jouë a faire vomir, sans ame, tout sur le meme ton, et scandant les vers pied a pied, comme la Frassinetty, c'est-a-dire, beaucoup plus mal que la Barnou.
>
> Mr Du Chatelet, a la lettre, n'a pas dit un vers qui en fut un, et en begayant. On souffloit le rôle, mot a mot, au petit Corasmin. Je jouois le papier a la main. Le reste alloit fort mal, Voltaire habillé comme un chianlit.
>
> Et malgré cela, de ma vie je n'ay tant pleuré a une tragédie, parce que le peu qu'il jouoit etoit divin. Il savoit fort peu, ou point, son rôle. Il estoit impatienté de ne le pas savoir, et il s'en prit a son valet de chambre, qui estoit nôtre soufleur: il s'imagina que c'etoit la faute de ce pauvre diable. Enfin, aprés l'avoir bien grondé de ce qu'il souffloit trop, du haut de la fierté ottomane, il luy cracha au nez pour l'avertir de souffler. Ce n'est point une plaisanterie, il luy cracha au nez avec fureur, et acteurs et spectateurs se mirent a eclater.

> *L'Enfant prodigue* ne fut pas mieux representé, et on s'y attendrit beaucoup. De toutes les pieces que Voltaire a joué avec nous, il n'a pas su une fois son rôle.[30]

The contrast between the quality of the performance and the pleasure it gave is a remarkable feature of this account, but again, there is ample material for the intending satirist.

It may very possibly be scenes like this that Piron had in mind when he gave to Francaleu his obsession with reading to his guests and making them perform his plays. And if these aspects of the figure of Francaleu are aimed at mocking Voltaire, perhaps others are too. What of the tragedy in six acts, for example? Part of the joke about such a work is, of course, that it is something that no one, not even the most experimental of writers, had thought to write before. Any tragedy that fails to adhere to the traditional five-act structure is, to the conservative literary mind of the period, anomalous,[31] but the comic force of six acts is greater than that of a lesser number because it suggests an author who does not know when to stop, a play that goes on for too long — in short, an experience for the audience that is bound to be boring, particularly given what we know about Francaleu's literary talents. However, while the issue of the six-act structure cannot be an attack on Voltaire, who, of course, never wrote such a thing, if the jest is also intended to have the more general effect of ridiculing all tragedies written in other than five acts, what then might Piron have in his sights? Voltaire's three-act tragedy *La Mort de César* of 1735 seems the most likely candidate, and H. Gaston Hall points to the similarity in the formulation of the title of this play with that of Francaleu's tragedy, *La Mort de Bucéphale*.[32]

Another nice joke relating to theatrical convention is Damis's comment when Francaleu tells him that he will not be able to go ahead with the performance of his play, the play that turns out to be the comedy *L'Indolente*: 'Certes, les trois sujets étaient bons; c'est dommage' (*M*, I. iv). For the traditionalist who believes in the unity of action, this, like the tragedy in six acts, suggests something that does not respect the limits of effective composition, something overloaded, and the effect is again comic. However, it is much harder to relate this criticism to any specific contemporary author (with, as we shall see, a single exception), and there certainly seems to be no particular reason for seeing it as being aimed at Voltaire; true, his first play *Œdipe* of 1718 had rather overloaded the myth with the introduction of an extraneous love-interest for Jocaste, but that was by now very stale news, and his subsequent tragedies are not particularly vulnerable to the same criticism. His first five-act comedy, *L'Enfant prodigue*, received its anonymous first performance only in October 1736, the same month in which *La Métromanie* was given its first reading at the Théâtre Français, and so clearly had no influence on the original conception, and is, in any case, not at all characterized by a complex plot,[33] and neither is the earlier one-acter, *L'Indiscret* (1725). However, in this context we can usefully examine the complexities of *La Métromanie* itself. It has at its heart the traditional Plautine plot so common in both French and Italian comedy of the classical era, in which the father acts as obstacle to the union of the lovers, often proposing his own rival suitor, although here Francaleu only ever half-heartedly plays the traditional role as paternal obstacle to his daughter's love — and initially only because Lisette tricks him into doing so — and Damis is only ever a rival in the imagination of others. This plot is combined with at least two other strands: Damis's love for the Breton poetess based on the original Malcrais de La Vigne affair, and his rejection of the profession of lawyer insisted on by his uncle in order to pursue a career as a poet. Bearing this in mind, Piron is not in a particularly strong position to criticize anyone else. But perhaps that is the point.

In the preface of 1758, Piron writes at length of his own desire to become a poet, and of his failure to find a more stable career, culminating in an abortive attempt to take up the law as a profession.[34] So, we can see in Damis not only a depiction of Voltaire and his role in the affair of Mlle Malcrais de La Vigne, but also of Piron himself in his youth. Hence, no doubt, the nobility of the character that Piron points out, but we must not exclude the humour from this autobiographical side of the character either. After all, Piron was more than capable of directing his wit against himself as well as others. It is never entirely clear just how much self-deprecating good humour and how much bitterness there is in what is surely the most famous example of this, the epitaph he wrote for himself:

Ci-gît Piron, qui ne fut rien,
Pas même académicien.

The fact remains, however, that it is Piron himself who is the butt of the humour. And it is not the only example of self-mockery to have come down to us.[35]

We have Piron's own word for the fact that, even if he denies that the character is an actual portrait,[36] whatever else Damis might be, he does have an autobiographical basis, and, in that light, it seems quite probable that the depiction of someone whose supreme confidence in his own abilities disappears completely in a bout of first-night nerves — a feeling Piron tells us all authors will recognize[37] — is an affectionate self-portrait, for he had experienced precisely this feeling himself quite recently when, as he tells us in his brief introductory note to *L'Amant mystérieux*, he realized shortly before the first performance of that comedy at the Théâtre Français in 1734, rightly as it turned out, that the work was likely to be a failure.[38] The sense of relief experienced by Damis when he is told that his play has flopped, presumably because anything is better than being on tenterhooks, is a particularly subtle piece of psychology which surely speaks of an author who knows what he is talking about. And if there are elements of Voltaire in both Damis and Francaleu, the same could be true of Piron, so it is likely that the comment about the comedy with three subjects is an amused reflection on *La Métromanie* itself.[39]

As Piron warns us in the later preface, then, it is impossible to identify any single character with a real-life equivalent, be it Voltaire, Le Franc, Piron himself, or indeed Nivelle de La Chaussée or anyone else. It is, however, harder to accept his contention that no one is portrayed in the play at all, and Voltaire and Piron do seem to be the principal models. Instead, elements of them are mixed together in characters who also have a significant fictional basis and may additionally contain references to others. The identities of the characters reflect those of real people, but are far from being equivalent. Nevertheless, for the original audience, clearly part of the piquancy must have been the mockery of Voltaire, and he and his circle certainly found enough of this to feel that he had been significantly ridiculed; Voltaire-baiting was, after all, one of Piron's favourite pastimes.

However, the complexities of the exploration of identity and personality within Piron's play do not stop here, and the aspect most closely related to the issues we have been discussing is the inclusion of a play within a play, *L'Indolente*, which, like *La Métromanie*, has its roots in reality — although here it is the internal 'reality' of Piron's play — without being a direct imitation of it, for the eponymous character is intended to be a close enough impersonation of Francaleu's daughter Lucile for her to recognize herself and learn from what she sees to be a less impassive personality. So, although *La Métromanie* itself seems principally to be a satirical work, lacking any of the didactic aims of 'plaire et instruire' that we associate with classical comedy — even if we may suspect that many authors merely pay lip-service to them — they are there aplenty in the case of the play within a play.[40]

For Pascale Verèb the function of this play within a play is to increase the realism of the play itself:

> Ce procédé de la pièce interne ou 'a play within the play', permet, par distanciation d'une fiction seconde, de transformer la fiction première, aux yeux des spectateurs, en une réalité de premier plan. [...] La fonction de *L'Indolente* est pareillement de faire oublier que la première pièce est une fiction. La pièce interne renforce 'l'effet de réel', chaque personnage de *La Métromanie* en devenant acteur de *L'Indolente* y gagne en réalité.[41]

But is this necessarily the effect? Just as Piron's treatment of the Malcrais de La Vigne affair will inevitably lead spectators to compare the dramatization with the real event and to be amused by its transformation, consequently reminding them of a reality external to the play,[42] so the play within a play reminds them that they too are in the theatre watching a play. Piron insists on reminding us of the theatrical milieu not just through this play, but by much else too: a significant amount of the latter part of the action revolves around the performance of another play (indeed, the only play — unless we count *La Métromanie* itself — to be performed, albeit off stage, during the course of the action, for *L'Indolente* never is), that is Damis's play, and there is also more than one reference to Francaleu's tragedy in six acts. Other references to plays and the world of play-acting and literature abound too. For instance, playwrights, poets, and other writers of previous eras are mentioned, including: Sappho (*M*, II. viii), Mme Deshoulières (*M*, II. viii),[43] Molière (*M*, II. viii), Corneille, including a specific mention of *Le Cid* (*M*, III. vii), Racine (*M*, III. vii), and Homer (*M*, III. vii). As well as numerous references to acting and plays, even advice on how to act, that relate to the performance of the play within the play, the terminology of acting is also used in metaphorical contexts, where it again has the effect of drawing attention to the theatrical illusion. 'Je suis las de jouer, pour vous, la comédie' (*M*, I. vi), complains Mondor to Damis of the performance he is forced to put on to get rid of his master's creditors; 'Donnons-nous à notre aise ici la comédie' (*M*, IV. vii), says Lisette to herself of the trick she intends to play on Dorante when she is disguised in clothing like Lucile's. We find a particularly interesting example when Damis asks Dorante, 'D'où vient tant d'*aparté*' (*M*, I. iii), after the latter has indulged in a number of asides to express his suspicions as he becomes increasingly convinced that Damis is a rival for the love of Lucile. The strangeness of this remark derives from the fact that, while people do 'put on an act' for various reasons in real life, hence the use of 'jouer la comédie' in metaphorical contexts, the same cannot be said about the aside. People may mutter under their breath, but this is surely never the equivalent of the aside as used by Dorante, in which he repeatedly speaks out loud the suspicions that arise from Damis's remarks with no intention that he be overheard or even that his interlocutor notice he is speaking. On stage the device is used, of course, because the author needs to communicate the character's thoughts to the audience,[44] and authors will generally use the convention only in a context where, as here, the emotion of the character justifies the loss of self-control which makes him express his thoughts out loud rather than keep them to himself. But the device is no less a stage convention for that: anyone who behaved in such a way in real life would surely be noticed and questioned by his interlocutor much sooner than Damis does with Dorante, and would also almost certainly raise doubts about the balance of his reason. The oddity here is twofold, that Piron should have Damis notice at all that Dorante has been uttering these comments out loud (in most plays the asides would not be noticed),[45] but also that, when he does so, he should have him refer to them by the appropriate theatrical term *aparté* rather than choose a less loaded expression. If our willing suspension of disbelief allows us to accept theatrical conventions precisely because they are conventions, this ceases to be the case when the characters begin to notice them themselves and point them out to us. At that point a breakdown in realism occurs which draws attention to the theatrical illusion in a way that is a common source of comedy in farce, but is not generally found in *grande comédie*. Is Piron deliberately signalling the artificiality of the theatrical experience?

Another interesting use of theatrical vocabulary occurs at the end of III. v. Francaleu has arranged a rehearsal between Damis and his uncle, Baliveau, and, before Damis's arrival, is explaining the plot of his play to Baliveau. He tells him that the scene to be rehearsed is a surprise meeting between father and son, and so suggests that the rehearsal should begin the moment Damis arrives. He says of the scene in his play: 'C'est un coup de théâtre admirable' (*M*, III. v). But when Damis enters, he finds himself faced with the uncle he has been avoiding, while Baliveau discovers in his rehearsal partner the nephew he has been looking for. The scene is almost as much of a surprise for the audience, since the only warning they have had of what is about to happen occurs just some eleven lines earlier when Francaleu sends a servant to summon M. de L'Empirée — we, of course, know this to be Damis's adopted name, but Baliveau does not. So, given the little preparation the audience has been given, we may feel that this scene which is described as a 'coup de théâtre' in the play within a play also constitutes a 'coup de théâtre' in the play proper, only slightly less of a surprise for the audience than it is for the characters.

This is not the only time we find correspondences between the internal 'reality' of the play and the plot of the play within a play. Most obviously, the title character, 'l'indolente', is a portrait of Lucile, and the actress will be dressed in clothing just like hers; Dorante will even find himself mistaking the costumed actress for the real thing (*M*, IV. vi–vii). Francaleu also tells us that an actor needs to feel the emotions of the role he is playing in order to be able to portray the character correctly, and he declares himself satisfied with Dorante's suitability to play the 'jeune premier' in his play only when he has established that his situation in real life corresponds with that of the character in the plot:

M. FRANCALEU *à Damis*
Il a d'un amoureux tout à fait l'encolure.
DAMIS
Le jeu bien au-dessus encor de la figure.
M. FRANCALEU
Mais il s'agit ici d'un amant maltraité;
Et peut-être Monsieur ne l'a jamais été.
Or il faut, quelque loin qu'un talent puisse atteindre,
Éprouver pour sentir, & sentir pour bien feindre.
DAMIS *avec un rire malin*
Aussi n'ira-t-il pas se chercher en autrui.
Le rôle qu'il accepte est modelé sur lui.
Le pauvre infortuné meurt pour une inhumaine,
Sans oser déclarer son amoureuse peine;
De façon qu'il en est encore à s'aviser,
Quand peut-être quelqu'autre est tout prêt d'épouser.
DORANTE *outré*
Ma situation sans doute est peu commune,
Et je sens en effet toute mon infortune.
M. FRANCALEU
Bon! tant mieux! vous voilà selon notre désir. (*M*, I. iv)[46]

However, in the rehearsal scene that follows the 'coup de théâtre' mentioned above, we seem to be in more ambiguous territory than ever. In III. vi Francaleu mistakes for acting what is, in fact, the genuine surprise of Damis and Baliveau at seeing each other. Since the mistake is Francaleu's, not that of the audience — much of the comedy derives from the dramatic irony arising from the audience's understanding of the error — we might expect that the confusion between acting and reality will come to an end when Francaleu leaves the two to rehearse in private, but this is not really what happens. III. vii seems to begin clearly enough, with Damis calling Baliveau 'mon oncle' — the role he is playing in the play within a play is the father of Damis's character — but, when Baliveau replies, Damis interrupts him to ask: 'Est-ce vous qui parlez, ou si c'est votre rôle?' (*M*, III. vii). Again, the reply seems unambiguous: 'C'est moi qui parle, & qui parle à Damis' (*M*, III. vii), but Damis shortly interrupts him with the following observation:

Un peu de patience.
Imitez-moi. Voyez si je romps le silence
Sur mille questions, qu'en vous trouvant ici,
Peut-être suis-je en droit d'oser vous faire aussi.
Mais c'est que notre rôle est notre unique affaire;
Et que de nos débats, le public n'a que faire. (*M*, III. vii)

Which 'public'? On the literal level Damis is obviously referring to the potential audience for *L'Indolente*, but it is the real audience, not they, who are witness to these 'débats', which would clearly not be repeated in the performance of the fictional comedy even if they do replace the rehearsal here. The levels of illusion are being blurred. Baliveau raises his cane to threaten Damis, but the latter refuses to abandon the idea of the rehearsal, and insists that because they are actors no hierarchy exists between them. Baliveau begins to weaken, and when Damis pursues the joke, calling him 'camarade', he laughs, thus clearing the way for a more relaxed discussion: 'J'ai ri. Me voilà désarmé' (*M*, III. vii). Damis has, in fact, been proposing that they get on with the rehearsal:

> Répétons donc en paix. Voyons, mon camarade.
> Je suis un fils ... [...]
> Et vous, un père ... (*M*, III. vii)

Baliveau's response to this is clearly intended to be confusing:

> Eh oui, bourreau! tu m'as nommé.
> Je n'ai que trop pour toi des entrailles de père. (*M*, III. vii)

Not only does he identify himself with his role in the play within the play rather than in the internal 'reality' of the main action, he also does so in a way that suggests the conventional language of drama rather more strongly than much of the rest of Piron's dialogue, with the exclamatory first phrase and the use of the words 'bourreau' and 'entrailles'. Consequently, we may well be forgiven for thinking that this refers directly to the role in *L'Indolente*, and therefore represents the beginning of the rehearsal, although the comment in the second line that he has 'des entrailles de père' perhaps already warns us that he is not claiming actual paternity, and the next two lines duly confirm that Baliveau is still speaking as his 'real' self:

> Et ce fut le seul bien que te laissa mon frère.
> Quel usage en fais-tu? Qu'ont servi tous mes soins? (*M*, III. vii)

From this point on, the ambiguities cease, and the conversation continues as what it has, in effect, always been — a 'real' discussion between uncle and nephew about whether the latter will make his future in law or in literature, rather than a rehearsal for a play — but with all the blurring of roles that has gone on up to this point, who could say that, particularly on first seeing the scene (or even, as it is more likely to be nowadays, on first reading), this is crystal clear? Moreover, this very long scene continues to be characterized by a more self-consciously literary style than the rest of the dialogue, as for instance this lapse into allegory:

> Je ne mets point de borne à ma reconnaissance;
> Et c'est pour le prouver, que je veux désormais
> Commencer par tâcher d'en mettre à vos bienfaits;
> Me suffire à moi-même, en volant à la gloire;
> Et chercher la fortune, au Temple de Mémoire. (*M*, III. vii)

Or the symmetrical use of metaphor in the following:

> Que la Fortune donc me soit mère ou marâtre;
> C'en est fait: pour barreau, je choisis le théâtre:
> Pour client, la Vertu: pour loix, la Vérité;
> Et pour juges, mon siècle & la postérité. (*M*, III. vii)

And not only the imagery, but also the firmly classical frame of reference of:

Que peut, contre le roc, une vague animée?
Hercule a-t-il péri sous l'effort du Pygmée?
L'Olympe voit en paix fumer le mont Etna.
Zoïle, contre Homère, en vain se déchaîna;
Et la palme du *Cid*, malgré la même audace,
Croît & s'élève encore au sommet du Parnasse. (*M*, III. vii)

When the interview is over and Baliveau has left, Damis will himself speak of it in his subsequent monologue as if it has been a scene in a play:

La scène est théâtrale, unique, inopinée.
Je voudrais, pour beaucoup, l'avoir imaginée.
Mon succès serait sûr. Du moins profitons-en;
Et songeons à la coudre à quelque nouveau plan. (*M*, III. viii)

Yet even here, if certain aspects of the style invite us to see this scene as an imitation of the conventionally dramatic, and hence make it seem at times to belong to the play within a play, there are little reminders that this is not a rehearsal, but a 'real' dialogue between the characters, such as the reference to *Le Cid* in the last extract but one, a detail from real life too recent, no matter how much of a classic it had already become, to fit entirely with the conventionally literary classical references that precede it,[47] or Baliveau's parenthetical deflation of Damis's image of the 'Temple de Mémoire':

Ce temple prétendu
(Pour parler ton jargon) n'est qu'un pays perdu. (*M*, III. vii)

One factor that adds to the constant ambiguity between 'reality' and rehearsal in this dialogue is that, because we never learn anything about the plot of *L'Indolente*, we can never be sure whether or not a dialogue such as that between Damis and Baliveau, uncle and nephew, could have any place in it as a dialogue between the father and son they are supposed to be playing.[48]

Pascale Verèb refers, quite rightly, to the relationship between the play and the play within a play as a 'jeu de reflet',[49] and it is a term that could be extended to the relationship between the play and the real-life events on which parts of its plot are based, but it is important to note that we are dealing with distorted reflections. Just as the correspondence between the actual Malcrais de La Vigne affair or Piron's life and the plot-lines that are based on them are only approximate, so Piron makes clear that the same is true of the relationship between the internal 'reality' of *La Métromanie* and the plot of the play within a play, *L'Indolente*. Hence, in the scene we have just examined, the dialogue is between uncle and nephew, not father and son, no matter how much it may confuse us about whether it belongs to the play or the play within a play; Dorante may think he has all the essential correspondences with the 'jeune premier' of *L'Indolente* to provide the precise identification between actor and character demanded by Francaleu, but he is mistaken — he has misread the signs in his dialogue with Damis, and, in fact, has no rival for the hand of Lucile, a principal requirement of the role. The character of the 'indolente' may be based on Lucile, but, even though it could have been played by Lucile herself — indeed, given Francaleu's views on acting she should have been the obvious choice — the didactic aim of the play will, it appears, be better served if she sees herself portrayed by someone else. Lisette explains:

> Enfin, je veux si bien représenter l'idole,
> Qu'elle se reconnaisse à la fadeur du rôle;
> Et, comme en un miroir, s'y voyant traits pour traits,
> Que l'insipidité l'en dégoûte à jamais. (*M*, II. ii)[50]

So we have a structure of shifting identities where we can see similarities but not equivalences, but where it is not always easy to see where the resemblances end and the differences begin: as the beginning of III. vii shows, Piron quite clearly sets out to confuse, to blur the edges. Perhaps he is setting out to show us that literature can never be a precise reflection of reality, that the writer must adapt and transform his material in order to create from a true story a viable work of art. Hence, through the treatment of the play within a play, he is able to make within his text points about the relationship between fiction and reality that are also apparent in his actual adaptation of reality to create the main plot-lines of *La Métromanie*. Yet in having Damis stress in his conversation with his uncle the importance of the play — that is the only thing the public are interested in, not the 'real-life' conversation of Damis and Baliveau — Piron also stresses the importance of art; indeed, the main issue discussed in III. vii is whether law or literature is of more value and which will better earn the individual the regard of posterity, in other words the great debate about the values of 'la belle page' and 'la belle action'. However, by defending literature as a school of virtue, not a new idea but one that would gain increasing prominence during the eighteenth century, Damis takes the argument onto a different plane by showing that literature can be both 'belle page' and 'belle action':

DAMIS

> De mes mœurs bientôt j'instruirai tout Paris.

M. BALIVEAU

> Et comment, s'il vous plaît?

DAMIS

> Comment? Par mes écrits.
> Je veux que la vertu plus que l'esprit y brille.
> La mère en prescrira la lecture à sa fille. (*M*, III. vii)

Ultimately, of course, it is Damis's poetic vocation that will prevail. Furthermore, the fictional roles allotted to these two protagonists turn out to be a more accurate reflection of their relationship than those they have in 'real life', for Baliveau really does feel more like a father to Damis than an uncle — 'Je n'ai que trop pour toi des entrailles de père' (*M*, III. vii). Hence, literature can be a more effective reflection of truth than reality.

A significant feature of this play about poets and playwrights, then, is its examination of the value of literature and of how literature works. However, the question of play-acting and role-playing in the literal sense, as seen in the issue of the play within a play, is linked by an event in III. vii to the wider subject of personal identity. When Damis makes Baliveau laugh, the latter is unable to continue behaving as the angry father-figure: 'J'ai ri. Me voilà désarmé' (*M*, III.

vii). The choice of vocabulary is revealing, for it tells us that Baliveau was using his anger as a weapon, and both this and the fact that he can be made to laugh so easily — given Piron's usual wit, the fact that Damis's jest is not particularly funny must surely be deliberate — prove that it is a persona he has adopted, that his affection for Damis outweighs his anger, that he is having to work at being angry: in short, that he is playing a role.

This is perhaps the most psychologically subtle example of such role-playing, but it is far from being the only one, and the fact that others come more obviously into the realm of stock comic plotting techniques — in the same way as the various games of who is who that we find in *L'École des pères* for instance — does not prevent them making some psychological comment on the characters involved. For instance, Damis's change of name may be a gibe at Voltaire and owe a debt to *L'École des femmes*, but that does not prevent it also suggesting that Damis is someone who is dissatisfied with his own station in life, that he feels his talents make him superior to the rank he was born into, or quite simply — and this may correspond more accurately to Piron's view of Voltaire — that he has ideas above his station.

Lisette's disguise as Lucile is perhaps an even more common device, and yet its use here is far from straightforward. Piron, from the outset, causes us to wonder what Lisette's motivation is for helping Dorante win the hand of Lucile, and she is, let us remember, a singularly loyal, skilful and ultimately successful ally, who continues to support Dorante even when he questions her motives. In most comedies, she would simply be serving the ends of her employers, and often her own too, for traditional plotting often rewards the servants of the young lovers for their successful scheming by a marriage of their own, as Mondor reminds Lisette and us in II. vi:

MONDOR
Lisette, ai-je un rival ici? Qu'il disparoisse.
LISETTE
S'il me plaît.
MONDOR
Plaise ou non; tu n'es plus ta maîtresse.
LISETTE
Comment?
MONDOR
Tu m'appartiens.
LISETTE
Et de quel droit encor!
MONDOR
Lucile est à Damis; donc, Lisette à Mondor. (*M*, II. vi)

In terms of comic convention — which, of course, has nothing to do with realistic human emotions — it is difficult to see why Lisette would reject Mondor, since, as the only male servant in the play, he is the only available potential spouse for her, but clearly her championship of Dorante's cause is more important to her. Why? Not out of loyalty to her mistress, who shows no preference at all among her suitors until Lisette manipulates her into an attraction to Dorante. Not for her master Francaleu either, for although he is almost as open-minded as Lucile about the choice of her spouse, preferring, unlike the majority of fathers in comedy, to let her choose the suitor she wants, he does express to Lisette a personal preference for Damis (*M*, II. iv); later he will even begin to behave like a traditional father in comedy and insist on this choice, although he quickly retracts when Lucile expresses an alternative preference (*M*, V. iv–viii). She is equally aware that Dorante has against him the fact that his father is involved in a court case against Francaleu, who therefore regards him as an enemy. It is also interesting to note that when Mondor asks Lisette if she has an alternative suitor, she answers in a way that, although vague, seems to suggest an affirmative, for although she makes no answer at all to the direct question 'Lisette, ai-je un rival ici?', her response to Mondor's order that she get rid of said unconfirmed rival elicits the response that she will do so only if it pleases her. So has she a suitor or not? The explanation for the ambiguity may perhaps be found as early as I. ii, her first encounter with Dorante, for it is a scene that has some odd features. Take the very opening:

LISETTE

Dorante ici! Dorante!

DORANTE

Ah Lisette! ah, ma belle!
Que je t'embrasse! Eh bien, dis-moi donc la nouvelle!
Félicite-moi donc! Quel plaisir! L'heureux jour!
Que ce jour a tardé longtemps à mon amour!
De la chose, avant moi, tu dois être avertie.
Que ne me dis-tu donc que Lucile est sortie?
Que je vais ... que je puis ... Conçois-tu? ... Baise-moi. (*M*, I. ii)

The first scene and her costume[51] have already made clear Lisette's status as a servant, and final confirmation, if confirmation be needed, is provided by her conventional name, which we learn here for the first time. Dorante's name provides equally sure confirmation of his superior status. Consequently, the very physical expressions of affection in his address to Lisette are bound to be surprising, and they become the more so when we realize that the reason for his joy is his love for a woman of his own rank. The dialogue will subsequently reveal continued physical contact between them: 'Laisse-là tes mains' (*M*, I. ii), comments Dorante at one point. Yet their intimacy is clearly dominated by Dorante's love for Lucile, despite the fact that he seems to know about her only what Lisette has told him: 'Je vous l'ai dit cent fois; c'est une nonchalante' (*M*, I. ii). The use of pronouns is interesting: despite Dorante's effusive greeting, the usual proprieties are observed in the use of the second person, with Dorante addressing Lisette in the *tu*-form and she replying in the *vous*-form, but use of the first-person plural is more interesting. Dorante uses it straightforwardly to refer to the team of conspirators formed by Lisette and himself, for example: 'Enfin, depuis un mois, sachons où nous en sommes' (*M*, I. ii), and Damis is 'notre poëte' (*M*, I. ii). Lisette uses it in the same way, but she also uses it in such a way as to identify herself with Lucile, suggesting that she is directly involved in the romantic liaison, when in fact she remains an outsider. So, Lucile's father becomes Lisette's father too:

Croyez-vous donc, Monsieur, vous seul avoir un père?
Le nôtre y voudra-t-il consentir! (*M*, I. ii)

Or Lisette, as well as Lucile, is the recipient of the poetry Dorante is sending:

> Elle aime éperdument ces vers passionnés,
> Que votre ami compose, & que vous nous donnez. (*M*, I. ii)[52]

Lisette, who is acting so selflessly to help Dorante, seems to be living this love affair — of which, bear in mind, at this stage Lucile is still ignorant — vicariously through the others. What is her motive? If the opening of this scene surprises even before we learn that Dorante's intentions are fixed on Lucile, it is because it seems like a lovers' greeting between characters of different ranks, between whom a romantic association is impossible. Of course, such *mésalliances* would become a feature of both sentimental comedy, which was beginning to develop at this period, and subsequently the *drame*, and there they would be resolved by a recognition scene revealing that the character thought to be of humble origins was in fact of higher birth. In real life, the habit of members of the master classes debauching servant girls was rife, but such things are not usually discussed in comedy, partly because of the *bienséances*, but also because comic plots tended to respect the rigorous separation of master and servant characters. Lesage could allude to such practices as early as 1715 in a play such as *Colombine Arlequin; ou, Arlequin Colombine*, but this is at the Fairs, and even then the servant girl (in fact Arlequin in disguise, which significantly defuses the situation, particularly since he is clearly inventing the story) describes how she has protected her virtue and given her would-be seducers the brush-off;[53] the awareness of such habits also underlies the plot of *Le Jeu de l'amour et du hasard*, first performed at the Théâtre Italien in 1730, but the fact that all the characters are disguised as their social opposites means that Dorante is not actually making advances to a real servant girl. Could it be that as early as 1738, at the Théâtre Français where the *bienséances* were most jealously guarded, Piron is implying a sexual attraction between Dorante and Lisette — or, even more daring, an actual sexual relationship — which, because of Lisette's servant status, can find its only long-term fulfilment in her obtaining for him a bride of his own social rank? There certainly seems to be a good chance that this is the case — otherwise how do we explain their behaviour in this first encounter between them? — and this gives particular poignancy to the scenes in which Lisette, in disguise, tricks Dorante into thinking she is Lucile, for this is the closest she will ever get to forgetting her rank and living her fantasy.

Francaleu too fulfils a fantasy by taking on the persona of the Breton poetess, for the ridiculed amateur poet finds his work not only admired, but admired by a professional poet such as Damis. It is this that means we cannot oversimplify this play into a straightforward contrast between the 'honnête homme' who cannot write poetry and the poet who is nevertheless an 'honnête homme' discussed in Piron's preface (*M*, préface, p. 38), for while the play written by the true poet Damis flops, so the ridiculed amateur manages, by dint of the gimmick of becoming a woman, to make a public success. Piron, of course, makes the contrast between Francaleu's failure and the success of his *alter ego* greater than it was in real life — Desforges-Maillard was merely mediocre, not the incompetent we see in Francaleu — but the success is genuine in both cases. Who is the great poet and who the failure, who is to identify the genius for us? It is a lesson that arises from the original Malcrais de

La Vigne story, but, since there are elements of Voltaire and Piron in both Damis and Francaleu, perhaps Piron is also comforting himself over the modesty of his own success in comparison with that of his rival Voltaire.

How, then, does Piron depict his poet? This is, after all, the idealized portrait that Piron thought beyond the aspirations of any actual poet,[54] and that Jacques Truchet sees as prefiguring the Romantic view of the poet, an interpretation about which Pascale Verèb is right to be sceptical and which H. Gaston Hall shows to be oversimplified despite having some elements of truth.[55] The fact is that his personality is oddly fragmented, he seems to lack a clearly defined identity. Indeed, the whole of the first scene consists of an attempt to identify him which succeeds (and only partly at that) only after an extended description that shows the relative impossibility of describing someone who has no fixed identity:

LISETTE

Sa mine? Ses habits? Son état? Sa façon?

MONDOR

Oh! c'est ce qui n'est pas facile à peindre, non.
Car, selon la pensée où son esprit se plonge,
Sa face, à chaque instant, s'élargit ou s'allonge.
Il se néglige trop, ou se pare à l'excès.
D'état, il n'en a point, ni n'en aura jamais.
C'est un homme isolé qui vit en volontaire;
Qui n'est bourgeois, abbé, robin, ni militaire;
Qui va, vient, veille, sue, & se tourmentant bien,
Travaille nuit & jour, & jamais ne fait rien;
Au surplus, rassemblant dans sa seule personne,
Plusieurs originaux qu'au théâtre on nous donne;
Misanthrope, Étourdi, Complaisant, Glorieux,
Distrait...[56] ce dernier-ci le désigne le mieux;
Et tiens, s'il est ici, je gage mes oreilles,
Qu'il est dans quelque allée à bayer aux corneilles,
S'approchant, pas à pas, d'un haha qui l'attend,
Et qu'il n'apercevra qu'en s'y précipitant.

LISETTE

Je m'oriente. On a l'homme que tu souhaites.
N'est ce pas de ces gens que l'on nomme poetes. (*M*, I. i)

He is a man who loses his sense of self in the act of poetic creation, and loses contact with the outside world when he is involved in his art. What he says about love seems equally well to apply, in his view of things, to everything else, that is to say that illusion is as important to him as reality:

En fait d'amour, le cœur d'un favori des Muses
Est un astre, vers qui l'entendement humain
Dresseroit d'ici-bas son télescope en vain.
Sa sphère est au-dessus de toute intelligence.
L'illusion nous frappe autant que l'existence.
Et, par le sentiment, suffisamment heureux,
De l'amour seulement nous sommes amoureux.
Ainsi le fantastique a droit sur notre hommage:
Et nos feux, pour objet, ne veulent qu'une image. (*M*, II. viii)

This may well be the *furor poeticus* or poetic fury of the ancients,[57] but, in keeping with the relationship of the original expression to madness, it is presented in a way that is not without ridicule, for Mondor's description ends with the poet falling into a ditch because of his detachment from the real world. We see equally comic evidence of this same trait on his first appearance in I. iii, when Dorante is unable to gain the attention of a Damis too intent on talking of his most recent composition and, like Francaleu, determined to read it even to an unwilling audience.[58] And if at the end of the scene between Mondor and Lisette the identification remains uncertain, it is because of another example of the dispersal of his identity, his change of name, something which is known to and recognized by some but not by others, resulting in the mistaken belief by those not in the know that he is two different people; he is even asked to obtain a *lettre de cachet* against himself. Of course, we could interpret his new name, M. de L'Empirée, as representing the poet's striving for higher things, hence contributing to the idealistic portrait of the true poet, but, again, this is undercut by comedy as a result of its sheer ludicrousness and the revelation that the change is inspired by pure snobbery (*M*, I. vi). Even the poet's gender is subject to a certain degree of fluctuation, for, although this work for the Théâtre Français attempts nothing as daring as the sexual ambiguities of the Fair plays *Tirésias* and *Le Claperman*,[59] there are ambiguities of gender inherent in the source, where the male poet's female persona attracts the romantic admiration of other male poets. In the play it is Francaleu who most obviously adopts the opposite gender, and Damis who attempts to woo her/him, but there is evidence of similar ambiguity in Damis himself, for we are told that Dorante's father loves Damis not only like a son, but also like a wife, the latter emotion appearing to be stronger:

> Mon père en est épris jusqu'à l'aimer, je croi,
> Un peu plus que ma mère, & presque autant que moi. (*M*, I. ii)

Connected with this is Damis's curious inability to relate to the opposite sex other than through the medium of poetry. He tells Mondor of his romantic experiences with women in II. viii: his first love was entirely a product of his imagination; the second was a real woman, but with whom he conducted an entirely imaginary love affair of which even she knew nothing; the third is a woman he believes to be real, but whom he knows only through her writings — as Francaleu's invented poetess, she has no existence apart from the writings. The narcissistic aspect of this is clear, and even if we do notice a tendency gradually to move away from the purely narcissistic to seek love with someone other than himself, his most recent infatuation is still with someone forged in his own image, an illusion created around the one thing that is important to him, poetry. So it is obviously no accident that his most recent poetic creation is on the theme of 'Daphnis et l'Écho', since Echo, the figure who in mythology fell in love with Narcissus, although having a separate female identity, remains simply an aural reflection of the self, analogous to the visual reflection with which Narcissus falls in love, and so is the closest the narcissist can get to a partner of the opposite sex who is, nevertheless, himself. Unfortunately for Damis, as Dorante reminds him, even Echo has a measure of independence, and so cannot be entirely relied upon, for, with Dorante's help, she provides an unexpected and unwanted echo to the first line of Damis's poem:

> DAMIS *avec emphase*
> *Écho, que je retrouve en ce bocage épais ...*
> DORANTE *d'une voix éclatante*
> Paix! dit l'écho. Paix! dis-je; une bonne fois: Paix! (*M*, I. iii)

Similarly, his third great love fails to provide the ideal narcissistic partner he seeks by inconveniently turning out not to exist, which is clearly just as well, for as Echo discovered to her cost, it is a waste of time falling in love with Narcissus. It is a logical outcome of all this that he should end by forgoing love altogether and seeking solace in his art (*M*, V. ix). Nevertheless, during the course of Damis's discussions of his love-life with his servant, the latter, who sees marriage with Lucile as the surest way of sorting out his master's finances, attempts to shift his affections from the Breton poetess by suggesting that, since Damis has no idea of the appearance of his beloved, he imagine her to look like Lucile:

> MONDOR
> Mais prenez un conseil. Votre esprit s'exténue
> A se forger les traits d'une femme inconnue.
> Peignez-vous celle-ci sous quelque objet présent.
> Lucile a, par exemple, un visage amusant ...
> DAMIS
> J'entends.
> MONDOR
> Suivez, lorgnez, obsédez sa personne.
> Croyez voir & voyez en elle la Bretonne ...
> DAMIS
> C'est bien dit. Cette idée, échauffant les esprits,
> N'en portera que plus de feu dans mes écrits. [...]
> On se peint, dans l'objet présent & plein d'appas,
> L'objet qu'on idolâtre & que l'on ne voit pas. (*M*, II. viii)

Despite Damis's enthusiastic espousal of this ploy, Mondor's attempt to inspire love for a real person, in the shape of Lucile, fails. Perhaps all Damis's romantic experiences suggest that love has nothing to do with reality, that the idealized object of our love may be as much the product of our imagination as of the actual identity of the beloved, but it is at its clearest here, where we see him constructing an inamorata from features of two different people, Lucile's looks and the Breton poetess's mind.

Lucile too falls in love with a similar construct, but in this case it is not she who invents the object of her love, but her suitor Dorante and his supporter Lisette, for just as we can misrepresent the identity of others to ourselves, as Damis does, so they can misrepresent themselves to us. Hence, in a plot-line that anticipates that of *Cyrano de Bergerac*, Lucile falls in love with Dorante at least as much for his poetic abilities as for his person, despite the fact that the poetry she has been led to believe to be by him is in fact by Damis. Dorante soon experiences the inconveniences of this; what is the point of being loved if it is not for oneself — indeed, in such a situation, can one really say that one is loved at all?

LUCILE *tirant des vers de sa poche*
L'auteur seul de ces vers a su toucher mon cœur:
Je l'avoue, & pour lui me voilà déclarée.
DORANTE *apercevant Damis*
On nous écoute.
LUCILE
Eh! c'est Monsieur de l'Empirée!
Lisons-les lui, ces vers; il en sera charmé.
DORANTE *à part*
Est-ce lui, juste Ciel! ou moi qu'elle a nommé? (*M*, II. ix)

Dorante even begins to feel his own identity being fragmented as a result of the composite persona that Lisette has imposed on him:

L'auteur seul de ces vers a su toucher son cœur,
Dit-elle! encore un coup, je n'en suis point l'auteur.
Supposé qu'on la trompe, & qu'elle me le croie;
Où donc est encor là le grand sujet de joie?
Je jouis d'une erreur; & j'aurais souhaité
Une source plus pure à ma félicité!
Un mérite étranger est cause que l'on m'aime;
Et je me sens jaloux d'un autre, dans moi-même! (*M*, III. ii)

Dorante's discomfort is increased by the fact that, as a result of a jealous misreading of the signs, he has constructed in the person of Damis a purely imaginary rival, and not until the end of the play will he understand that his invention has no basis in reality.

Ultimately, the traditional comic dénouement will demand that such deceptions and self-deceptions are sorted out. Damis remains true to his artistic idealism and so, when he discovers that the poetess who is the true object of his love does not exist, he does not transfer his affections to Lucile, the physical envelope in which he has clothed her. Lucile, rather more practical than either Damis or Rostand's Roxane, realizes that the most important thing about the poems she has received is that, in sending them to her, Dorante has awakened her ability to love, regardless of whether he wrote them himself or not:

Votre sincérité mérite qu'on vous aime,
Dorante; aussi pour vous suis-je toujours la même.
Tel enfin est l'effet de ces vers que j'ai lus:
J'étois indifférente, & je ne le suis plus;
Et je sens que, sans vous, je le serois encore. (*M*, IV. viii)

That last quotation leads us to another interesting point about the depiction of Lucile. In what is perhaps another of Piron's references back to *L'École des femmes*, she is, like Agnès, a young woman who has just emerged from a convent education, and, although in her case there has been nothing like the sinister attempt to keep her predecessor in Molière's work ignorant, she is a purely passive personality, seemingly incapable of reacting with the outside world:

Je vous l'ai dit cent fois; c'est une nonchalante
Qui s'abandonne au cours d'une vie indolente;

> De l'amour d'elle-même éprise uniquement,
> Incapable en cela d'aucun attachement.
> Une idole du Nord, une froide femelle,
> Qui voudrait qu'on parlât, que l'on pensât pour elle.
> Et, sans agir, sentir, craindre, ni désirer,
> N'avoir que l'embarras d'être & de respirer. (*M*, I. ii)

The other characters regard her as a blank canvas on which they can paint the personality they choose, although Francaleu is a sort of anti-Arnolphe who regards ignorance as a dangerous state and wishes her to be educated to the point where she can choose her own husband:

LISETTE

> Monsieur, excusez; mais vous & votre femme,
> Vous avez fait un corps où je veux mettre une âme.

M. FRANCALEU

> L'indolence en effet laisse tout ignorer;
> Et combien l'ignorance en fait-elle égarer?
> Le danger vole autour de la simple colombe;
> Et sans lumière enfin, le moyen qu'on ne tombe!
> Tu feras donc fort bien de la morigéner.
> Qu'elle sache connoître, applaudir, condamner.
> Qu'à son gré d'elle-même elle dispose ensuite.
> Le penchant satisfait répond de la conduite. (*M*, II. ii)

Lisette too proves a more shrewd judge of character and psychology than Arnolphe, and realizes that if she wishes to manipulate Lucile into doing what she wants (that is, falling in love with Dorante), this is better achieved not by direction, but by contradiction, for the self-centred nature of her unformed character will cause her to rebel against any directions: 'l'indolence est toujours indocile' (*M*, II. iv). So, by the end of the play Lucile has developed into a woman who can make her own decisions, although Lisette and Dorante have done a rather better job of making her choose what they want than Arnolphe manages with Agnès.[60] So Lucile's identity develops, but it does not develop independently of its context: she is influenced, whether positively or negatively, by those around her.

Mondor suggests a similar influence when he comments that servants are like their masters: 'Ne dit-on pas, telles gens, tel patron [...]?' (*M*, IV. i), and Francaleu speaks of another in the character traits we may inherit from our parents: 'Des sottises d'un père, un fils n'est pas garant' (*M*, IV. iv).

However, it is not just identity that is subject to external influences; so is the perception that others have of that identity, which may cause them to adopt a view that differs from reality. So determined is Francaleu to hate the offspring of his enemy —

> Mais le tort que me fait ce plaideur, est si grand,
> Que je puis, à bon droit, haïr jusqu'à sa race. (*M*, IV. iv)

— that the discovery that Dorante is that enemy's son causes him to reassess his opinion of him completely, so that, when Damis asks 'Dorante n'a-t-il contre lui que son père?' (*M*, IV. iv), he receives the following reply:

> Pardonnez-moi, Monsieur; il a son caractère.
> Je lui croyais du goût, de l'esprit, du bon sens;
> Ce n'est qu'un étourdi. Cela tourne à tous vents.
> Cervelle évaporée, esprit jeune & frivole
> Que vous croyez tenir au moment qu'il s'envole;
> Qui me choque, en un mot, & qui me choque au point,
> Que chez moi, sans ma pièce, il ne resteroit point. (*M*, IV. iv)

So, Francaleu says, we can be mistaken about character. But which version of Dorante is correct, the opinion that Francaleu held of him before he knew the identity of his father, or the reconstructed version created under the influence of that knowledge? The answer seems to lie in the fact that it takes no more than a promise by Dorante's father to end the court case for Francaleu to be instantly prepared to accept Dorante as a suitable son-in-law. We have also noted how Dorante's jealousy causes him to misjudge Damis in a way that, at the end of the play when he learns his error, he is thoroughly ashamed of, adopting a view of himself as 'un monstre' (*M*, V, ix), which, Damis has to explain to him, is similarly mistaken.

It is not just in the case of people that judgements may be similarly distorted: we may note how Damis's initial confidence in his play changes completely as a result of author's first-night nerves (*M*, V, i), while Francaleu's and Baliveau's opinions of the same play are entirely determined by their existing prejudices either in favour of or against poetry (*M*, V, ii).

La Métromanie, then, is not just a play about the Malcrais de La Vigne affair, not just an attack on Voltaire, and neither is it just an autobiographical essay examining the nature of Piron's own poetic vocation and the differences between the true poet and the incompetent versifier, but it is a work that takes these elements, combining and distorting them in such a way that they remain recognizable and yet cease being historical fact. These plot-lines are mingled with an examination of the nature of theatrical illusion and its link with reality, which acts almost like a theoretical discussion of the way Piron has adapted his sources. And the rich mixture also contains numerous examples of that favourite theme of Piron's, the precarious nature of personal identity. So identities, whether of characters or facts, are constantly shifting.

Very near the opening of the play Piron introduces a remark we have already quoted that draws attention to itself by the very oddity of the vocabulary involved. Mondor is speaking of Damis:

> Et tiens, s'il est ici, je gage mes oreilles,
> Qu'il est dans quelque allée à bayer aux corneilles,
> S'approchant, pas à pas, d'un haha qui l'attend,
> Et qu'il n'apercevra qu'en s'y précipitant. (*M*, I. i)

'Haha' is one of those picturesque words that classical style usually eschews, and its force is intensified by the fact that it appears to have been a comparatively rare word in eighteenth-century France.[61] Hence, its quaintness ensures that we notice it. A ha-ha is a ditch with a perpendicular drop on one side, supported by a retaining wall, and a gentle slope on the other.[62] Examples would generally be found on country estates, such as Francaleu's, as a way of separating the formal gardens from the parkland in order to stop livestock and other undesirables straying into the gardens, but without obstructing the view. So, on the park side, animals can wander down the slope with no danger to themselves, but cannot proceed further because of the wall, while on the garden side, which is where Damis is, nothing is visible until the walker arrives close to the barrier, at which point he will either, as the word tells us he should, utter the exclamation of surprise 'Ha ha!' or, if like Damis he is not paying attention (although clearly this was never the intention), he will fall in. The ha-ha is something that is not what it seems, that gives a false impression, that conceals its identity, and its presence at the beginning of Piron's play tells us to beware of taking anything at face value.

Notes to Chapter 1

1. An abbreviated version of this chapter has appeared in the *Modern Language Review*, 101 (2006), 62–74, under the title 'Alexis Piron's Ha-ha: Shifting Identities in *La Métromanie*', and I am grateful to the editors for permission to re-use the material here.
2. Voltaire, *Œuvres complètes / Complete Works*, ed. by Theodore Bestermann and others, 135 vols (Oxford: Voltaire Foundation, 1968–), IX (1999), 480–81. Unless specified, subsequent references, abbreviated to *Œuvres complètes*, are to this edition. Quotations from Voltaire's correspondence also come from this edition, but will follow the usual convention in being identified by the D number and date.
3. *Œuvres complètes*, IX, 485–86.
4. D845 (probably February 1735).
5. D851 (probably March 1735), D888 (probably June 1735).
6. *Œuvres complètes*, CXVII (1974), 122.
7. D1431 (22 January 1738).
8. D1436 (25 January 1738).
9. D1471 (22 March 1738).
10. D1471 (22 March 1738). For more on Le Franc, see below.
11. D19905 (7 February 1776).
12. See on this subject Jacques Truchet in *Théâtre du XVIIIe siècle*, 2 vols ([Paris]: Gallimard, 1972–74), I, 1456, n. 1.
13. In *Théâtre du XVIIIe siècle*, I, 1460.
14. He says he has given him 'quelques petits ridicules essentiels à la profession' (*M*, préface, p. 36) and later describes him as 'honnêtement fourni des ridicules de son état' (*M*, préface, p. 38). Comic elements like Mondor's description of his changeability and of how he is not to be trusted to look after himself when in the grip of poetic composition (*M*, I. i), or the scene in which he is determined to read his poem to Dorante despite his opposition (*M*, I. iii) are discussed below. In an interesting and detailed article, H. Gaston Hall also draws attention to his dual nature, seeing a possible influence in Desmarets de Saint-Sorlin's *Les Visionnaires* (1637), which remained popular in the first part of the eighteenth century, and had been reprinted in 1735 and 1737. He also draws attention to the presence of a poet who, in contrast to Molière's usual practice, is not absurd, in *La Comtesse d'Escarbagnas* (1671), and traces a connection with the Fairs in the admirable poet who is the title character in Lesage, Fuzelier, and D'Orneval's *L'Ombre du Cocher Poète* (1722). Ultimately, though, Hall says, it is a comedy from two years later than *La Métromanie*, Cerou's *L'Amant auteur et valet* (1740), that provides a more convincing eighteenth-century example of an entirely serious poet in a comedy. See 'From Extravagant Poet to the Writer as Hero: Piron's *La Métromanie* and Pierre Cerou's *L'Amant auteur et valet*', *Studies on Voltaire and the Eighteenth Century*, 183 (Oxford: Voltaire Foundation, 1980), 117–32.
15. H. Gaston Hall also makes this comparison with Molière and his satire of Thomas Corneille, linking the incident with the '*topos* of "usurped nobility"' (pp. 131–32), but does not make any comparison with Voltaire.

16. For information on Le Franc see Theodore E. D. Braun, *Un ennemi de Voltaire: Le Franc de Pompignan, sa vie, ses œuvres, ses rapports avec Voltaire* (Paris: Minard, 1972).
17. Braun, *Un ennemi de Voltaire*, pp. 21–24.
18. *Œuvres complètes de Voltaire*, ed. Louis Moland, 52 vols (Paris: Garnier, 1877–85), XXIV (1879), 461–62.
19. See Verèb, *Alexis Piron, poète*, p. 66.
20. *Alexis Piron, poète*, p. 141.
21. See Verèb, *Alexis Piron, poète*, pp. 111 and 638.
22. See Braun, *Un ennemi de Voltaire*, p. 17.
23. See Braun, *Un ennemi de Voltaire*, pp. 50–51.
24. See *Alexis Piron, poète*, p. 558.
25. We learn later (*M*, III. iv) that this six-act play is, in fact, a tragedy, and then, later in the same act (*M*, III. xi), that its title is *La Mort de Bucéphale*.
26. See *M*, II. i. The claim, which seems highly probable given that Piron knew La Chaussée well, is found in Gustave Lanson, *Nivelle de La Chaussée et la comédie larmoyante* (Paris: Hachette, 1887), p. 23, and is referred to in Truchet, *Théâtre du XVIIIe siècle*, I, 1463.
27. This aspect of the character may however also be linked to an event retold by Pierre Dufay. When the young Piron was employed as a copyist by the Chevalier de Belle-Isle, the Chevalier's secretary Blin read to him the first act of a tragedy he had written. Apparently Piron's criticisms were such that the unfortunate author read no more and burnt his creation (introduction to *Œuvres complètes illustrées de Alexis Piron*, ed. by Pierre Dufay, 10 vols (Paris: Guillot, 1928–31), I, p. xx).
28. Initially Mme de Graffigny was delighted to be at Cirey and in the presence of Voltaire, but at the turn of the year she was subjected to a dreadful scene when Mme Du Châtelet, who had been opening everyone's incoming mail, deduced (wrongly) from a remark by Mme de Graffigny's correspondent Devaux that she had copied for him part of the text of *La Pucelle*, a work that, at that time, Voltaire did not want in the hands of the public. She had, in fact, only summarized the content. Although Voltaire seemed more ready to believe her explanation than Mme Du Châtelet, she still felt obliged to ask Devaux to send her the original letter to use as evidence in her defence. Mme de Graffigny found herself in a house where she now knew that her outgoing as well as her incoming mail was being opened and scrutinized, and, although relations improved, they never entirely returned to normal, but, since she had neither the financial nor the practical means to escape, she was forced to remain until she could be rescued by a friend in mid-February. Understandably the tone changes between her initial letters and those written after the disagreement; however, the most forthright observations on the dramatic activities are to be found in two letters signed jointly with her lover (and on this occasion her rescuer) Léopold Desmarest and written after their departure, and come from his pen, not hers. Her stay is chronicled in letters 60 to 91 of the first volume of her correspondence (*Correspondance de Madame de Graffigny*, ed. by Elaine Showalter and others, 15 vols (Oxford: Voltaire Foundation, 1985–), I, 192–319).
29. *Correspondance de Madame de Graffigny*, I, 315–18.
30. *Correspondance de Madame de Graffigny*, I, 318, 12 February 1739. The whole of the passage quoted is in Desmarest's hand, and since, in the same letter, he declares himself well pleased with his stay — 'Je n'ai jamais passé dans ma vie des jours si agréables que les six derniers que j'ai été a Cirey' (*Correspondance de Madame de Graffigny*, I, 319) — there seems no danger that the more satirical parts of the description are inspired by malice, as they might have been if, given her unfortunate experience, they had come from the pen of Mme de Graffigny.
31. The five-act opera with prologue, which was a standard form, is, of course, more or less equivalent to six acts, but the fact that the prologue in such works stands apart from the action makes this, in classical terms, perfectly acceptable, quite different from a work literally in six acts. La Motte, who is usually given to questioning all the traditional tragic conventions, in his *Premier discours sur la tragédie* (*Les Œuvres de théâtre de M. de La Motte* (Paris: Dupuis, 1730)), as part of his attack on the unity of time, sketches a work in four acts, but, surprisingly, far from providing any commentary on the unusual structure, does not even mention its unconventional length; in his *Troisième discours* (1730) he defends the conventional division into five acts. Russell

Goulbourne, in an interesting discussion of the issue in 'The Eighteenth-Century "querelle des vers" and Jean Du Castre d'Auvigny's *La Tragédie en prose*', draws attention to the one-act tragedy that formed one of the acts of d'Aigueberre's *Les Trois Spectacles* (performed in 1729), and also to the joke in the comedy by d'Auvigny performed in 1730 that forms his main subject: that the only objection to a tragedy in eight acts is that all tragedies should have an odd number of acts (*Studies on Voltaire and the Eighteenth Century*, 2000.5 (Oxford: Voltaire Foundation, 2000), 371–410 (pp. 382–83, n. 4)). Nevertheless, these discussions had little impact on the general expectation that comedies (those intended for the Théâtre Français, at least) should be written in one, three, or five acts, and that the norm for all tragedies was five acts.

32. 'From Extravagant Poet to the Writer as Hero', p. 125.
33. According to Adrien-Jean-Quentin Beuchot, one paradoxical result of the anonymity of the first performance of *L'Enfant prodigue* is that, although Voltaire was one of those suspected of authorship, Piron found himself being one of the others, along with Destouches and La Chaussée, to whom it was attributed. Voltaire tried to pass it off as the work of Gresset, much to the latter's irritation when he got wind of it (see Beuchot's *avertissement* to the text reproduced in *Œuvres complètes de Voltaire*, ed. by Moland, III (1877), 441).
34. See *M*, préface, pp. 11–20.
35. See, for instance, the anecdote relating to the failure of *L'Amant mystérieux* recounted in Chapter 5.
36. This denial is not taken seriously by everyone; Pierre Dufay comments quite simply: 'Damis [...] représente Piron lui-même' (introduction to *Œuvres complètes illustrées de Alexis Piron*, I, p. lxxviii).
37. See *M*, préface, pp. 22–23.
38. His first tragedy *Callisthène* had also failed, but less spectacularly than *L'Amant mystérieux*.
39. H. Gaston Hall also assumes an autobiographical link between Piron and both Damis and Dorante ('From Extravagant Poet to the Writer as Hero', p. 119).
40. Examples of the device of the play within a play in French neo-classical theatre go back more or less to its beginnings, with two of the most inventive and famous examples being Corneille's comedy (with a mock tragedy intercalated into the final act) *L'Illusion comique* (1635) and Rotrou's tragedy *Le Véritable Saint-Genest* (1645). There are examples of the device throughout the century, although, in many cases, it principally provides a means of introducing divertissement elements, as in the *comédies-ballets*; Molière's most famous contribution not to fit into this category is *L'Impromptu de Versailles*. Examples can also be found in the *Théâtre Italien* of Gherardi, and the Fair theatres; indeed, the Fairs often introduce programmes with prologues that have the effect of transforming the plays that follow into plays within a play. Nevertheless, there is less evidence of the use of the technique in works for the Théâtre Français at this period, and it may be significant that in *La Métromanie*, perhaps the most interesting use of the device during the first half of the eighteenth century, no play within the play is actually performed. For more on this subject see Georges Forestier, *Le Théâtre dans le théâtre sur la scène française du XVIIe siècle* (Geneva: Droz, 1981), and David Trott, *Théâtre du XVIIIe siècle: jeux, écritures, regards* (Montpellier: Espaces 34, 2000).
41. *Alexis Piron, poète*, p. 547.
42. This is similar to the way in which other parasitic art forms such as parody or impersonation work: no matter how funny the entertainment may be in its own right, its main point, its *raison d'être* even, is the way it treats the original that it is imitating — often to comic ends, although we may, for instance, be impressed by the accuracy of an actor's impersonation of a real person in a serious drama, and serious adaptations of myths or other well-known stories are also frequently found — and hence such forms depend for their effect on the spectator's ability to compare the performance with something external to it. Consequently the performance depends on our *not* being drawn into it to the extent of setting aside external reality.
43. This could be a direct reference to Voltaire, who compares Mlle Malcrais de La Vigne to Mme Deshoulières in the *épître* quoted above, just as Damis does here.
44. I am disregarding here the use of the term *à part* to indicate lines addressed confidentially by one character to another without the other characters present hearing. This is a much more usual feature of real conversation, even if it is sometimes used to an implausible extent in the theatre,

but it is not a true aside, or *aparté*, and is more properly indicated in French by the formula 'bas à ...'. Piron also uses *à part* in *Les Courses de Tempé*, xiv, to denote lines spoken by a character to herself as a monologue, but which, in a scene that may well have been inspired by *L'École des femmes*, IV. ii, are overheard and replied to by another character.

45. A similar, although less developed incident, is to be found in *L'École des pères*, when Pasquin's asides reacting to Nérine's comments are overheard by Grégoire despite not being aimed at him:

PASQUIN *à part*

J'enrage!

GRÉGOIRE *sans se retourner*

Heim! Quoi?

PASQUIN *à part*

Quel contretemps!

GRÉGOIRE

Tu crains lé contretan? Gnien aura pas, te dis-je. (*ÉdP*, II. ix)

46. This notion that the actor should correspond as closely as possible with the character is found in a slightly different form in *La Fausse Alarme*, in which the constant shepherd Lysis is persuaded by Hylas the inconstant shepherd to take on in a divertissement a role more appropriate to Hylas. The discomfort of Lysis is so pronounced he eventually refuses to take the part (*FA*, vi–xii).
47. References, usually satirical, to absolutely contemporary literature abound in Piron's work for the Fairs, particularly *Arlequin-Deucalion*, but here Corneille, Molière, and Racine are the most recent authors to be mentioned. Perhaps he felt that the world of *grande comédie* required some sense of detachment, or perhaps he simply felt that in a work that sets out largely to praise poetry and the poet, none of his contemporaries was worthy of inclusion.
48. A more straightforward version of this sort of confusion of drama and 'reality' is found in the pastorale *La Fausse Alarme*, in which a shepherdess, eavesdropping on her beloved's rehearsal of a monologue for a divertissement, believes him to be expressing his own opinions.
49. *Alexis Piron, poète*, p. 547.
50. For other views on Lisette's disguise and also on Francaleu's assumption of a female identity, see Sharon Diane Nell, 'Trading Places: Dialogical Transvestites and Monological Gender Politics in Alexis Piron's *Tirésias* and *La Métromanie*', *European Studies Journal*, 17–18 (2000–01), 131–46.
51. But see Jean Emelina, *Les Valets et les servantes dans le théâtre comique en France de 1610 à 1700* (Grenoble: PUG, 1975), pp. 396–400.
52. Other uses, when Lisette uses the first-person plural to refer to Francaleu's household or the female sex or when Dorante refers to his family, are clearly too straightforward to require attention here.
53. See *Colombine Arlequin*, vii.
54. Mocking those poets who complained that Damis was a portrait of them and denying that he was intended to be a self-portrait, Piron comments: 'Le caractère moral de *M. de l'Empirée* l'emportant sur notre prétendu mérite littéraire, autant que la belle âme l'emporte sur ce qu'on veut bien appeler bel esprit, se plaindre ici de la *personnification*, c'est moins se plaindre que se glorifier; c'est moins jouer le rôle d'un homme offensé, que celui d'un *fier en fat*' (*M*, préface, p. 37). That Voltaire is uppermost in Piron's mind is indicated by the reference to the Président de Fierenfat, a character in *L'Enfant prodigue*, which, although written too late to influence the first version of Piron's play, was completed in time to feature in the preface.
55. For Truchet's comments see *Théâtre du XVIIIe siècle*, I, 1460, for Verèb's, *Alexis Piron, poète*, p. 545, and for Hall's analysis, 'From Extravagant Poet to the Writer as Hero'.
56. *Le Misanthrope* and *L'Étourdi* are, of course, both by Molière; *Le Complaisant* has been attributed to both de Launay and Antoine de Ferriol, comte de Pont-de-Veyle; *Le Glorieux* is by Destouches and *Le Distrait* by Regnard.
57. Piron uses the expression in a slightly different sense in the preface to *La Métromanie*: 'Je ne me donne que pour ce que je suis, que pour un de ces esprits trop ordinaires, qui reçoivent le jour, non sous l'astre bénin dont l'influence est si rare, mais sous cet astre pestilentiel & non moins dominant, qui fait qu'on a la fureur d'être poëte, & souvent, qui pis est, celle de se le croire' (*M*, préface, p. 11).

58. Piron had already used the same joke of the over-insistent author in the *opéra-comique L'Âne d'or* (I. x), in which there is no suggestion that the poet is anything other than a comic figure, since he is played by the *commedia dell'arte* character Scaramouche, and goes by the name of M. Gloriolet. In another *opéra-comique, Le Caprice* (xi–xii), we find a dialogue between father and son about the latter's decision to become a poet rather than taking up more gainful employment which prefigures that between Baliveau and Damis, but, despite the fact that the scene clearly draws on the same personal recollections as that in *La Métromanie* and also raises the issue that poetry can be a better instrument for teaching virtue than the law, the poet in that play would appear to be simply one of a succession of characters who are seen to behave foolishly under the influence of the god who gives the work its title; we may be tempted to sympathize with him and even agree with the final verdict: 'Voilà ce qui s'appelle un héroïsme poétique' (*Cap*, xiii), but the remark is entirely devalued by being put into the mouth of Le Caprice.
59. In *Tirésias*, see in particular the sequence beginning at II. vi, where two female characters disguised as men woo Tirésias — transformed into a woman, but still played by a male actor — and his/her entirely female companion, or, in *Le Claperman*, II. ix and xiii, where cross-dressing leads to mistaken identity.
60. Of course this comparison is oversimplified in that Dorante, despite his manipulations, is a desirable partner, and hence, according to comic convention, an acceptable husband for the *ingénue*, while Arnolphe clearly is not.
61. That its unusualness was considered somewhat outlandish is seen in the fact that, in some editions, it is replaced by the word 'fossé' (see Truchet, *Théâtre du XVIIIe siècle*, I, 1460–61), although this clearly diminishes the force of the line. The word did exist earlier in French with other meanings (in particular, 'une vieille haha' was an old, ugly woman), but this particular English borrowing is found in a dictionary for the first time in the Littré of 1738, where Piron's text is quoted, confirming the importance of his use. The Dictionnaire de L'Académie failed to include it in the third edition of 1740, but did list it in the fifth in 1762.
62. Littré defines it as follows: 'Ouverture faite au mur d'un jardin avec un fossé au dehors afin de laisser la vue libre', and the Académie Française definition is virtually identical. Although the general idea is clearly the same as in Piron, by being centred on the opening with a view, they have moved slightly away from the meaning obviously intended by Piron, which, like the original English term, applies more properly to the walled ditch itself.

CHAPTER 2

❖

A First *Grande Comédie*

L'École des pères

Although the plot of Piron's earlier comedy *L'École des pères* (1728)[1] is less complex than that of *La Métromanie*, lacking the multiple strands of the later work and conforming more straightforwardly to the unity of action, it anticipates the later comedy's interest in the problem of identity, most obviously in the double misrepresentation of Angélique's identity which is central to the mechanisms of the plot. Hence, Géronte fails to identify her to his sons as the impoverished woman he wants one of them to marry, while Nérine tells them she is a wealthy countess. The resultant infatuation of the sons with the rich and titled woman, contrasted with their comic attempts to avoid doing their duty and marrying their father's poor protégée, carries a clear message that others' perception of our individual worth will frequently be influenced by things not always within our personal control — in other words, that considerations such as wealth and rank are just as much a part of the impact we have on others, and therefore our identity, as more personal qualities like character, morality, or appearance. Indeed, for the brothers, the former turn out to be the more important criteria for choosing a woman with whom to fall in love, for they reject Angélique on the basis of her lack of money without even having met her, despite the fact that we know her to be every bit as desirable as their countess on the personal level, since she is one and the same person.

In the event, therefore, this double identity tells us much more about the three sons than it does about Angélique. The play will teach us to value those who judge an individual by his or her personal qualities, and not those like the sons whose judgement is based entirely on considerations like rank or, most important in their case, wealth, a message reinforced by the fact that their values lead them to a foolish obsession with a fictional creation, whereas the other characters value the real individual.

If we learn little of Angélique from the events surrounding her double identity it is because this is a plot device, rather than an aspect of the subject of the play. Indeed, she turns out not to be a particularly interesting character: she is an ideal, a woman who appreciates virtue and goodness, no matter where it is found, and is not taken in by mere appearance, so that her name tells us virtually all we need to know about her personality.

The true focus of interest is Géronte, the exploration of his obsession with his three sons, and, as the title tells us, the lesson he learns about them. Before we meet the sons, there is potentially a mystery surrounding their personalities: are they the reprobates identified by the *raisonneur*, or should we believe the excuses Géronte makes for them? But the conventions of classical comedy are such that we are never in any doubt that the *raisonneur* will be right and the eponymous central character wrong; as the title warns us, the play will be about the learning process undergone by the father. The views of the *raisonneur* have also been confirmed by the servant Pasquin — an example of the sort of sensible domestic whose views are usually to be trusted in comedy — before we meet the three sons.

> Tous les trois sont égaux; le financier habile
> Est un vrai financier, un Arabe, en un mot;
> Le capitaine un fat; & l'auditeur un sot.
> Tous trois enfin, soit dit sans offenser mon Maître,
> Les trois plus francs vauriens que vous puissiez connoître.
> (*ÉdP*, I. iv)

Hence, the behaviour of the odious sons may be a source of comedy, but it will never be a mystery. Any suspense in the play derives not from what the sons are like, but from whether Géronte will see them for what they are.

Piron makes in his depiction of the sons an interesting comment on the question of nature versus nurture in the matter of character development. They have quite distinct characters, as outlined in the remark by Pasquin quoted above, yet they share certain traits, chief among which are a lack of respect for their father and an obsession with money. Piron makes it clear to us in the first scene that these characteristics are a result of Géronte's indulgence. Interestingly, although he puts into the mouth of the *raisonneur* Chrisalde some indications of how we are to read the father's speech, it is mainly from his own mouth that we learn the details of his treatment of his sons which has led to their character defects:

> De tout ce que j'avois, j'ai fait part à mes fils:
> Oui, mon frère; & je fis fort bien, quand je le fis.
> Le poids de la richesse, à notre âge, importune.
> A peu de passions, suffit peu de fortune.
> De l'or & de l'argent, sources de tous plaisirs,
> La jouissance est due à l'âge des désirs.
> Devois-je, à votre avis, thésaurisant sans cesse,
> Imiter ces vieillards, tyrans de la jeunesse,
> Qui, la faisant languir, sans être plus heureux,
> La privent des plaisirs qui sont perdus pour eux?
> Et que devient souvent le bien d'un père avare?
> L'héritier est frustré, l'usurier s'en empare,
> Cette peste publique ayant, à notre insu,
> Dévoré l'héritage, avant qu'il fût échu;
> Ou, si le fils échappe à ce désordre extrême,
> Le père est détesté. Je veux, moi, qu'un fils m'aime;
> Et ne soit pas réduit, pour voir changer son sort,
> Au déplorable point de désirer ma mort. (*ÉdP*, I. i)

By comparing this speech with the subsequent behaviour of the sons, we will see how the father's actions have had the opposite of the intended effect. Such are the dangers of trying to mould the personality of another; one cannot always predict the effect one's actions will have. But, of course, as Chrisalde points out, Géronte's foolishness goes further: his failure to see the effects of his behaviour, persisting instead in seeing his sons as paragons of filial devotion, continues to make them worse and worse. For his own good, Géronte must be made to see the monsters he has created, and it is this process of discovery that is the subject of the play.

Of course, it would be possible in this context to see the sons as victims of a bad upbringing, but this is not Piron's concern. It is on the feelings of the father that the play concentrates, and, indeed, it is he who, in its later stages, will appear to be a victim; the initial impression of him as ridiculous is never really sustained, and, towards the end of the comedy, as he begins to realize his sons' true natures, the play turns in the direction of sentimentality — a development which rather dismayed Piron, as he tells us in his preface, since he disapproved of the fashion for *comédie larmoyante.*[2] What techniques, then, does Piron adopt to reveal the unpleasantness of the sons to the audience? After all, although filial ingratitude is in itself an unpleasant enough characteristic, particularly for an age which laid such stress on paternal authority, the opposition of sons to their fathers' wishes, particularly in the matter of arranged marriages, is an accepted tradition of classical comedy.

To begin with, he introduces us first to the father, showing him to be well-meaning and charitable, despite his foolishness, while the appearance of the sons is delayed, Tartuffe-like, in order to allow the secondary characters to present them in a negative light. This also gives him time to invert the usual expectations relating to the potential spouses chosen by the father and by the sons themselves. Apart from her financial impoverishment, Angélique is shown to be desirable and virtuous; indeed, as Nérine points out in I. v, the sons are in fact smitten by her before their father proposes the match to them:

> Trois cavaliers, l'un de l'autre jaloux,
> Me viennent, tour à tour, d'embrasser les genoux.
> Le tout pour vos beaux yeux. (*ÉdP*, I. v)

However, the combination of Nérine's lie about Angélique's identity, passing her off as a countess, and the father's decision to preserve her anonymity means that they do not know that the woman they are refusing is the same person as the object of their affection. Consequently their choice of spouse is devalued both because she is a figment of their and Nérine's imaginations, and because, since all three are rivals, she could not in any case be available to all of them. The fact that she is fictional also means that their love is not reciprocated — generally an essential ingredient setting out the true couple from the unsuitable rivals. Nevertheless, lest we should see them as being idealists, a more disagreeable element is to be found in Nérine's account of the brothers' love for their fictional countess: although they have been attracted to Angélique without knowing who she is, a significant issue is raised that shows their priorities to be determined by their base natures, and it is to this that Nérine is responding when she attributes to her a title and wealth:

> Mais comment croyez-vous qu'ils avoient débuté?
> Par exalter Madame, ou leurs feux? Bagatelle.
> Au solide. Son nom? Qu'aura-t-elle? Qu'a-t-elle?

Que répondre, Madame, à ce début galant?
Saisie aussi pour vous d'un dépit violent,
J'ai payé d'impudence; &, vous faisant comtesse,
J'ai, d'un front provençal, vanté votre noblesse;
Nommé tous vos aïeux, barons ou chevaliers;
Et fait monter la souche à quinze ou vingt quartiers.
Item, je vous ai faite une grande héritière. (*ÉdP*, I. v)

In other words, they would not be interested in their father's choice of spouse even if they knew her to be the same person they have chosen themselves, since their attitude would be entirely modified by the fact that she is impoverished. Hence, Angélique is seen to be a worthy spouse, but the sons are clearly not worthy of her.[3]

Nevertheless, Piron gives us an example of how Géronte can be taken in by these unpleasant characters, for actions are not always what they seem. Pasquin is puzzled by the generosity of these money-obsessed individuals when they bribe Nérine with diamonds to persuade her to intercede with Angélique on their behalf. But Nérine, a typical *soubrette* and so shrewder in such matters, gives the surprising explanation:

Ne vous étonnez pas d'un si grand sacrifice;
Leur générosité vient de leur avarice. (*ÉdP*, I. v)

She shows their behaviour to be motivated by her telling them that Angélique is a rich heiress, for them even more important than the fact that Nérine has also passed her off as a countess:

Item, je vous ai faite une grande héritière.
A cette qualité, qui passe la première,
J'ai vu, pleins d'une ardeur qu'ils ne pouvoient couvrir,
De l'avide trio les six grands yeux s'ouvrir,
Comme on verroit des loups, quand la faim les fourvoie,
Les gosiers affamés s'ouvrir sur une proie.
Ils se sont séparés. De là, sans s'être vus,
Tous trois, l'un après l'autre, à moi sont revenus;
Ont très-éloquemment brigué mon assistance;
M'ont offert (à regret) ces bijoux d'importance. (*ÉdP*, I. v)

Piron uses other means to ensure our disapproval and dislike of the sons. When in Act II Géronte returns from his mission to consult them about one of them marrying Angélique, he has not seen them, but knows that the three are dining together at the house of the youngest brother, Éraste. Despite Géronte's excuses on their behalf, Chrisalde guesses that he has been refused entry. It is a petty insult which indicates a casual and habitual lack of respect for their father that is, in certain respects, worse than their subsequent defiance over the choice of a spouse. The incident is brought up again when Pasquin has tricked the brothers into thinking that Géronte has unexpectedly come into money: all three assume that their father wishes to pass on the money to them; their clearly empty praise of him is immediately followed by an attempt on the part of the elder two to shift the blame for the insult onto their youngest and less bright sibling (*ÉdP*, II. xii). They show similar disloyalty to each other when the elder brothers try to cheat Éraste of a share of the money they think they are about to get from their father, or try to browbeat each other into being the one to marry their father's poor protégée (*ÉdP*, III. vii). They are disloyal to others too: when Géronte complains to them about being turned away from Éraste's door, they join together to shift the blame to their servants, with Valère even striking the lackey who naively blurts out the truth (*ÉdP*, III. v). In high comedy this sort of violence against servants always reflects badly on a character.

Hence, the combination of a lack of respect for their father, avarice, cowardice, disloyalty, and even violence, coupled with an infatuation with a non-existent beloved, are used by Piron to ensure that we take a negative view of these characters. His task is made harder by the fact that our normal expectation in any comedy in which a father opposes the romantic aspirations of his offspring in order to force a marriage of his own choosing is to side with the son (or daughter), no matter how outrageous the stratagems he and his servant come up with to outwit the father. In other words, Piron's characters, in being sons of an obsessive father who reject his proposed marriage in favour of their own choice, conform to an expected dramatic type, and yet, in all other details, thwart our expectations.

The other major complication in the action is Pasquin's denial of his father to Nérine in order to claim for himself less humble origins. This thread is clearly related to the central issue of the relationship between Géronte and his sons, and Piron tells us in his preface that he had originally thought of including it in the main plot, but, thinking it would be going too far to have his main characters behave in such a way, transferred the idea to the servant characters:

> Rien, comme on conçoit bien, ne se présentoit plus naturellement à l'imagination dans un portrait de fils ingrats, qu'une scène où, par une sotte vanité, & du haut de leur opulence, ils méconussent & désavouassent leur malheureux père appauvri. Aussi cet incident fut un des premiers qui me vinrent à l'idée, lorsque je jetai les fondemens de ma fable.
>
> [...] Je rejetai cet incident comme une image infâme & scandaleuse, dont on ne devoit soupçonner la réalité nulle part. Je trouvai cette bassesse & cet excès aussi indignes d'être mis au théâtre, qu'au rang des choses vraisemblables, & surtout dans des enfans que je supposois avoir des sentimens d'honneur, d'après quelque éducation.
>
> Cependant ne me pouvant résoudre à renoncer totalement à ce petit avantage de mon triste sujet, je le fis valoir comme je pus, en me rabattant sur les personnages subalternes du paysan père, & du valet fils. Non que le caractère paternel ne soit également sacré dans toutes les conditions; & que je ne sache bien qu'un paysan doit être le roi de sa famille, comme un roi doit être le père de son peuple; mais c'est que l'indignation naïve d'un père tel que le paysan, & la ridicule impudence d'un fils tel que Pasquin, devenoient, selon moi, compatibles avec cette espèce de comique faite pour une sorte d'auditeurs, dont nos maîtres ont cru ne devoir pas négliger le suffrage & la satisfaction. En un mot, l'état vil & grossier de ces personnages, me sembloit demander grâce pour quelques messéances que je n'imaginois insupportables que dans des gens d'une condition plus relevée. (*ÉdP*, préface, pp. 7–8)

Whatever Piron's explanation for this decision, it has the effect of reinforcing the idea that all sons potentially share common feelings when it comes to their fathers.

To an extent, this is already present in the inclusion of not one but three sons for Géronte, but since, despite Piron's individual characterization of them, they are treated in relation to their father and the demands of the plot more generally almost as a single character, the point is reinforced very significantly by duplicating it in a different father–son pairing. Hence, the play illustrates a trend, not a single isolated example, and a trend that may be found in an amiable character like Pasquin as well as in the unpleasant sons. So Piron is depicting the impulse to reject the father that, in a post-Freudian world, we will inevitably identify as Oedipal.

Piron's contention that the rejection of the father seems less dreadful in a servant character than in those of the master class fits with the general theatrical convention which, rightly or wrongly, attributes less emotional depth to those characters, but this is perhaps not the only reason the action seems less reprehensible when performed by Pasquin than it would be if performed by Géronte's sons. The latter show at their first entrance that their contempt for fathers is general (*ÉdP*, II. xi); Pasquin shows support for Géronte and condemnation of the behaviour of his sons from the outset, for although he criticizes Géronte's foolishness, his affection and support for him are never in doubt.[4] Pasquin's good nature and moral attitude to paternity have thus been established before his denial of his own father. This is seen as being an action arising almost in the heat of the moment:

PASQUIN
Ma foi! j'ai bien aimé des filles en ma vie;
Mais pas une, à mes yeux, n'a paru si jolie.
NÉRINE *reprenant l'air aisé*
J'ai bien eu d'amans; mille d'entr'eux m'ont plu;
Mais je ne m'en remets pas un qui t'ai valu.
PASQUIN *se redressant à son tour*
Je le crois. Entre ceux qui cherchoient à te plaire,
Tu ne pouvois choisir qu'un valet ordinaire,
Un valet né pour l'être: &, sans faire le fat,
Je suis bien au-dessus de ceux de mon état.
J'ai, par libertinage, endossé la mandille:
Mais je n'en suis pas moins un enfant de famille,
D'un riche procureur l'héritier & l'aîné;
Et l'on se sent toujours, tiens, de ce qu'on est né. (*ÉdP*, I. vi)

He has been carried away by his own boasting, in a way that is typical of his comic type. We forgive him because, unlike his master's sons, he has scruples. His boast to Nérine takes place in the final scene of the first act; already in II. i he is feeling ashamed, attempting to reassure himself with self-justification and worrying about the repercussions when, inevitably, he is found out. Various comic scenes arising from his discomfiture add to the sense that his lie is foolish rather than malicious. He is even made to suffer by Nérine, who, cleverer than he is, sees through his lie (*ÉdP*, IV. iii) and teases him before making sure that the truth is revealed and that Pasquin's father finds out what he has said (*ÉdP*, V. iii–iv). His contrition and the earthy good humour of his father's reproaches allow us to feel that no real damage has been done (*ÉdP*, V. v). Hence, the link between action and identity is not inevitable: good characters may perform bad actions, but we will judge those actions differently in relation to the general character of the individual. The act of denying their father in the case of Géronte's sons, whose behaviour is generally reprehensible, might be too dreadful for a comedy, but in the case of Pasquin it is merely comically foolish not just because of his rank, but also because he is otherwise of good character.

The theme of appearance and reality may be seen in a number of other details of plot centred mainly on Pasquin's attempt, with the help of Grégoire, to trick the sons into revealing their true natures. Accordingly, Pasquin lies to them that ships have come in bringing wealth to their father, while lying to Géronte that his country house has burnt down (*ÉdP*, II. vi). When the sons meet their father in III. v expecting him to distribute the windfall among them, he passes on in good faith his news that he has lost everything and tells them he expects one of them to marry his impoverished protégée. After the sons have reacted in the expected manner by refusing, Pasquin invents a further lie, telling them that this was a test: Géronte had begun to believe criticisms of them, and so had made up the story of the burning of the house in order to discover whether they were worthy of his intention to distribute his new-found wealth to them (*ÉdP*, III. ix). Chrisalde too indulges in a lie about ships bringing home a fortune, this time money belonging to Angélique's late father, but, in this case, for the opposite reason: it is the only way he can make Angélique accept money which is, in fact, a gift from him. These lies lead Géronte's sons to compete for the hand of Angélique in the penultimate scene of the play, thinking to receive both her new-found wealth and their father's. They are punished by her refusal of their offers and then the revelations in the final scene, from which she is absent, that their father has come into no money and that the gift Angélique has received from Chrisalde is only a part of what she will eventually receive, for he has disinherited Géronte's sons, his nephews, in her favour.

One incident in all of this has special significance. Pasquin and Grégoire stage a scene in which the latter is found counting what Géronte's sons believe to be their father's money. However, we are told in advance that only the money Grégoire is seen counting is real, a single bag of *louis d'or* obtained from Chrisalde; the rest of the bags are stuffed with straw (*ÉdP*, IV. xv). These fake money-bags are another of Piron's symbols, like the ha-ha in *La Métromanie*, which stand for the theme of appearance and reality that runs right through the play. In this earlier comedy, Piron is less prepared to leave it to chance that we will make the connection, and so has Grégoire point it out to us in the final scene, when he draws the moral by informing the sons that they are like those worthless bags:

GRÉGOIRE
(*Rendant un sac à Chrisalde qui sort*)
Vlà le sac aveuc quoi j'avon fait no recrue,
Et le biau filet d'or où j'avon pri lé grue.
(*Aux trois frères*)
Léz aute sacs, Messieu, qu'on reluquiais de loin,
En lieu d'or & d'arjan, n'étion plein que de foin.
I vous ressemblion: fausse & belle apparance.
Vote père dans vous boutoit son espérance;
Il a vu dans le fond que vous ne valiais rian. (*ÉdP*, V. viii)

Yet, if the closest comparison is to be made with the sons, whose appearance of worth in the eyes of Géronte conceals a worthless interior, they are also related to all things that are not what they appear, and, as we have seen, the entire plot is constructed of people or ideas whose exterior conceals a different internal identity or truth. The concealed identity of the sons is revealed by plots that are themselves based on things that are not what they seem.

It is perhaps fitting, then, that this is a play which itself seems to have an identity crisis. It has had two titles during the course of its existence: *Les Fils ingrats*, under which it was initially performed and published[5] and so tended to be known in the eighteenth century, and *L'École des pères*, the title of the revised version that appeared in the *Œuvres* of 1758.[6] This change betokens some indecision on Piron's part concerning the true focus of the plot, and he expresses his regret in the preface of 1758 that the original version centred on the immoral behaviour of the sons:

> L'ancien titre annonçoit un vice horrible; & [...] c'étoit, pour ainsi dire, tendre de noir l'entrée d'un lieu de plaisance. Le but de la Comédie fut toujours d'inspirer le plaisir & la gaîté, loin de faire naître l'horreur & la pitié. (*ÉdP*, préface, p. 5)

The new title focuses on a ridicule, which is the true role of comedy, whether as a source of laughter or as an instrument for moral education:

> [La Comédie] ne doit donc offrir sur la scène que de riantes peintures des ridicules; & n'en est-ce pas un, que ce fol entêtement qui égare un père, & qui l'aveugle sur les impertinences de ses enfans, jusqu'à le rendre quelquefois un enfant lui-même? (*ÉdP*, préface, pp. 5–6)

Hence one issue centres on the whole question of what comedy is or should be. Interestingly, though, it is precisely this question that becomes problematic when we focus on the role of the father, for Géronte, despite what Chrisalde and Pasquin say near the beginning of the play, is not a conventionally ridiculous comic character. Alongside the ridicule of his behaviour towards his sons, we are presented with his humane treatment of Angélique, and it is this that dominates the opening of the play, since, until we actually see them together in II. iv, we do not witness his relationship with his offspring in action. By this time, we have met the sons and are aware of their cynical attitude to their father, so that, although their efforts to avoid doing their father's bidding while attempting to force one of their brothers to do it instead are undoubtedly comic, it is comedy with a bitter edge, since the result for both Géronte and Angélique is humiliation.

While we may find satisfaction in the humiliation of an unpleasant character, this is not how we respond in the case of these characters. Hence the comedy turns in the direction of sentimentality, and this will remain a feature of the play. In certain respects, this puts Piron at the forefront of fashion: when *Les Fils ingrats* was first performed in 1728 the sentimental was a relatively new arrival in the theatre; La Motte's sentimental tragedy *Inès de Castro* had received its first performance in 1723, but Voltaire's effort in the same genre, *Zaïre*, would not be performed until 1732, and the creator of *comédie larmoyante*, Nivelle de La Chaussée, would not begin his theatrical career until the following year. By the time Piron wrote his preface in 1758, the fashion had not exactly run its course, but it was already undergoing its transformation into the *drame* with the publication of *Le Fils naturel* in 1757 and *Le Père de famille* in 1758 itself.

Despite the sentimental elements in *L'École des pères*, it seems unlikely that the fashion for *comédie larmoyante* was much to Piron's taste: it does not particularly coincide with the sense of humour found either in his poetry or in his works for the Fairs, and *La Métromanie*, despite being written when the movement was at its height, shows virtually no influence. So it is perhaps not surprising that in 1758 he shows significant distaste for the genre and the fact that his play contributed to it: 'Le plus grand défaut que je me reproche [...], est [...] cette partie sombre du poème, qui excite à la commisération pour un père abandonné par des enfans sans naturel, sans pudeur' (*ÉdP*, préface, p. 18).

Nevertheless, Piron finds himself in a difficult situation, for he is forced to admit that this aspect of the play was one of the principal reasons for its success, and not only to deplore, but also to warn against pandering to the poor taste of the public that caused this and has led to the success of subsequent sentimental comedies:

> Ce défaut toutefois, à la honte du goût, ou si l'on veut, à l'honneur des bons cœurs d'à présent, ce défaut, dis-je, qui domine surtout dans le dénouement, est l'endroit de la pièce qui intéressa le plus, &, par conséquent, celui qui réussit le mieux aux représentations. Mais c'est précisément pour cette raison que j'en parle comme je fais, afin de détourner, s'il se peut, nos jeunes poètes d'une route où les égareroit le chant des Syrènes, je veux dire, la dangereuse mélodie des applaudissements de la multitude, qui, depuis ce temps-là, n'en a que trop séduits. (*ÉdP*, préface, p. 19)

Writing with the benefit of hindsight, Piron could have proclaimed himself the pioneer of a new form of comedy, but such is his dislike of the genre that he criticizes those who based their plays entirely on what is simply one unfortunate aspect of his:

> L'erreur commune là-dessus, va pourtant jusqu'à honorer du nom de *nouveau genre de comédie*, des drames hétéroclites uniquement composés de ce qui dépare ici le mien. Comme si, composer toute une pièce de ce qui forma la moindre partie (& même la plus vicieuse) de quelques autres, c'étoit mériter le titre éminent d'*inventeur*: comme si corrompre c'étoit créer! Non assurément. (*ÉdP*, préface, p. 20, Piron's italics)

Another aspect of the change of title concerns its relationship to the action. Again, Piron's own analysis is of interest: it is, he tells us, the father who learns something during the course of the action, not the sons. The combination of their refusal to marry the woman chosen for them by their father and their failure to come to his aid when they believe he has lost everything after having given most of his fortune to them (the 'indigne procédé' in the quotation that follows) at last forces him to admit their true nature:

> Leur refus, aggravé de l'indigne procédé dont je viens de parler, lui dessille enfin les yeux: il se désabuse; il les reconnoît pour tels qu'ils sont; revient ainsi de ses préventions paternelles, se reproche sa facilité passée; & ressaisi de ses biens, redevient le maître des ingrats qui venoient de l'abandonner. C'est-là le dénouement de la pièce; &, par conséquent, l'*École des Pères* en est le vrai titre. (*ÉdP*, préface, p. 7)

On the other hand, perhaps Piron has been guilty of being too timid in his depiction of the sons, since the general impression given by them was not that they portray filial ingratitude, but that they are simply selfish individuals:

> Parce que ne peignant pas sans répugnance quelque chose d'aussi détestable que l'ingratitude filiale, je craignois que le coloris ne fût trop vif, ou l'expression trop forte. Il a résulté de cette crainte assez raisonnable, que ces fils, en tout, représentent moins, *dit-on*, des enfans ingrats, que des enfans et des hommes, faits à peu près comme tous les autres; c'est-à-dire, des enfans & des hommes uniquement occupés d'eux-mêmes & de leurs intérêts particuliers. (*ÉdP*, préface, p. 6, Piron's italics)

He goes on to protest that, for him, their actions do single them out as ungrateful sons, but concludes that if society does not think likewise, then he cannot use the original title for his play:

> Ainsi, tout l'accommodement que j'y trouve, c'est de continuer à croire, en mon particulier, ces fils, des fils ingrats & très-ingrats, mais sans permettre à cette qualification d'intituler désormais, ou de caractériser ma pièce. (*ÉdP*, préface, p. 7)

This is the same sort of old man's disgust with modern morality as would appear in *Le Salon*, published some four years later.

This, then, is a comedy that is problematic from a number of points of view. It is not entirely the comedy its author wanted to write, for it contains sentimental elements which he regarded, and continued to regard, as out of place in a comedy, even though changes in taste since the play was written effectively legitimized them. Furthermore, his depiction of the sons failed to provoke the moral outrage he expected. Partly, although not entirely, as a result of this, he came to realize that the play had two possible centres of attention, and that the original title did not highlight the one that was actually central to the action.

Despite this, *L'École des pères* is in many respects a fairly conventional classical comedy. For instance, it conforms to the three unities: the issues of time and place are unproblematic here; the two sides of the plot illustrated by the two titles are nicely bound together by the fact that the father's proposed bride for the sons and the countess they are pursuing are the same person, and the issue of Pasquin's denial of his father is never allowed enough independence to develop into a sub-plot. Hence, although the plot is relatively complex, there is none of the unconventional multi-layering we will later find in *La Métromanie*. This plot is based on the traditional Italianate model of the father as obstacle to his son's marriage, although with some interesting variants provided by the fact that there are three sons, that the true object of their affections turns out to be not only an invention, but the same person as the father's preferred spouse, and the final twist that, in promoting a marriage his sons do not want, the father has, in fact, been acting as an obstacle to his own marriage, not theirs. We end with the conventional marriage for master and servants, achieved by a stratagem devised by the servant, aided by the *soubrette* and the *raisonneur*.

Nevertheless, there is a less conventional side too, signalled by the revised title. For what are we to make of a play called *L'École des pères* which begins with a scene between its principal male character and a *raisonneur* called Chrisalde? This cannot fail to remind us of something else; even allowing for the conventional nature of characters' names in the classical tradition, it can surely be no accident that Piron has chosen for his *raisonneur* the same name, apart from a minor spelling variant, as the equivalent character in *L'École des femmes*,[7] a play which, as we have already seen, Piron would also later echo in *La Métromanie*. The first scenes of the two plays also set up similar situations: the central character finds himself in charge of the daughter of a friend and plans her marriage. However, while Molière's Arnolphe, who will discover the identity of his charge only at the dénouement,[8] plans to marry her himself, despite warnings of the folly of this from the *raisonneur* and the comic convention that the *senex* never marries the ingénue, Piron's Géronte reveals that he has considered this course of action, but rejected it:

> Touché de sa beauté, d'abord, malgré mon âge,
> Je formois, je l'avoue, un projet si peu sage;
> Et laissois naître en moi, sous ombre de pitié,
> Des sentimens plus vifs que ceux de l'amitié.
> De là vient qu'à mes fils, qui lui rendent visite,
> J'ai caché, quelque temps, mes pas et ma conduite,
> Et que, de ce qu'elle est, loin d'avoir nuls soupçons,
> Ils ignorent encor que nous nous connoissons.
> Mais je me suis bientôt reproché ma foiblesse.
> La jeunesse est pour être unie à la jeunesse:
> Et l'offre de ma main tiendroit plus, en effet,
> De l'abus du malheur, que du prix d'un bienfait. (*ÉdP*, I. i)

In his unselfishness, Géronte reveals himself to be the opposite of Molière's insensitive and self-centred character. The *raisonneur*'s response to this is surprising, since it contradicts the comic convention we have just mentioned: he tells Géronte that his age is less of a problem in relation to his love for Angélique — his conventional name specifically draws attention to his advanced age — than his poverty. For if Géronte is in certain respects an anti-Arnolphe, he is also an anti-Harpagon, who has given all his money to his sons. While there is no equivalent in *L'École des pères* of Arnolphe's change of name in *L'École des femmes* — except, perhaps, the passing reference to the fact that Géronte's sons have changed their names — the speech just quoted sets up the possibility of a play of double identities just as in Molière's play, but here it is the ingénue rather than the central character who has two identities. Like Arnolphe, Géronte has a plan, not to marry Angélique himself, but to marry her to one of his sons, and, like Chrysalde, Chrisalde predicts that the plan will fail.

As the intriguing valet, Pasquin is a conventional figure, equivalent to the clever first *zanni* of the *commedia dell'arte*, but there is also one significant way in which he defies comic convention: he is working on behalf of the father, not the sons — he even remarks that he is different from this theatrical stereotype:

> Oh! je veux des valets être le vrai modèle.
> Non, ces fripons qu'on voit sur la scène, à Paris,
> Toujours prêts à tromper les pères pour les fils ... (*ÉdP*, I. iv)

When fathers, or father-figures like Arnolphe (or indeed Géronte, as far as his relationship with Angélique is concerned), do have servants, they tend usually to conform to the type of the stupid second *zanni*. Consequently, Arnolphe is saddled with the foolish pair Alain and Georgette.

At first sight, this role of the second *zanni* might appear to be taken by Grégoire, since, as a general rule, while not all stupid characters in comedy necessarily have comic accents, characters with comic accents do tend to be stupid. Is it pure coincidence that he has a speech containing the base word 'potage', even if in a more literal context than the sexual image of Alain's speech in *L'École des femmes* thought to be such an offence against the *bienséances*?[9]

> Au bout d'eun tams st'ami meurt; &, pour tout potage
> Ne laisse à son enfan qu'un petit héritage. (*ÉdP*, IV. viii)

His first appearance too shows all the characteristics of the second *zanni*, as he rushes in obviously bringing bad news, but then, in his absurd stage-peasant language, keeps everyone waiting, while he tells them it was not his fault, or makes comments like, 'Ça va vous mettre en chaleur' (*ÉdP*, II. vi), bearing in mind that the news concerns a fire. Other characteristic features include the use of picturesque exclamations — 'patatrâs!', 'tatigué!' — or over-long enumeration:

> Meubles, chevaux, bestiaux, l'écurie & l'étable,
> Et la grange, & la paille & le blé, tout au diable! (*ÉdP*, II. vi)

And yet, Grégoire too fails to conform exactly to the type to which we initially assume he belongs. This first impression is subverted when we discover that we have witnessed a carefully calculated performance; we know that Pasquin has plans, but have no idea that this is one of them until after the event:

> Heim! Jeannot, qu'en dis-tu? Sais-je baillé dé colle?
> Comme je m'y sis pris tout d'abord par bricole,
> Afin qu'i gobît mieux par après le marlan! (*ÉdP*, II. viii)

No conventional foolish second *zanni* he. When later he complains about the fact that Pasquin treats him as if he is stupid — 'Mais tu me pranra don toujou pour eune bête?' (*ÉdP*, IV. xv) — instead of laughing at his naivety, as we usually would with a second *zanni*, we find his complaint quite justified.

Another unconventional feature is the fact that all the brothers are equally disagreeable. Apart from Pasquin, who gets his Nérine, not one of the young men in this play is suitable husband material. And yet, we still arrive at the usual happy ending of a marriage, and a marriage which is not entirely unexpected, since it has been prepared by remarks scattered through the dialogue from the first scene, but which, nevertheless, completely subverts the conventional expectations of comedy, for the ingénue marries her guardian, Géronte the *senex*. This inverts the ending not only of *L'École des femmes*, but also of just about every other comedy to use this traditional plot. But that is not to say that it is entirely without precedent: in Molière's other 'école' play, *L'École des maris*, there are two brothers, Sganarelle, the proto-Arnolphe, who fails to marry his ward, and Ariste, who at something in the region of sixty makes his brother and Arnolphe, who are both about forty, look positively young,[10] but through his generous behaviour wins the love of his ward and weds her. While Molière reworked the Sganarelle plot of this play for *L'École des femmes*, Piron seems, for Géronte's relationship with Angélique, to have gone back to the Ariste plot.

One other small detail of the plot is also worth attention, for it constitutes yet another subversion of expectation. It is a convention of classical theatre that any character or thing pronounced missing at the beginning of the play will turn up before the end. In the first scene of this play we discover that the impoverishment of Angélique's late father, and consequently hers too, was caused by a ship going missing:

> De la fortune ainsi tourne, ici-bas, la roue.
> Depuis un an entier, la perte d'un vaisseau
> A causé sa ruine, & l'a mis au tombeau. (*ÉdP*, I. i)

Our knowledge of classical convention will lead us confidently to assume that the ship will turn up, making Angélique wealthy, and solving everyone's problems. Pasquin's lie to the sons that a ship has come in, making their father wealthy (*ÉdP*, II. xi), grows naturally from this, but does not form a logical conclusion to it, for we are never in any doubt that it is a fabrication; unlike the lie about the burning of the country house, where we are not let in on the secret until after Géronte has been duped, in this instance Pasquin's intended fib is revealed to us before he tells it (*ÉdP*, II. viii). But then our expectation is apparently fulfilled when, in V. i, we are told that Angélique's father's ship has come in with his riches, only to to be thwarted when we learn that this too is a fabrication, a stratagem by Chrisalde to persuade Angélique to accept his money. The promised boat fails ever to arrive in the way that it would in any normal comedy.

It would certainly be going too far to see this play as an anti-comedy, a sort of *Cantatrice chauve avant la lettre*, for its general structure and the impression it makes are too conventional for that; and yet, it has a strong tendency to invert the conventions that it uses, so that they surprise us despite their conventionality. It would also be going too far to see it as an anti-*L'École des femmes*, although there, too, there are a number of occasions, particularly the first scene, and particularly with the revised title, where it seems that play is being evoked only to be contradicted.

And this play which is in some ways an anti-play is preceded, again in the revised version, by an anti-*art poétique*. For, while there is enough in the preface to *L'École des pères* about Piron's theory of comedy for Pascale Verèb to call it 'son unique discours sur ce genre dramatique',[11] Piron also spends a significant amount of it telling us why we should mistrust the motives and the conclusions of those who write *arts poétiques*; he is not going to allow himself to be easily pinned down.

Notes to Chapter 2

1. At its first performance in 1728 the play bore the title *Les Fils ingrats*; this was changed when the play was revised for the collected edition of 1758.
2. See *ÉdP*, préface, pp. 16, 18–20.
3. Pascale Verèb points out, although unfortunately without giving any specific references, that, despite Piron's efforts, the sons' refusal to marry Angélique was not generally seen as unreasonable (*Alexis Piron, poète*, p. 528).

4. Although Pasquin joins in with the sons' criticism of fathers in II. xi, it soon becomes apparent that it is simply a way of gaining their confidence in order to put into action his plot against them.
5. The first performance was in 1728; it was first published in 1729, then in 1733 and 1738. The next (and last) individual edition, which appeared in 1763, bore the new title, but preserved the original as a subtitle.
6. Pascale Verèb interestingly sees the two titles as representative of two types of comedy between which Piron is torn, 'la comédie de mœurs ou de caractère dénonçant les ridicules du temps et la comédie dite "bourgeoise" proposant un idéal moral' (*Alexis Piron, poète*, p. 534), a tension she also identifies in *La Métromanie*. Nevertheless, while *Les Fils ingrats* does tend to point in the direction of the former type, it is not clear that *L'École des pères* does not imply a *comédie de caractère* just as strongly as a moralizing comedy.
7. So irresistible is the comparison that Pascale Verèb uses Molière's spelling, Chrysalde, to refer to Piron's character (*Alexis Piron, poète*, pp. 528, 535), and it also appears twice as a misprint in Dufay's edition (pp. 43, 107).
8. It will be recalled that he has obtained his ward from an impoverished peasant woman, but she turns out to be the daughter of the sister and brother-in-law of his friend Chrysalde.
9. We will recall the character in *La Critique de 'L'École des femmes'* who, typifying a particular critical response to Molière's play, says: 'J'ai pensé vomir au *potage*' (iii). Even without the sexual connection, the very banality of the word makes it alien to conventional ideas of the correct linguistic register for comedy.
10. Molière gives the ages of his characters quite near the beginning of the plays, although in *L'École des maris* the details are rather vague: we are first told by Sganarelle that his brother is about twenty years older than him (I. i) and then later that he is nearly sixty (I. ii). Even if we are intended to assume a degree of exaggeration on the part of the unpleasant Sganarelle, who clearly enjoys baiting his brother about his age, the figures still give us a general idea of the relative ages of the characters, placing Sganarelle somewhere in his early forties and Ariste in his late fifties. The information in *L'École des femmes* is more precise: Chrysalde asks Arnolphe why on earth he has taken it into his head to change his name at the age of forty-two (I. i).
11. *Alexis Piron, poète*, p. 511.

CHAPTER 3

A Tragic Success

Gustave Wasa

One of the most interesting issues relating to the use of transformation in Piron's theatre, which also sheds light on his dramaturgy, is the relationship of *Gustave Wasa* (1733)[1] to the source identified by Piron, *L'Histoire des révolutions de Suède* by the Abbé Vertot.[2] To what extent can Piron's Gustave Wasa be identified with his historical prototype, or at least — and this is what must concern us here — with that prototype as presented by Vertot, and how has Piron modified what he took from that source?

The young Gustav Vasa[3] was certainly an attractive character, heroic and swashbuckling, 'with as many hairbreadth escapes and desperate adventures to his credit as Bonny Prince Charlie', as one noted historian puts it.[4] Vertot gives an animated account of his colourful escapades, during which he sometimes dons disguises to escape detection; of the way his charm would lead strangers — sometimes female — to help him; and of his ability to win over the rebellious peasants of the region of Dalarna.[5] Clearly Piron has been inspired by this figure, and has responded enthusiastically in his dramatic re-creation.

Piron has also made a brave attempt to fill in the complex political background so carefully set out by Vertot. Gustav's campaign brought to an end the Union of Kalmar, officially consecrated in 1397 when Erik of Pomerania became King of Denmark, Norway, and Sweden. During the period of the Union the Swedes had often had their own regent, with Sten Sture the younger[6] taking this role from 1512 until 1520, when Kristian II bloodily asserted his right as King of Denmark to govern Sweden. The Bloodbath of Stockholm[7] is the most famous of his atrocities but is far from being the only one, and it is undoubtedly the cruelty of his rule that allowed Gustav to gather such overwhelming popular support. Hence, the sanguinary character depicted by Piron in his Christierne is true to historical fact.

A particularly striking aspect of Piron's characterization of Christierne in his opening scene, clearly aimed at underlining the brutality of his nature, is the callousness of his reaction to the news of the death of his wife, left as regent in Denmark during his absence:

> Tu m'annonces le sort d'une épouse importune,
> Dont l'époux, dès longtemps, méditoit l'infortune:
> Oui, la mort la frappant de ses traits imprévus,
> Rompt des nœuds que bientôt le divorce eût rompus. (*GW*, I. i)

The explanation for this reaction is given immediately: Christierne is passionately in love with his prisoner Adélaïde, daughter of Sténon. Thus we are faced with the paradox of the brutal tyrant enslaved by love, a figure who, despite his decidedly literary resonances,[8] can have real-life counterparts too, as is shown by the case of the historical Kristian. As we shall see, there was no real-life equivalent of Christierne's love for Adélaïde, but Vertot attributes to the historical figure a no-less-complex domestic arrangement. According to his narrative, the queen[9] accompanies Christiern when he first leaves for Sweden (V, I, 155) and is still with him when, after his defeat in Sweden and rejection by the Danes, he goes into exile (V, II, 21) — this is Vertot's last mention of her; in fact, she died in 1526, some three years after her husband's exile began. So not only did she not die during the period depicted in the play, she was not left in Denmark as regent either. However, Vertot's Christiern has his own grand passion, for Sigebritte, described by Vertot in the following terms:

> C'était une femme hollandaise déjà âgée, et qui sans naissance et sans beauté était parvenue, par sa seule habileté, jusqu'à se faire aimer éperdument de ce prince. Sigebritte le gouvernait avec un empire absolu, et faisait elle seule le destin de la cour et de tout le royaume; rien ne résistait à son crédit: elle donnait et ôtait les charges et les dignités, sans égard pour les lois du pays, et selon son caprice: elle entreprenait même souvent des choses injustes, simplement pour faire paraître son pouvoir; mais quoi qu'elle entreprît, Christiern, malgré son âge et ses défauts, approuvait toujours sa conduite, et se faisait un mérite d'être le premier ministre de ses volontés. (V, I, 149–50)

It is she who remains in Denmark while Christiern is in Sweden, possibly, although Vertot is uncertain, as unofficial regent:

> Sigebritte ne fut point du voyage, soit qu'elle craignît de s'exposer à la raillerie des seigneurs suédois, qui plaisantaient souvent sur la passion extravagante de Christiern, ou que ce prince eût trouvé plus à propos de la laisser en son absence à Copenhague, pour veiller sur la conduite du sénat. (V, I, 155)

She is still with Christiern when he and his family go into exile (V, II, 21).[10]

It may have been the privilege of kings in Piron's time as in Kristian's openly to keep mistresses, but, the *bienséances* and the demands of the plot both requiring Christierne to express his love for Adélaïde through a desire to marry her, it is necessary for him in the play to be wifeless, hence the need for Piron to bring the death of his wife forward.[11] However, that Piron should choose to include the detail in the action proper, rather than the pre-play action, is surely because it is useful for rapid character-building. That he should have changed completely the identity of Christierne's beloved from what he found in Vertot is unsurprising. The *mésalliance* implied by the differences in both age and rank would again have strained the *bienséances*, but these details also, as Vertot so strongly suggests, make the match unrealistic, even if he was under the impression that it was real. Since Piron's plot requires no fewer than three principal male characters to be in love with the same woman, they need a more plausible object for their affections, and, by making her the daughter of the previous ruler of Sweden, he complies with the usual requirement of tragic universality, according to which love never exists in isolation, but is linked to the political plot of the play. Hence, even this most colourfully *romanesque* aspect of Christierne's character has some link, however tenuous, with Vertot's retelling of history.

That, however, is where Piron's historical fidelity ends. Other events and characters are more loosely based on Vertot's narrative or are complete inventions. Frédéric has his roots in Fredrik von Oldenburg,[12] Duke of Holstein, subsequently Fredrik I of Denmark, the uncle of Kristian II, who was asked by the Danes to accede to the throne when they staged their own revolt against Kristian. He played no part in Kristian's exploits in Sweden, and, far from being the generous character of the play who gives up everything for Gustave, as soon as he became King of Denmark he began unsuccessfully to assert his own claim to the Swedish throne, albeit by diplomatic rather than military means. Piron's character has waived his rights to the throne because of a desire for a quiet life:

> Je n'eus d'autres vertus que l'amour du repos.
> Je ne méprisai point les droits de ma naissance:
> J'évitai le fardeau de la toute-puissance,
> Je cédai sans efforts des honneurs dangereux,
> Et le pénible soin de rendre un peuple heureux.
> D'un noble dévouement je ne fus pas capable. (*GW*, I. iv)

This has no historical precedent, and seems to have been inspired by a single remark in Vertot: 'Ce prince vivait tranquillement dans les terres de son apanage, et il n'avait fait paraître jusqu'alors aucune ambition' (V, II, 19). Admittedly this is our first introduction to him, and is, in consequence, striking, but the impression that this historical figure might in any sense have been similar to the character that this sentence inspired Piron to base on him is immediately dispelled by what follows:

> Cependant la vue d'une couronne l'éblouit: il écouta avec plaisir les propositions des mécontens: il traita avec eux, et il consentit à dépouiller son neveu [Kristian II]; il crut aisément et il se flatta que la conduite violente et toutes les cruautés de ce malheureux prince justifieraient ses armes, et empêcheraient qu'on ne le regardât comme un usurpateur. Il leva des troupes dans toutes les terres de ses dépendances pour appuyer les mécontens. (V, II, 19)

Piron's character, with his strange combination of self-interest and generosity, whose failure to shoulder his responsibilities in the past has made him to some extent responsible for the events depicted in the tragedy by permitting Christierne's reign, but who will eventually rise to the occasion and resolve the conflict, is much more interesting than his historical counterpart but risks being less credible, with the complexity of the role adding to the already convoluted circumstances that have to be communicated to the audience in the exposition. Interestingly, Piron suppresses the detail that Fredrik was the uncle of Kristian II, leaving us with the impression of a younger character,[13] whose final decision to depose Christierne and shoulder his responsibilities seems, as we shall see, to represent a sort of coming of age. His presence in Sweden is also an invention of Piron's: the historical figure, who is mentioned by Vertot for the first time in relation to his acceptance of the throne of the deposed Kristian, did not form part of his retinue there.

The only other characters to bear the names of figures found in Vertot do not appear, but form part of the pre-play or off-stage action, such as the important figure of Sténon, or a more minor figure like Othon.[14] The other characters generally have some sort of connection with historical fact but often very distant.

Although they are required by the plot to be unrelated, the suggestion of a mother and daughter relationship between Gustave's mother Léonor and his beloved Adélaïde recalls the pairing of the mother and sister of Vertot's Gustave. However, since they are mentioned in Vertot only in relation to Christiern's threat to kill them and their subsequent murder, it is only in the episode in the play in which Léonor's life is threatened that either has any concrete link with Vertot's narrative. In Vertot, Christiern, in his anger, had the women thrown into the sea in a sack (V, I, 228); it seems more likely that the episode where Léonor is held hostage on a ship was inspired by the incident in which Gustav himself, a number of years before the events depicted in the play at the time that Sten Sture was still administrator of Sweden, was kidnapped by Kristian and taken by ship to be imprisoned in Denmark (V, I, 114–15).[15] Incidentally, Gustav's mother, although unnamed by Vertot, was called not Léonor but Cecilia.

This same mother and daughter pairing, given Adélaïde's status as daughter of Sténon, will also remind us of Kristina Gyllenstierna,[16] the widow of Sten Sture who held out against Kristian II in Stockholm, and her two young sons, whom Gustav Vasa took under his protection, but this is as close as we will get historically to the character of Adélaïde and the nature of her relationship with Gustave, for Sten Sture had no daughter.

Casimir perhaps stands for all those Swedes who were forced, as an act of self-preservation, to appear to support Kristian, but returned to their true loyalties when Gustav's revolution got under way. Nevertheless, we may feel that his behaviour is rather too specific to be no more than this. Perhaps there is a link with Vertot's Severin de Norbi, the historical Soren Norby, who Vertot tells us saved the life of Sténon's widow when Christiern ordered that she be drowned, since Vertot says of him:

> Cet homme était en apparence esclave de toutes les volontés de son maître; mais sous cette feinte complaisance il méditait secrètement de hauts desseins: il était persuadé qu'un gouvernement aussi violent que celui de Christiern ne pouvait pas durer. (V, I, 166)

This is where the similarity ends, however, since he was a Dane,[17] and no supporter of Gustav. Neither the names nor the behaviour of the two remaining characters, Rodolphe and Sophie, link them to any particular historical individuals.

What of the authenticity of the events depicted? Christierne's holding Adélaïde prisoner is true to fact, even if Adélaïde herself is not, although the unity of place necessitates one significant modification: the imprisoned female relatives of those Kristian had executed in the Stockholm Bloodbath, including Gustav's mother and sister and the widow of Sten Sture,[18] were held in Denmark and not Sweden (V, I, 167). It is also true that it was Gustav, with the help of Fredrik, who secured the release of the surviving women, but by much more prosaic methods than the dramatic rescue of Léonor in the play — in any case, Gustav's mother had already been murdered by Kristian by that time — and with Fredrik's actions being based on a pragmatic approach to the situation, rather than generosity and heroism:

> L'envoyé de Gustave étant arrivé à la cour de Danemarck, demanda publiquement au roi la liberté de la princesse et des autres dames suédoises. (V, II, 36)
>
> Fridéric comprit bien [...] que Gustave était plus puissant que l'archevêque ne le lui avait voulu faire croire: il reconnut qu'il n'était pas temps de faire revivre d'anciennes prétentions, qui attireraient la guerre dans son pays; il offrit à cet envoyé de convenir à l'amiable de tous ses différens avec Gustave, et de faire une ligue offensive et défensive avec lui contre Christiern; et pour gages de son estime et de son amitié, il lui renvoya, avec une escorte honorable, la veuve de l'administrateur, et toutes les autres dames suédoises qui étaient prisonnières en Danemarck depuis le massacre de Stockholm. (V, II, 37–38)

The most striking historical event to feature in the play, however, is the battle on the ice, which takes place in the interval between Acts IV and V and is narrated by Adélaïde:

> Sur ces bords, dont l'hiver a glacé la surface,
> Mes ravisseurs fuyoient; & franchissant l'espace
> Qui semble séparer le rivage & les eaux,
> M'enlevoient vers la rade où flottoient leurs vaisseaux.
> J'en croyois Frédéric; & je m'étois flattée
> De voir, en sa faveur, la flotte révoltée;
> Mais plus nous approchions, moins j'avois cet espoir;
> Tout ce que j'aperçois, paroît dans le devoir.
> Laissant donc pour jamais Gustave & ma patrie,
> Je demandois la mort, quand ce Prince en furie,
> Du palais où ses yeux ne me rencontroient point,
> Entend mes cris, me voit, vole à nous, & nous joint.
> On se mêle. Je veux regagner le rivage;
> Partout je me retrouve au centre du carnage.
> La fortune se joue en ce combat fatal.
> Sur la glace, long-temps, l'avantage est égal;
> Elle nuit à la force, elle aide à la foiblesse;
> Et chaque pas trahit la valeur ou l'adresse.
> Parmi des cris de rage & de mourantes voix,
> Un bruit plus effrayant, plus sinistre cent fois,
> Sous nous, autour de nous, au loin se fait entendre.
> La glace, en mille endroits, menace de se fendre,
> Se fend, s'ouvre, se brise, & s'épanche en glaçons
> Qui nagent sur un gouffre où nous disparoissons. (*GW*, V. i)

The geography of Stockholm means that naval action played a considerable part in the efforts to conquer it, but there is no record in Vertot, or indeed anywhere else, of a battle like this on the frozen sea. Two events, however, have distinct similarities, one of which takes place at about the same point in the chronology of events as Piron's battle — in other words, shortly before the defeat of Kristian II. This is Gustav's attempt to burn Norby's ships when they are stuck in the ice:

> Norbi espérait renouveler le combat le lendemain; mais, des présages de gros temps l'ayant obligé de se retirer, il relâcha le soir auprès d'une petite île,

> dont le fond était sûr, et qui n'était pas cependant éloigné du bord de la mer. Il y fut surpris la nuit par une gelée extraordinaire, et si violente que tous ses vaisseaux se trouvèrent pris et arrêtés dans la glace. Gustave en ayant été averti, résolut de les aller brûler; il prit avec lui les troupes de Lubeck, qui campaient de ce côté-là [...]: il fit passer les soldats sur la glace jusque dans l'île, avec ordre de s'avancer à la faveur des ténèbres le plus près qu'ils pourraient des vaisseaux ennemis. (V, II, 14–15)

After a battle, this is how the incident ends:

> Mais le général de Lubeck arracha lui-même la victoire des mains de ses soldats; il fit sonner la retraite au milieu du combat; et malgré les prières et les menaces de Gustave il ramena ses troupes sur terre sous prétexte qu'elles étaient trop exposées au feu des ennemis. [...] Comme la saison n'était pas encore fort avancée, le soleil parut le matin, il fit fondre la glace, et un vent du sud s'étant levé en même temps, acheva de la dissiper; Norbi mit aussitôt la voile. (V, II, 16)

The excitement of this episode is similar to that of Piron's narration, but of its most striking feature, the breaking of the ice, there is no sign; it stays firm until the weather changes, then melts. Piron may also have had in mind another episode in Vertot, one of the most famous incidents in Swedish history of this period, an earlier event concerning not Gustav, but Sten Sture: the battle on a frozen lake during which he was mortally wounded. This is how Vertot describes it:

> Othon,[19] à la vue de l'armée suédoise, fit paraître quelque frayeur; il se retira avec une précipitation apparente sur le lac Weter[20] qui était glacé, et il y campa avec toute son armée: Sténon, emporté par son courage, poursuivit avec plus d'ardeur que de précaution un ennemi qu'il croyait trouver en désordre et épouvanté: il laissa son infanterie et les paysans suédois dans les bois, où ils s'étaient retranchés, et avec sa cavalerie il chargea les Danois, qu'il rencontra proche Bogesund. (V, I, 122)[21]

The subsequent description of events makes no further mention of the location of the battle, and here again the ice, unlike that in Piron's battle, remained securely intact.

Like the ha-ha in *La Métromanie* and the fake money bags in *L'École des pères*, the ice seems to stand as a symbol for the theme of appearance and reality that runs right through the play: what appears solid, substantial, disintegrates to reveal that all is not what it appeared, just as the characters constantly reveal that they are not what we, and other characters, thought.

Piron avoids in his tragedy the most inherently comic indicator of the unreliability of appearance as proof of identity, disguise; but numerous others are used, and perhaps the closest to disguise is found when Gustave appears before Christierne pretending to be his own killer. This scene even includes some dark dramatic irony which gets perilously close to being that very unclassical device of comedy in a tragic context, albeit very black comedy, as Gustave speaks in double meanings appreciated by the audience but not by Christierne. Christierne asks the 'killer' if he is the man who brings with him Gustave's head; Gustave replies that he is. Christierne enquires why he is not carrying it in his hand; Gustave replies that, if it were not in his power, he would not appear with such assurance before

Christierne. Gustave sidesteps enquiries about his name by saying that a name is worthless unless it is known to everyone, but he hopes it soon will be. Christierne asks how he saw through Gustave's disguises; the 'killer' replies that he knows Gustave too well to be taken in by any disguise. And the conversation continues in similar vein. This refusal to lie, even to his enemy, sets Gustave out as a hero; in contrast to Christierne, he is scrupulously truthful, even to the point of rashness. But it also shows how our preconceptions about identity influence our responses: Christierne is incapable of understanding the real meaning behind what Gustave says because he hears what he wants to hear, as Gustave later explains to him (*GW*, IV. vi). Piron adds to Gustave's heroism by having him declare that he would use concealment of his identity only for noble ends: it was necessary for his attempt to rescue Adélaïde, but he would not have used it to facilitate an assassination attempt on Christierne. Had he succeeded in the rescue attempt, he would have revealed his true identity and met him in open combat. He makes similar comments at the moment his identity is discovered, making no attempt to deny or explain away Christierne's suspicions that he is Léonor's son:

> Oui, je le suis. Je fais cet aveu sans contrainte.
> Pour d'autres que pour moi, j'eus recours à la feinte:
> Mais mon propre péril me défend d'en user;
> Et je le sens trop peu pour daigner t'abuser. (*GW*, IV. v)

So Gustave takes a moral attitude to concealment of identity: it may be used for noble purposes, but not as a substitute for heroic action. Moreover, it is Christierne's base nature which prevents him from seeing through his act of concealment. Given the reputation of the mythologized historical figure of the real Gustav for the use of disguise, which is alluded to in Piron's text, this may seem a rather high-minded attitude, but it is clearly intended to give tragic dignity to this potentially comic theme of concealed identity.

The character who comes closest to Gustave in this matter of hiding her true identity is Léonor, who conceals the fact that she is Gustave's mother. Like Gustave, she is depicted as a strong and noble character, and the way she speaks in her first major scene[22] suggests that her destiny is linked to that of her son, so that her survival is for his sake and not her own:

> Un fils m'est aussi cher que vous l'est un amant;
> Et je ne voudrois pas lui survivre un moment. (*GW*, I. vi)

Later, when she believes that Gustave is indeed dead, she changes her ground slightly — she will survive to support Adélaïde — but there is still a sense that her importance to Léonor is as a last reminder of Gustave:

> Qu'il vive en votre cœur! ne l'oubliez jamais:
> Je vivrai du plaisir d'adoucir vos regrets. (*GW*, III. iii)

This resolve, however, is short-lived; her subsequent actions return to her initial reluctance to survive her son, and in an outburst of anger provoked by an insult to the son she supposes to be dead, she reveals her identity in a grand gesture that Adélaïde, Léonor herself, and the audience believe to be an act of suicide. Although Christierne's desire to curry favour with Adélaïde saves her at this point (*GW*, III.

iv), threats against her continue, and in IV. iv we find her lamenting the fact that her execution has still not brought an end to her suffering. Of course, once she has discovered that Gustave is safe, her attitude changes, and in V. v, after her rescue from Christierne, she speaks in entirely positive terms. Hence Léonor's concealment of her identity is strongly linked to the fate of Gustave and Adélaïde, and so again has a noble purpose that goes beyond simple self-preservation.

Christierne represents the other side of this moral issue. He does not conceal his identity, but he does conceal his feelings for Adélaïde from all but his confidant Rodolphe, even encouraging everyone, including Adélaïde herself, to believe until the last moment that it is to Frédéric and not Christierne that she is to be forcibly married. This is clearly reprehensible; Christierne well knows that Adélaïde, while not wishing to marry Frédéric, would find marriage to himself even more abhorrent. He is also aware that Frédéric is in love with Adélaïde, and would wish to wed her with her consent, but does not want to force her into marriage against her will. So both Adélaïde and Frédéric are tortured by the knowledge that she is to be forced to marry, but Christierne knows that his last-minute revelation that he is to be the groom will make matters even worse.

This is not his only act of deceit: he leads Léonor to believe that she is to be executed in order to make her more compliant with regard to Adélaïde, and stages another mock execution, that of Gustave, to trick her into giving away his identity. Christierne's use of pretence is neither selfless nor heroic, like that of Gustave and Léonor, but is selfish and cruel.

And yet, as Gustave says, along with this selfishness goes the inability to judge properly the true character of others. We have seen how this prevents him seeing through the assumed identity of Gustave himself, so obsessed is he with the idea that the man before him is the killer of Gustave, but this is not his only failure. His extreme prejudice against Adélaïde because she is his enemy prevents him from even noticing her until after he has made public his plan to marry her to Frédéric. This is how Christierne describes his first sight of her during his attack on the palace:

> Mourante entre les bras d'une femme éperdue,
> Adélaïde alors fut offerte à ma vue
> Sa pâleur, à mon œil de colère enflammé,
> Déroba mille appas qui m'auroit désarmé.
> D'un mortel ennemi je ne vis que la fille,
> Que le reste d'un sang funeste à ma famille.
> Les armes de son père ont fait périr mon fils;
> Et cette image alors fut tout ce que je vis. (*GW*, I. i)

He does not see her again until a visit inspired by Frédéric's failure to persuade her to marry him:

> Je vis Adélaïde. Ah! Rodolphe, peins-toi
> Tout ce qu'a la beauté de séduisant en soi!
> Tout ce qu'ont d'engageant la jeunesse, & des grâces,
> Où la tendre langueur fait remarquer ses traces!
> Jamais, de deux beaux yeux, le charme en un moment
> N'a, sans vouloir agir, agi si puissamment;

> Ni jamais, dans un cœur, l'amour ne prit naissance,
> Avec tant d'ascendant, & si peu d'espérance. (*GW*, I. i)

Hence, while, for the spectator, Adélaïde is the fixed point at the centre of this play, the constant in the midst of the other shifting identities, Christierne's initial failure to understand her means that even her identity is not entirely transparent. Others whom Christierne fails to understand fully, as we shall see, are Frédéric and Casimir. But we should not leave Christierne without drawing attention to another problem with his identity: that he is (as we have seen) a villain who harbours unexpected emotions, the paradoxical hard man who is in love. Although this is revealed very near the opening of the action, Piron still exploits the element of surprise inherent in it by first taking care to give the impression of someone who is ruthless, even, it would appear, devoid of emotion: Rodolphe announces to Christierne the death of his wife as if it were important only for its political implications; Christierne responds by apparently talking politics himself for some sixteen lines, before eventually commenting that, had his wife not died, he would have divorced her. This response turns out to be more logical than at first appears, since the political issue Christierne is alluding to is the unifying effect of the marriage he is planning to Adélaïde, but the callousness of the response to his wife's death is intended to shock, and the revelation of his intention to marry Adélaïde, even if it does follow on logically from this speech, still comes as a surprise, particularly when we discover that it is motivated by a great passion and not simple political pragmatism. Of course, despite the paradox of the combination of cruelty and love, such figures are scarcely unknown either in reality or in literature, but, as with previous literary versions (Racine's Néron, for example, or Corneille's Cléopâtre, or perhaps even, in a comic context, Molière's Arnolphe), Christierne's love differs from the selfless passion of the heroic characters, who put the safety and feelings of the beloved before their own — as do Gustave, Adélaïde, Léonor, and Frédéric — by being entirely selfish, and not only showing indifference to the feelings of the beloved, but even relishing her suffering:

> Qu'eus-je opéré d'ailleurs sur cette âme inflexible?
> Que, de loin, dominoit un rival invincible?
> Je n'osai donc parler; mon feu se renferma;
> Mais, sous ce feu couvert, le dépit s'alluma.
> Du fugitif aimé, craignant l'audace active,
> Je resserrois toujours les fers de ma captive. (*GW*, I. i)

Even a usually positive emotion like love fails to have a positive effect on a morally corrupt individual.

Casimir, like Christierne, conceals his identity not by pretending to be someone else, but by dissimulating his feelings and opinions. But, like Gustave and Léonor, he has noble motives, underlined by the fact that, far from deliberately worming his way into Christierne's affections, it has simply been an accident of fate that he has been trusted by him. However, he has been able to profit from his position to do good work on behalf of Gustave and his supporters. Casimir also provides a further insight into Christierne's character, by suggesting that his own corruption is such that he is unable to trust others on any logical basis: his attachment to

Casimir is simply a whim, a 'caprice', and so is not dissimilar to his infatuation with Adélaïde:

GUSTAVE

Christierne, dit-on, est devenu ton Roi,
T'appelle à ses conseils, ne s'ouvre qu'à toi.

CASIMIR

A tous beaux sentimens une âme inaccessible,
D'aucune confiance est-elle susceptible?
Non, Seigneur, non; le traître, au crime abandonné,
Se croit, de ses pareils, toujours environné;
Et s'il me distingua, ce ne fut qu'un caprice
Qui fut une faveur pour moi, moins qu'un supplice.
J'en soutenois l'affront: mais le motif est beau.
Vos amis, sans cela, seroient tous au tombeau.
Je flattois, sans rougir, une injuste puissance
Qui souvent, à ma voix, épargna l'innocence;
Et vous devez, Seigneur, à ce zèle, à ma foi,
Ceux que vous avez cru plus fidèles que moi. (*GW*, II. iii)

The tone of injured innocence in the last couplet elicits a hurried apology from Gustave. It is not the only time he will be criticized for having insufficient confidence in one of those loyal to him: Adélaïde will also be offended that Gustave tests her continuing love for him rather than identifying himself to her immediately:

ADÉLAÏDE

Et d'erreur en entrant ne m'avoir pas tirée!
Avoir de mes regrets prolongé la durée,
Et, sur des fictions, laissé couler mes pleurs!

GUSTAVE

Ces pleurs m'étoient garants du plus grand des bonheurs.
Ils remettoient la paix dans une âme saisie
Des terreurs d'une aveugle & tendre jalousie.
Terreurs que j'avouerai comme un crime à présent;
Mais dont mon cœur alors ne pouvoit être exempt.
Le bruit de mon trépas, près de neuf ans d'absence,
Les feux de Frédéric, ses vertus, sa puissance,
Et dans le temple enfin son bonheur annoncé ...

ADÉLAÏDE

Ah! qu'un moment plutôt mon amour offensé,
A cette jalousie injuste & criminelle,
Opposoit un témoin bien cher & bien fidèle! (*GW*, III. vi)

Gustave may try to claim, both to exculpate himself from any accusation of deceit and to accuse Christierne of moral weakness, that the latter's inability to see through his disguise was proof of his moral corruption, but his own failure to place absolute trust in Casimir and Adélaïde proves that identity is not transparent, even to the good man. Christierne might, as Casimir points out, be guilty of judging every one by his own corrupt standards, but Gustave too is aware enough of the imperfections of the real world to recognize that his own sense of loyalty and morality will not be shared by all, even if he is mistaken in the two instances depicted in the play.

Frédéric raises interesting questions regarding identity, for here we have a man who, rather than concealing his true self, seems not to have found it himself. No longer the king's uncle, as he was historically, he has still been offered the throne of Denmark before Christierne, a detail which could suggest an older man, but turned it down in favour of an existence less plagued by responsibility. However, other factors seem to suggest his youth: he is unmarried, and makes a suitably ardent rival suitor to the hero, who is taken seriously by Adélaïde, in a way that an older suitor rarely is in drama (*GW*, I. v); he is a prince of Denmark, and yet defers to and is dependent on Christierne; and he is heir to the throne. But, above all, it is his gradual coming to terms with the responsibilities of life which he has previously avoided that seems, as we have noted, to imply a transition from adolescence to adulthood, a process of self-discovery.

We first hear of him in the opening scene between Christierne and Rodolphe, where the former sees him simply as the devoted but hopeless lover of Adélaïde, who could be disposed of by being sent back to Copenhagen as regent, whereas Rodolphe sees someone with the potential to be dangerous, who needs to be more carefully managed:

> Frédéric est encor vertueux & fidèle;
> Mais il est adoré dans le parti rebelle:
> Et des écrits publics font revivre des droits
> Que l'on prétend qu'il a de nous donner des loix. [...]
> N'exposez pas le Prince au danger trop visible
> D'oublier ses devoirs, en trouvant tout possible;
> Et surtout, au moment qu'environné d'amis,
> Son amour offensé se croiroit tout permis.
> Laissez-le, s'occupant de sa folle tendresse,
> Vainement soupirer aux pieds de la Princesse. (*GW*, I. i)

For Rodolphe, then, Frédéric is impressionable, but unlikely to cause trouble without the influence of others. He can be controlled simply by leaving him in his current position of lovesick suitor to Adélaïde, a view that suggests his immaturity.

Our first encounter with Frédéric himself makes it clear that things are more complex. We see him with Christierne, who both dominates him — as the interruptions show — and seems to trust him:

> CHRISTIERNE
> Frédéric, savez-vous le destin de la Reine?
> FRÉDÉRIC
> Seigneur, on me l'apprend: & le devoir m'amène ...
> CHRISTIERNE
> Vous a-t-on dit aussi, qu'infidèle à son Roi,
> Mon peuple ose, pour vous, s'élever contre moi?
> FRÉDÉRIC
> Ah! je le désavoue! & je n'ambitionne ...
> CHRISTIERNE
> Prince, on ne s'ouvre guère à ceux que l'on soupçonne.
> (*GW*, I. iii)

But he is much less compliant with regard to Adélaïde than Rodolphe predicts. Yes, he is in love with her, but her constant rejections have turned him to despair, so that when Christierne tells him that it is only to spare him the pain of separation that he has not sent him to Denmark to quell the uprising, Frédéric responds that to have parted him from her would have been a favour. The sincerity of his love is seen from his obvious concern for the feelings of the object of his hopeless passion, so that when Christierne tells him to pursue his wooing, this time it is Frédéric who interrupts, in a passionate outburst, saying that this would both increase his own despair and be a torment to Adélaïde. Part of the cruelty of this scene derives from the fact that the audience already knows that Christierne has no intention of allowing Frédéric to marry Adélaïde, but intends to wed her himself, and that he clearly does not share Frédéric's concern for her.

It is already evident that Frédéric is a more complex individual than either Christierne or Rodolphe has anticipated, but what follows complicates matters further. Christierne continues, telling Frédéric that he has news that gives him hope with Adélaïde: the death of Gustave. Giving Frédéric no opportunity to respond, he exits, leaving him with Casimir, who reveals immediately something that is news to the audience: that he is a patriot and sympathizer of Gustave; yet, surprisingly, Frédéric has clearly been aware of this for some time. He is no loyal follower of Christierne, but sees the murder of Gustave as a blot on the honour of his people, something that makes Christierne unworthy to be king (*GW*, I. iv), and he indulges in a lengthy bout of self-criticism when Casimir suggests it is Frédéric's modesty that has allowed Christierne to behave in this way. He sounds like a man who is beginning to take responsibility for his actions, but this impression is weakened when we see that his main preoccupation is that he is the person designated by Christierne to inform Adélaïde of Gustave's death. He even contemplates running away to avoid this, and, although prevented by Adélaïde's arrival, still leaves her without having fulfilled his task of conveying the news — she guesses it from the manner of his departure. So this is the picture we have of him by the end of the first act: he has a political conscience, but it is subordinated to his romantic aspirations; he is weak when forced to confront his responsibilities, even where his beloved is concerned.

Act II finds him again bemoaning his fate to Casimir, and again the principal focus of his complaints is his love life: because he was the one who told Adélaïde about the death of Gustave, she will implicate him in the crime. However, he ends with what sounds rather more like a call to arms:

> C'est trop mettre à l'épreuve un Prince au désespoir,
> Qui, hors de l'équité, méconnoît tout pouvoir:
> Qui peut briser un joug qu'il s'imposa lui-même.
> Je ne reponds de rien, blessé dans ce que j'aime.
> Tant de méchancetés, d'injustices, de sang,
> Ne rappellent que trop Frédéric à son rang. (*GW*, II. ii)

But his next act is to run away again; this time in order to avoid meeting the man he believes to be Gustave's murderer, because it would upset him. This is a man who knows his duty, but lacks the strength of character to fulfil it.

When we next meet him, a significant change has occurred. Yes, Adélaïde seems to be the main focus of his resolve, and it is also true that his plan is to leave Sweden, but the sense of going back to do the duty he owes to the Danish people has significantly strengthened; he no longer appears simply to be running away from an unpleasant situation (*GW*, III. ix). By the end of Act III he will even have been persuaded to stay and act directly against Christierne by rescuing Léonor. He attempts to do this not by actions, but by interceding with Christierne; he is, however, unable to convert his intentions into reality. As the exchange becomes more and more furious, Christierne eventually reveals that it is he, not Frédéric, who is to marry Adélaïde, and the true limitations of Frédéric's new-found assertiveness are revealed when his subsequent outburst succeeds only in having him placed under house arrest. As Christierne comments: 'En imprécations, l'impuissance est féconde' (*GW*, IV. ii).

This is the last time we see him, but not the last we hear of him. He keeps his promise to Adélaïde by rescuing Léonor, but in the only way likely to work with Christierne, by deeds not words. The various threads come together in his farewell, quoted to us by Léonor. He relinquishes all claims not only to Adélaïde, but also to Sweden, as he goes to do his duty as the new King of Denmark. We have seen the strengthening of his resolve to return to his own country, but, for the first time, he can do it without leaving us with the suspicion that he is running away from problems. Now the situation in Sweden is stable, and it is logical for him to leave power entirely in the hands of the new ruler, Gustave. Hence, Piron does not bring him back on stage to pronounce his own farewell. This is how Piron, via Léonor, reports his final actions in the drama; he progresses from prince to king during the course of the narration, but, in a final sigh, the last word still goes to his unrequited love:

> Tous les chefs de la flotte, & le Prince à leur tête,
> Les armes à la main, volant sur notre bord,
> Fondent sur le tillac où j'attendois la mort.
> Rodolphe, trop fidèle aux volontés d'un traître,
> Glorieux & puni, meurt aux yeux de son maître.
> Je demeure sans force aux pieds de l'inhumain.
> Le nouveau Roi m'aborde; & me tendant la main,
> Honteux de mes liens, les détache lui-même.
> *Pour prémices*, dit-il, *de mon pouvoir suprême,*
> *Madame, je vous rends à votre illustre fils.*
> *Que son épouse & m'aime & m'estime à ce prix.*
> *Allez, & de la paix soyez le premier gage.*
> *Mon cœur n'en goûtera de long-temps l'avantage.*
> *C'est pour l'y rétablir que je vais m'éloigner:*
> *Et ne mettre mes soins désormais qu'à régner.*
> Frédéric à ces mots, qu'un soupir accompagne,
> Me laisse, & fait partir la flotte qu'il regagne.
> (*GW*, V. v, Piron's italics)

Nevertheless, in a speech where he is otherwise identified by rank, that sigh is the only action attributed to him by name, and his promise that henceforth he will devote himself entirely to his duties as king suggests that it is the final act of a part of him that is to be left behind.

In many respects Frédéric is the most interesting character in the play, since, during the course of the action, he is the only one who truly changes; others keep and reveal secrets that change them in the perception of the audience and of other characters, but they remain fundamentally the same. Only Frédéric develops inwardly, and so his discovery of his true destiny and mature identity makes him the most complex character in the tragedy. Although he is not the central character, the play is about his coming of age.

Another incident worthy of note in Léonor's narration is the death of Rodolphe. Adélaïde is the stable figure who provides the focus of attention for the three main male characters, but even she is open to misinterpretation by both Christierne and Gustave. Around her are characters who are almost all subject to changing identity in one way or another, with only two exceptions: Sophie, such a minor character that she barely interests us, and Rodolphe. In a play in which the instability of the characters is the norm, the last character we would expect to be constant even to the point of dying for his master is the villain's servant, particularly in view of Casimir's comments about the dubious nature of Christierne's relationship to his retinue.[23] Rodolphe's death, which is certainly not essential to Léonor's narration, seems to be included to surprise us: even inconstancy cannot be relied upon; constancy can be found where we least expect it.

To end, we should examine how Piron exploits these changes of identity in dramatic terms. Take first the fact that Léonor is Gustave's mother. She first appears in I. v, also Adélaïde's first appearance, and a dialogue between her and Frédéric. Léonor contributes only two part-alexandrines towards the end of the scene, and is unlikely to attract significant attention, appearing rather to fulfil the conventional role of confidante. Consequently, when Adélaïde identifies her in the opening speech of the subsequent scene as Gustave's mother, there is little sense of surprise, since we have scarcely been given any reason to be interested in her or her identity. Piron goes on to exploit the suspense of whether she will be found out by the villains, even making a *coup de théâtre* of the moment when her secret is revealed by unexpectedly having her do it herself, but, for the audience, he makes no mystery of her identity. A similar underplaying of dramatic effect can be observed in the revelation of Casimir's true loyalties.

The issue of the death of Gustave and the identity of his murderer is rather more drawn out, but, again, Piron does not exploit the mystery as much as he could. True, the initial announcement of his death immediately follows the news of the death of Christierne's wife, a death that we have no reason to believe to be anything but genuine, which encourages us to believe that Gustave's death is also real, but two other factors have a stronger impact. The first is that the play is called *Gustave Wasa*. It is not usual for classical writers to name plays after characters who are dead before the action begins; furthermore, the audience would be expected to know that, historically, Kristian was defeated by Gustav. So it is unlikely that the news of his death will be taken seriously; however, Piron allows us to appreciate, perhaps with a sense of superiority, some interesting scenes based on this theme — the gloating of Christierne and Rodolphe, the despair of Casimir and Frédéric, the latter's unsuccessful attempt to break the news to Adélaïde and her subsequent grief — before introducing another trick to reinforce our doubts about the veracity of the report: the prophetic dream. Interestingly, however, Léonor's dream is only the last in a whole list of reasons she gives for not believing the news: enemies are often over-confident; this would not be the first time Christierne had tried to deceive them (an incorrect explanation, since Christierne believes the news himself at this stage); Christierne may be guilty of believing a false report because it is what he wants to hear (the correct explanation); if rumours are to be believed, Léonor herself is dead; her feeling of confidence that he is still alive is a good sign. And then there is the dream, or, in fact, not one, but two dreams:

> Deux fois le Ciel, deux fois cette nuit à mes yeux,
> Ce Ciel au châtiment trop lent à se résoudre,
> A présenté Gustave ayant en main la foudre.
> De la pourpre royale il étoit revêtu:
> Tandis que, sous ses pieds, Christierne abattu,
> Cachant dans la poussière un front sans diadème,
> Restoit dans cet opprobre, en horreur aux siens même.
> Est-ce nous annoncer mon fils privé du jour? (*GW*, I. vi)

This is a prediction not only that Gustave will turn up alive, but also of the eventual outcome of the drama, and the fact that it coincides with historical fact, coupled with our knowledge of classical convention, should convince us that it is true. Adélaïde is convinced enough to have her hope restored.

If Gustave is not dead, who then is the man who claims to be his murderer? If we are in any doubt, his behaviour on his first appearance, when he tries to conceal his identity from Casimir,[24] should give us the final clue. Hence, for most spectators, the issue in this scene is not the murderer's identity, but whether Casimir might mistakenly kill Gustave, although even this is not exploited at any length by Piron; it is resolved and Gustave identified definitively in the space of some seven lines (*GW*, II. iii). As with Léonor, the source of interest quickly becomes not who he is, but whether his identity will be discovered. The moment of discovery is, however, handled a little differently, for while, as we have seen, the revelation of Léonor's identity to Christierne comes as a momentary surprise, in the case of Gustave, tension is built up over a longer period. In IV. iii Rodolphe tells Christierne not only that Gustave is not dead, but that he suspects that the man posing as his murderer is himself Gustave. Since this suspicion is correct, our anxieties are awakened and continue as the two men hatch their plot to see if his mother will give away his identity at a mock execution, then bring in Léonor followed by Gustave himself. Yet, when the moment arrives, one is struck by how little time Piron spends on it. The suspense before the execution could have been drawn out; Léonor might have denied that her reaction proved the stranger to be her son; Gustave could have continued the pretence about his identity. Instead, from the appearance of Gustave, it is all over in a mere five lines:

CHRISTIERNE

> Tiens, regarde ces fers.
> Est-ce là donc un prix digne de tes reproches?
> Suis-je accusable encor du meurtre de tes proches?

Qu'il périsse; & qu'enfin ce coup nous rende amis.
Qu'on l'immole. Frappez!

LÉONOR *retenant le bras du garde*

Arrête!

CHRISTIERNE

Ah! c'est ton fils.

GUSTAVE

Oui, je le suis. (*GW*, IV. v)

Again, Piron prefers the heroic gesture to a potentially less noble wringing of the emotions.

One scene which Piron does draw out to increase the emotional effect — perhaps the only example in the play of him doing this — is that in which Gustave uses his assumed identity as his own killer to gain an interview with Adélaïde and then, instead of identifying himself, tests her by observing her reactions. Perhaps the difference in treatment is due to this being a scene that inspires pity, while the other instances we have looked at often have elements of terror, but perhaps it is also important that the issue here is not just Gustave's concealed identity, but Adélaïde's too: we need the test to establish the constancy of her character much more than we do on occasions when a concealed identity is revealed. It is also important, though, that, as usual, the revelation of Gustave's identity is a surprise only for Adélaïde, not for the audience. Piron prefers to exploit the more drawn-out emotions we experience by appreciating the dramatic irony of the situation rather than the fleeting surprise of a *coup de théâtre*.[25]

We have noted too the paradox in Christierne's character of the brutal man who is hopelessly in love, but we may also feel that, as elsewhere, Piron reveals this contradiction too quickly for it to come as a surprise. We have barely had time to familiarize ourselves with his character, even though Piron spends his opening speeches making his cruelty obvious, before the contradiction appears, and, since we have not yet been introduced to Adélaïde, the revelation of the identity of the beloved makes less impact than it might have done had Piron delayed the revelation.

So, even though *Gustave Wasa* has a potentially sensationalistic plot, studded with revelations about hidden identities of one form or another — most of them his own inventions, rather than matters of historical fact — Piron prefers to exploit more noble tragic emotions of pity and terror (this latter achieved more by suspense than horror) rather than the sensationalism of surprise, and so repeatedly underplays the moments of revelation. It is significant that the only thread concerning identity to be sustained through the whole play is the story of Frédéric's gradual process of self-discovery, for such psychological development is the proper subject matter for classical tragedy.

Notes to Chapter 3

1. For a consideration of Prévost's accusations of plagiarism in relation to this play, see my 'Piron, Prévost and a Case of Plagiarism: *Gustave Wasa* and the *Mémoires et aventures d'un homme de qualité*', *British Journal for Eighteenth-Century Studies*, 27 (2004), 189–201.

2. René Aubert de Vertot d'Aubœuf, *Histoire des révolutions de Suède* (Paris: Brunet, 1695). The most accessible edition is the facsimile of the edition of 1819, 2 vols (Paris: Ménard et Desenne, 1819), available on the Bibliothèque Nationale's Gallica website <http://gallica.bnf.fr/>, and it is from this that references are taken, identified in the text by the abbreviation V.
3. This is the authentic spelling of the name Vertot and Piron spell Gustave Wasa. The issue of names here is not entirely straightforward: Vertot Gallicizes all names in his history, but Piron sometimes further modifies them in his play. I have retained their forms when referring specifically to their texts, but have gone back to original spellings when referring to the historical figures. Even this, however, is not without complications, for Swedish history often has its own variants for the names of non-Swedes, as in the case of Kristian, who is Christian in his native Danish, and becomes Christiern in Vertot and Christierne in Piron's text. I have preferred to use the Swedish forms in my main text, but notes give other variants and also point out the links between these forms of the names and those used by Vertot and Piron.
4. Michael Roberts, *The Early Vasas: A History of Sweden, 1523–1611* (Cambridge: Cambridge University Press, 1968), p. 20. The first part of this study, 'The end of the Union of Kalmar' (pp. 1–24), provides a useful, concise summary of the relevant events depicted in Vertot.
5. Although Vertot's history is certainly largely accurate in its overall telling of the story, it is less clear how many of the colourful and very precise details are based on absolute fact, but that need not concern us here.
6. Vertot's Sténon Sture, who becomes simply Sténon in Piron's text.
7. The term generally used in English for Kristian II's beheading on 8 November 1520 of 82 people, with more in the following days; Vertot calls it simply 'le massacre de Stockholm'; the more colourful English expression refers directly to the Swedes' own name for the event — 'Stockholms blodbad' — although 'the Stockholm Massacre' is found in some English sources.
8. The works of Racine feature more than one example.
9. Nameless in Vertot, she was Isabella, also known as Elisabeth, Infanta of Spain, and with a number of other titles to her name.
10. Since it is this version of events that is found in Piron's source, it is the most important to us here. Vertot's account of this relationship is not entirely correct, however, although the reality is no less rum than what he describes. It was not Sigbrit Villoms who was the mistress of Kristian, but her daughter Dyveke. He had begun his relationship with her before his marriage, and it continued until Dyveke died some two years later. But even if this means that Kristian was not guilty of the gerontophilia of which Vertot accuses him, everything else in his account is accurate, from Sigbrit's nationality and social rank to the power she wielded: Kristian made her a councillor, and she even claimed to have telepathic power over him; neither does her influence appear to have abated with her daughter's death.
11. This device is less likely to draw the audience's attention to the alteration to historical fact than the introduction of an invented detail like a divorce, even if this possibility is mentioned in the text, or making Christierne an unmarried man.
12. Vertot's Fridéric d'Oldenbourg.
13. While the fact that he is Kristian's uncle is not in itself conclusive proof that he is his senior, the contrary is sufficiently unusual to suggest that Vertot would have given some indication had it been the case; in fact, Fredrik was some ten years older than Kristian — he celebrated his fiftieth birthday in the year after the Bloodbath of Stockholm.
14. Othon Crumpein in Vertot, historically Otto Krumpen.
15. This issue is considered in more detail in my 'Piron, Prévost and a Case of Plagiarism', pp. 191–94.
16. Christine in Vertot's index, although she remains nameless in the main text.
17. His forename is spelt Søren in his native Danish.
18. Sten Sture died before the Bloodbath, but, in a sense, Kristian still contrived to include him among those executed by exhuming and defiling his body.
19. Otto Krumpen was at the head of the Danish troops.
20. Lake Vättern, although most accounts place the battle to its west on the smaller Lake Åsunden, and it is indeed on the latter that the town identified here as Bogesund is to be found.

21. Bogesund, renamed Ulricehamn in 1741 in honour of Queen Ulrica Eleonora, is situated at the northern tip of Lake Åsunden.
22. I. vi. She is present in I. v, but speaks only two lines.
23. It is true that in I. ii Christierne expresses his absolute faith in Rodolphe, so his final fate is not a complete surprise, but, of course, Casimir provides proof that Christierne is not a reliable judge in such matters.
24. '*Gustave* [...] *détourne la vue à sa rencontre, & semble vouloir l'éviter*' (*GW*, II. iii).
25. Piron's preference coincides with Diderot's later criticism of the *coup de théâtre*. See the latter's *Entretiens sur 'Le Fils naturel'* for his dislike of the sudden surprise produced by *coups de théâtre* (*Œuvres complètes*, ed. by Herbert Dieckman and others, 33 vols (Paris: Hermann, 1975–), x (1980), 91–93), and his eloquent writing on the advantages of producing suspense by making the audience aware of what is going on rather than storing up surprises in *De la poésie dramatique* (*Œuvres complètes*, X, 368–71). Throughout this play Piron's aim seems to be to avoid the sensationalism of a sequence of *coups de théâtre* produced by recognition scenes that he had criticized in *Colombine-Nitétis* (1723), his parody of Danchet's *Nitétis* (see *CN*, iii, vii, ix, xii, xiii).

CHAPTER 4

❖

The Other Tragedies

Callisthène and *Fernand Cortès*

Piron's first and third tragedies, both much less successful than *Gustave Wasa*, share with it and with each other enough common features to make it sensible to consider them together. Nevertheless, in the matter of its treatment of its source text, *Callisthène* (1730)[1] does show significant differences from its successors, most obviously by being expanded from a very brief original, rather than compressed from lengthy histories as we have seen with *Gustave Wasa* and will encounter again with *Fernand Cortès* (1744). Although in all three of his tragedies Piron prefers historical to mythological subjects, the fact that for his debut he chose classical history, rather than the more exotic subjects of his later tragedies, makes the subject matter of *Callisthène* the most conventional of the trio.

Piron identifies its source as a single paragraph from the *Historiae Philippicae* of Marcus Junianus Justinus.[2] This is Piron's translation of that paragraph, which he also quotes in the original Latin, in the preface of 1758:

> Alexandre le Grand, irrité contre le philosophe Callisthène, de ce qu'il désapprouvoit hautement qu'il se voulût faire adorer, à la façon des Rois de Perse, feignit de croire qu'il trempoit dans une conspiration formée contre lui; &, sur ce prétexte, non content de lui avoir fait inhumainement couper les lèvres, le nez & les oreilles, ainsi défiguré & mutilé, il le faisoit traîner à sa suite, enfermé avec un chien, dans une cage de fer, pour être, à son armée, un spectacle d'horreur & d'épouvante. Lysimaque, disciple de ce vertueux personnage, touché de le voir languir dans une misère qu'il ne s'étoit attirée que par une louable franchise, lui fit tenir du poison qui le délivra de tant de tourmens & d'indignités. Alexandre l'ayant su, en fut si transporté de colère, qu'il fit exposer Lysimaque à la rage d'un lion affamé. Quand ce brave homme vit venir à lui le monstre prêt à le dévorer, il s'enveloppa le bras de son manteau, lui plongea la main dans la gueule; &, lui ayant arraché la langue, l'étendit mort sur la place. Un acte si courageux frappa le Roi d'une admiration qui le désarma, & qui lui rendit, depuis, Lysimaque plus cher que jamais. (*Cal*, préface, pp. 180–81; XV. iii. 3–9)

Horrible as this is, the original is even worse, for, although he includes it in his quotation of the Latin text, in the description of the mutilation of Callisthenes, Piron does not translate the phrase 'eumque truncatis omnibus membris' (*Cal*, préface, p. 180; XV. iii. 4) — 'il [...] lui [fit] tronquer tous les membres'.

This stated choice of source is in itself interesting: not only is Justinus less reliable and often more sensationalistic than many other historians, as Piron must have known,[3] this particular paragraph, included after the event to give the reader information about Lysimachus, is itself more highly coloured, not to say far-fetched, than the version included at the correct point in the chronological sequence:

> Il [Alexander the Great] adopta ensuite un usage qu'il avait différé d'abord d'emprunter à l'orgueil des rois perses, pour ne pas éveiller trop de mécontentement en les adoptant tous à la fois: au lieu de le saluer, il voulut qu'on se prosternât devant lui. Nul ne s'y opposa plus vivement que Callisthène. Ce refus lui coûta la vie, à lui et à beaucoup de nobles Macédoniens: ils furent tous mis à mort sous prétexte de trahison. (XII. vii. 1–2)

Piron would also have known that other accounts of the death of Callisthenes fail to back up as historical fact the details of his mutilation, his humiliation by being caged with a dog, Lysimachus's help to end his life, or, unsurprisingly, the latter's victorious fight with the lion.[4] The choice of this particular version is obviously a considered decision.

One of the significant advantages of the choice of a relatively brief text is that it is much easier to give a faithful representation of its events than with a longer narrative of the sort chosen for *Gustave Wasa* and *Fernand Cortès*, where the restrictions of length imposed by drama, to say nothing of the unities, make the inclusion of anything but the tiniest fraction of the events described impossible. How faithful a representation of that original paragraph, then, is Piron's play?

First, there is an omission that is at once odd and unsurprising; odd because it is perhaps the most striking feature of the original text, unsurprising because the *bienséances* would have made its inclusion impossible: that is, the details of Callisthenes' punishment. While it is true that it was never impossible to include descriptions of violence in narrations — the *récit de Théramène* includes some decidedly unpleasant details — Piron clearly judged Justinus's description much too sadistic to feature even in this form. Hence, Callisthène is simply threatened with unspecified torments (*Cal*, IV. viii, V. i, V. vii). It is perhaps also significant that these torments are never a reality, only a threat, for Callisthène kills himself before suffering them, not after, as in Justinus's narrative. Hence, one of the details that most strikingly sets this version of events apart from the retellings of other historians, and even from Justinus's own earlier narrative, is presented in the play only in a form so attenuated that it is barely recognizable.

This sheds interesting light on the role of the preface: we would probably expect Piron to allude to his source there, but not necessarily to quote it verbatim, particularly given the graphic nature of the material. Piron may have been obliged to protect sensibilities in the theatre, but it seems that he is anxious to share the sensationalistic details with readers of the 1758 collection. Perhaps he even saw in this a way of spicing up the events of his play, which had, of course, been a failure in the theatre. For it is impossible, having read the preface, not to see in the unspecified torments of the play text those specified there, rendering the threat to the eponymous character more terrifying. Perhaps even in the theatre Piron hoped that many of the audience would know the source text well enough to fill in the details for themselves. Hence the play ceases to be an autonymous entity, and is influenced by the spectator's or reader's knowledge of another text. Bearing this in mind, we may even feel that Piron has been selective in the way he has decided to impart his information to his readers: the translated version is horrifying, but the omission of one detail means that the full horror is revealed only to those who can read the Latin text — given the differences in the education of the sexes in the eighteenth century, it is not impossible that it was his female readers Piron aimed to protect from the original text.

The events of the rest of the paragraph are treated like building blocks; they are all there, but not connected in the way that they are found in the original. The original sequence of events can be expressed as follows:

a) Callisthenes refuses to support Alexander's introduction of prostration,
b) so Alexander falsely accuses him of plotting against him
c) and has him mutilated and humiliated.
d) Lysimachus provides Callisthenes with poison to put an end to his suffering;
e) Callisthenes kills himself,
f) so Alexander punishes Lysimachus by throwing him to a lion.
g) Lysimachus kills the lion.
h) Alexander is so impressed that he forgives Lysimachus.

Piron, whose subsequent tragedies are packed with events, clearly found this too straightforward to fill five acts, so he complicates things by repetition — a sequence of reprieves that increase the suspense over the fate of Callisthène. Some rearrangement is also needed to make Callisthène's death and not Lysimaque's triumph the denouement. In the list that follows events have the same letter code as those to which they are related in the source text; added linking events have no code, although relationships with the original tale are shown in brackets; since it is my intention here to highlight the treatment of the paragraph quoted in the preface, I have omitted from this synopsis any mention of additions that are unrelated to it:

b) Alexandre falsely accuses Callisthène of plotting against him
   and threatens him with execution. (Related to, but not identical with, c.)
   With the help of Lysimaque he is reprieved. (Related to, but not identical with, d.)
a) Callisthène refuses to support Alexandre's introduction of prostration;
c) Alexandre decides not to execute him, but to keep him alive in dreadful torments.
   (Although not carried out, as it is in the original.)
   Callisthène is reprieved on the intervention of Alexandre's wife Roxane.
   Lysimaque again supports Callisthène (related to, but not identical with, d),
f) so Alexandre punishes him by throwing him to a lion.
g) Lysimaque kills the lion.
h) Alexandre is so impressed that he forgives Lysimaque.
d) Still worried about Callisthène's fate, Lysimaque gives him the means to end his life before he is subjected to torture. (A dagger taken from Lysimaque by Callisthène, not the poison of the source text.)
c) Alexandre again threatens Callisthène with dreadful torments,
e) so Callisthène kills himself.
   Alexandre is overcome with remorse and forgives Callisthène. (Related to h, but there may be another source for this incident.)

We can see that by a system of rearrangement and near repetition Piron has drawn out the original into a longer, more complex sequence of events. We have already come quite a way from that original paragraph, but, so far, it is clearly the inspiration behind the main incidents. However, there is evidence that Piron did not limit himself to this single section of Justinus.

We have seen that Justinus's earlier narration of Callisthenes' death adds nothing to the events described in the later more elaborate version quoted by Piron, but there is another mention of him, the first and only other time we encounter him in Justinus's text. At a banquet, Alexander is bragging about the superiority of his exploits to those of his father:

> Mais un de ses vieux officiers, Clitos, confiant dans l'amitié du roi, où il tenait le premier rang, défendit la mémoire de Philippe et loua ses exploits. Le roi en fut si choqué qu'arrachant un javelot à l'un de ses gardes, il en perce Clitos au milieu du festin, puis, dans l'exaltation du meurtre, il reproche au mort de s'être fait l'avocat de Philippe et d'avoir loué le génie militaire de son père. Mais, lorsque, sa fureur assouvie, son cœur se fut calmé, et que la réflexion eut succédé à la colère, considérant tantôt la personne du mort, tantôt la cause du meurtre, il regretta ce qu'il avait fait. Il avait accueilli l'éloge de son père avec une colère que des injures mêmes n'auraient pas méritée; il s'affligeait de la perte d'un ami vieux et innocent, qu'il avait tué dans l'orgie d'un festin. Portant dans le remords la même fureur que naguère dans sa colère, il voulut mourir. D'abord il s'abandonne aux pleurs, il embrasse le mort, touche ses blessures, et fait l'aveu de sa démence, comme si Clitos l'entendait. Il saisit le javelot et le tourne contre lui-même et il se serait tué, si ses courtisans n'étaient intervenus. (XII. vi. 3–8)

The description of Alexander's despair continues at length and ends as follows:

> Aussi persista-t-il à ne pas manger pendant quatre jours. Enfin il se laissa fléchir aux prières de son armée entière, qui le conjurait de ne point porter le regret d'un seul homme jusqu'à les perdre tous, et, après les avoir amenés aux confins de la barbarie, de ne pas les abandonner au milieu de nations ennemies dont la guerre a irrité la colère. Ce qui contribua beaucoup à le fléchir, ce furent les instances du philosophe Callisthène, qu'il avait connu familièrement en suivant avec lui les leçons d'Aristote et qu'il venait d'appeler près de lui pour écrire l'histoire de ses exploits. (XII. vi. 15–17)

Although not integral to the plot like the events we have already examined, and so used more episodically, this incident is also exploited repetitively. There is a relatively straightforward allusion near the end of the play as Callisthène predicts that his death will satisfy Alexandre, so that Lysimaque and Léonide will have nothing to fear:

> Voyez-moi donc en paix terminer mes ennuis;
> Et craignez peu, pour vous, les horreurs que je fuis.
> La colère du Roi ne veut qu'un sacrifice;
> Le repentir en lui suit de près l'injustice.
> Quand du sang de Clytus il eut rougi sa main,
> Sans moi, du même fer, il se perçoit le sein.
> De mon sang répandu, ses vertus vont renaître. (*Cal*, V. v)

The compression of events, making Callisthène the person who prevented Alexandre's attempt on his own life rather than just the person who consoles him, is clearly a way of making the incident more striking as well as more concise, but we may also note that there is no explanation of the reasons for Alexandre's attack on Clytus. This is partly for dramatic reasons: it would be inappropriate to waste time on this anecdote as the play approaches its catastrophe, those who know their Greek history will be able to fill in the details from memory,[5] and, for those who do not, they are not essential to understand the point being made. But perhaps dramatic concision is not Piron's only concern, for he has already made use of the missing details elsewhere. During the scene that ends with Alexandre's decision not to kill Callisthène but to keep him alive to subject him to an even worse fate, Alexandre accuses him of spreading sedition, and asks him what he has been saying. This is Callisthène's reply:

Rien qui dût vous déplaire.
Quelqu'un, pour vous louer, déprimoit votre père;
Je ne crois pas Philippe un objet de mépris;
J'ai su le relever, sans abaisser son fils.
J'ai dit que sa prudence égala son courage;
Que vous avez, sous lui, fait votre apprentissage;
Que, si la mort ne l'eût surpris dans son projet,
Il eût pu faire un jour ce que vous avez fait;
Mais la Grèce vengée, & la Perse conquise,
Qu'il n'eût jamais poussé plus loin son entreprise
Et que ... (*Cal*, IV. vii)

Although Alexandre keeps his control in a way that his historical counterpart did not in the tale of his murder of Clitos, the very fact that he interrupts Callisthène signals a first step in the deterioration of relations between the two.

So, if Piron uses the events following the death of Clitos to make one point, he is vague about the reason for it because he has already made use of that in another context. When Callisthène makes his prediction that his own death will put an end to any danger for Léonide and Lysimaque, Piron stops short of having him predict that it will also lead to Alexandre's forgiveness of him — this would be to give away the ending — but, in fact, this is precisely what happens; just as in the tale of Clitos, as soon as Callisthène is dead, Alexandre realizes his mistake, forgives him, and ends the play with a speech expressing his despair and guilt. As I have suggested, there is a link with Alexander's forgiveness of Lysimachus after his victory over the lion, but the tale of Clitos is clearly a more direct source.

Just as Piron has taken Clitos's defence of Philip and attributed it to Callisthène, he also makes use of two other episodes from Justinus that, in the original, are unrelated to Callisthenes. One is treated straightforwardly: Justinus tells us that in Egypt Alexander bribed priests to identify him as the son of Ammon, the Egyptian god associated by the Greeks with Zeus;[6] in the scene in which Callisthène admits he has voiced support for Alexandre's father, he also responds to Alexandre's claim that he was proclaimed son of Jupiter by remarking that it was only because the priests had been bribed (*Cal*, IV. vii). The episode thus becomes yet another example of Callisthène's plain speaking. The other incident, however, is more interesting, for it again gives us an example of Piron's use of repetition, but here the repetition is strikingly combined in a single scene. This is the extract from Justinus

— Alexander is struck down with a severe illness as a result of jumping into a cold river when hot:

> Parmi ses médecins, un seul, Philippe [not to be confused with his namesake Alexander's father], proposait un remède; mais ce Philippe même était devenu suspect, à la suite d'une lettre que Parménion avait envoyée la veille de Cappadoce. Ignorant la maladie d'Alexandre, Parménion lui avait écrit de se garder du médecin Philippe, car il avait été acheté pour une grosse somme par Darius. Néanmoins le roi crut qu'il était plus sûr de se confier à la foi douteuse du médecin que de périr d'une maladie qui ne laissait aucun espoir. Il prit donc la coupe, remit la lettre au médecin et but, les yeux fixés sur son visage, tandis qu'il lisait. Le voyant calme, il se réjouit et recouvra la santé le quatrième jour. (XI. viii. 5–9)

Again, Piron links to Callisthène an incident that was not connected with his historical counterpart, but he also provides a clear statement of the original tale alongside it. We are at an earlier stage in the play: Callisthène has been declared innocent of the accusations of treachery for which he is imprisoned at the start of the action, but Alexandre is explaining why he suspected him. Just like the doctor, Callisthène is presented by Alexandre with a letter accusing him of treachery and told to read it; on being asked by Alexandre what he would have done in his place, Callisthène replies with the example of Alexandre's trust in the doctor, but with one addition to the original: it was he, Callisthène, who was behind Alexandre's decision to trust him:

ALEXANDRE

Aujourd'hui même encor, j'ai reçu ce billet.
On vous chargeoit: lisez; j'ai craint. Qu'eussiez-vous fait?
(*Pendant que Callisthène lit*)
O trône! ô triste siège environné d'abîmes!
Quiconque te remplit, craint, ou commet des crimes;
Un Roi les fuit en vain: l'indulgence ou l'erreur
Font qu'il en est toujours la victime ou l'auteur.
(*Reprenant le billet*)
Eh bien?

CALLISTHÈNE

Qu'eussé-je fait? Ce qu'au mépris des suites,
Dans les bras de la mort, vous-même un jour vous fîtes
En faveur d'un fidèle & sage médecin,
Faussement accusé d'un semblable dessein.
Votre grand cœur livra vos jours à sa science;
Vous les devez, Seigneur, à cette confiance;
Elle vous fit revivre, & revivre admiré:
La méritois-je moins, moi qui vous l'inspirai? (*Cal*, III. iv)

It is a striking scene, and, although the two seem to reach a reconciliation, Alexandre's failure to learn from his previous experience and trust Callisthène despite the letter is worrying. Ultimately he will continue to be plagued by doubts about Callisthène's loyalty to him, doubts which will be dispelled only by the former's suicide. Hence, the letter is this play's version of those concrete symbols that we have found in all the plays we have studied, an icon of the doubts that plague Alexandre about his faithful servant. Interestingly too, in this first tragedy, as in *L'École des pères*, his first comedy, Piron actually puts the symbol physically on stage; in the later plays the effect is more subtle, for in *La Métromanie*, *Gustave Wasa*, and *Fernand Cortès*, these concrete symbols are merely mentioned in the dialogue.

This effort to expand the limited material found in the source text leads to something we do not generally find in the later tragedies,[7] which is the inclusion of historical details not found there. Although claiming Justinus — indeed, a single paragraph in Justinus — as the sole source, Piron has also drawn on his wider knowledge of the history of Alexander the Great to flesh out that material. Perhaps the most significant of these additions is in Piron's exploitation of the figure of Anaxarque. The historical Anaxarchus is mentioned only once by Justinus, in a context unlinked to the story of Callisthenes; we see him advising Alexander in a way that could be linked to the flattery of his vanity we find in the play, but Justinus generally gives a positive picture of his views and his influence:

> Là, le philosophe Anaxarque lui persuada de mépriser les prédictions des mages, comme des choses fausses et incertaines, fermées à la connaissance des mortels, si elles s'accordent avec les destins, impossibles à changer, si elles sont dues à la nature. (XII. xiii. 5)

It is certainly not from this that Piron derives his role as antagonist to Callisthène, advising Alexandre to indulge his sense of superiority and causing him to mistrust the more austere views preached by Callisthène. Nevertheless, that view of him is not the playwright's invention, but is based on historical fact,[8] and provides him with a useful means of creating dramatic tension and suspense — the classic literary topos in which the man of power listens to the bad adviser and ignores the good — and helps Piron flesh out his action. Nevertheless, although the role of Anaxarque conforms for the most part to historical fact, his part in the love plot is pure fiction.

The reference to the criticism of the Lacedaemonians included by Alexander on an inscription[9] is no more than a point of detail adding to the sense of historical colour (*Cal*, III. iv), but another detail provides material for character-building towards the opening of the play. This is the fact that Hermolaus and the others with whom Callisthenes is accused of conspiring against Alexander do not implicate him in their plot.[10] Piron uses this in his first scene to indicate two things, the irrational nature of Alexandre's hatred of Callisthène, and the inevitability of a tragic outcome, since Alexandre will find evidence to condemn him whatever the truth:

LYSIMAQUE

Peut-être Hermolaüs, ou quelqu'un des complices
Vous l'a rendu suspect au milieu des supplices;
Mais, Seigneur, un coupable immole en ces momens
La vertu la plus pure à l'horreur des tourmens.

ALEXANDRE

Non, j'en ai vainement tenté la violence.
Les conjurés pour lui sont morts dans le silence.

LYSIMAQUE

Quel indice évident l'aura donc condamné?

ALEXANDRE

Me le demandez-vous? Leur silence obstiné,
Leur sacrilège audace à m'accabler d'injures;
Leur courage à braver la mort & les tortures,
Plutôt que de livrer à mon juste courroux
Le zélateur outré qui les séduisit tous. (*Cal*, I. i)

In fact, Alexandre has already given us an indication of his real motivation:

Du trône mille fois sa liberté hautaine
N'a-t-elle pas en moi blessé la majesté?
A ma gloire, à mes jours n'a-t-il pas attenté? (*Cal*, I. i)

So Callisthène's failure to massage Alexandre's pride is the real reason for his hatred, but the evidence will prove that the leap of faith that takes him from 'gloire' to 'jours' is unwarranted. This is a characteristic theme for Piron, and central to this play: appearances can always be misunderstood by someone determined to impose his own version of reality on the outside world.

Alongside this fidelity to historical sources, Piron makes two major distortions of historical fact: the invention of the character of Léonide, the object of the love of both Lysimaque and Anaxarque and the sister of Callisthène, and the love plot that surrounds her; and the decision to make Callisthène a Spartan.[11] However, since there are common features here with *Fernand Cortès* — and, in the case of the love plot, with *Gustave Wasa* too — we shall return to these issues after we have examined the relation of the former to its source text.

As Piron's career as tragic dramatist progressed, his subjects became more exotic, progressing from traditional classical history in his first tragedy to more modern history in the subsequent works, and from the unusual setting of Northern Europe in *Gustave Wasa* to the even more striking location of the New World for *Fernand Cortès* — Piron even refers near the beginning of this play to its wider horizons in comparison with those of his first tragedy, as Aguilar tells Cortès his achievements have exceeded even those of Alexander the Great (*FC*, I. iv).

Another progression we may note is that the relationship of the plots of the plays to their sources becomes less precise. Most of the events in *Callisthène* can be linked in some way with the source, even if this is not limited to the single paragraph quoted by Piron or even to Justinus's history. In the case of *Gustave Wasa*, the background material tends to be generally faithful to Vertot's history, but specific historical links with events in the action itself are less frequent and less specific. Nevertheless, as with *Callisthène*, apart from the female character at the centre of the love plot, there are a number of links between the major characters — and even some of the more minor ones — and the historical narrative. How does this compare with *Fernand Cortès*?

The 1758 preface to *Fernand Cortès* does not include an unambiguous statement of the source of the work, as those of the earlier tragedies do, but a footnote to Piron's reference to the motto on Cortés's coat of arms refers us to 'François Lopez de Gomara, *Histoire générale des Indes avec la conquête du Mexique et de la Nouvelle Espagne*'. *La historia general de las Indias* by Francisco López de Gómara was first published complete in 1554[12] and appeared in a French translation by Martin

Fumée[13] in 1569. It is the title of the augmented fifth edition of this translation of 1584 (reprinted 1605 and 1606) that corresponds most closely to that quoted by Piron in his preface.[14] Clearly this was one of Piron's sources, but there are at least two indications that, as with *Callisthène*, he may also have used another source or sources, or perhaps just drawn on his general knowledge of the historical facts. One sign is that the Gallicizations of the characters' names in the play are those that had become more common in French, rather than those used by Fumée: Fernand Cortès and not Ferdinand Cortés for Hernán Cortés, and Montézume rather than Fumée's Moteczuma.[15] The other is a comment in Cortès's speech urging the Spanish to go to battle against the Mexicans at the end of the fourth act:

> Imitons le Romain
> Qui se rendit l'effroi du rivage africain.
> Que notre flotte, espoir d'une honteuse fuite,
> Par nous-mêmes en cendre à leurs yeux soit réduite;
> Et que l'ennemi juge à cet embrasement,
> Si de sa fermeté l'Espagnol se dément ... (*FC*, IV. viii)

The city of Mexico was built on a lake, so this reference to the use of boats in the forthcoming battle is not out of place; however, Gómara includes no such detail in his narrative. Nevertheless, one of the most frequently repeated details in even the most concise tellings of the tale of Cortés is the fact that he burnt his fleet on landing in Central America to indicate that there was no possibility of turning back. Gómara's version of events is slightly different: his rather cryptic phrase suggests not that the ships were burnt, but that they were sunk by being turned side-on to the wind: 'Cortés commanda que les neuf vaisseaux qui lui restoient, donnassent à travers, à fin d'oster toute esperance à ses soldats de plus retourner en arriere' (G, p. 78b). Despite Piron's classical reference,[16] it would seem to be too much of a coincidence if his passage were not inspired by the more popular version of Cortés's action, but it also indicates that he must have known it from a source other than Gómara.[17]

Nevertheless, the key events of the play accord with Gómara's version of historical fact, the action beginning well after Hernán Cortés has disembarked in Central America and made his way, by means of a combination of warfare and diplomacy, to the city of Mexico, or Tinochtitlán,[18] forming an alliance with the Tlaxcalans and their leader Xicohténcatl[19] on the way. They have made a peaceful entry into the city of Mexico and won the confidence of Montezuma, but then, to end an uprising by the Mexicans, place him under house arrest and, for a short period, put him in irons. This is how we find him at the beginning of the play, and the events leading up to this action are reviewed in the first scene between Montézume and the Grand Prêtre, the representative not only of the Mexican religion, but of all that is anti-Spanish, and the only other Mexican character. This is how Gómara describes the events leading up to Montezuma being put in irons:

> Vingt iours après la prinse de Moteczuma, arriuerent ceux qui estoient allez querir auec son cachet Qualpopoca, lequel ils amenerent, & vn sien fils, & quinxe personnes, lesquels se trouuoient chargez. Apres que ceux ci eurent confessé la mort des Espagnols susdits, & mesme que [ç'auoit][20] esté par le

> conseil de Moteczuma, & apres auoir esté interrogez par plusieurs fois sur ce mesme fait, & y auoir persisté[,] Cortés les condamna tous à estre bruslez: ce qui fut executé en la grand place deuãt tout le peuple sans aucune esmotion: mais auec vn grãd estonnement de tous. Ce pendant qu'on menoit Qualpopoca au supplice[,] Cortés dit à [Moteczuma][21] que par la depositiõ de Qualpopoca son vassal il se trouuoit chargé de la mort des siens, & lui fait mettre les fers aux pieds. Mais le mesme iour après que Qualpopoca eust esté executé[,] il les lui osta, & lui donna liberté de s'en retourner à son palais. (G, p. 104b)

This is how Montézume describes his imprisonment and the reasons for it in the play:

> J'ai vu fondre sur moi cent guerriers plus qu'humains,
> Dont le moindre est l'effroi de mille Américains.
> Leur Général, aux yeux de ma garde interdite,
> Se venoit plaindre à moi d'un complot qu'on médite,
> Me demandoit raison de qui l'osoit trahir,
> Et, la foudre à la main, se faisoit obéir.
> J'ai cédé. Qui de vous m'a creusé cet abîme!
> Tu dis que l'infortune est un effet du crime:
> Celui-ci n'étant pas dans le nombre des miens,
> Serois-je par hasard, la victime des tiens? (*FC*, I. i)

There are a number of features to note. The actual uprising of the historical account has become merely a threatened action, a plot that has been discovered. The reason is presumably one of dramatic expediency: the tensions raised by the uprising during the Act IV–V interval would be significantly decreased if the play began with an indication that the Spaniards had already emerged victorious from another uprising. Neither, however, is there any indication, beyond Montézume being in chains, that the culprits have been punished; the fact that the uprising has not actually happened does not prevent the punishment of those who plotted it. This could be explained simply as the omission of details that are dramatically redundant, but it also has a significant impact on the characterization of the protagonist.

Two givens of the history of the conquistadors, which appear in any telling of the story, are that the Spaniards plundered the gold and silver of the Central Americans and that the Central Americans made human sacrifices to their gods. The extent to which each is stressed will depend on the point of view of the teller of the tale. Gómara, whose work was published very shortly after the death of Cortés in 1547, is clearly proud of his country's achievements, seeing no need to apologize for what for him are the justified actions of his compatriot — even the plundering of treasures from the conquered country is seen as a legitimate goal of the expedition — and he would have expected his readers to share this view. Nevertheless, some legitimization of violence perpetrated by his compatriots can be seen in the fact that he does not spare us details of the cruelty of the Central Americans' religious rites. Piron cannot rely on such patriotism, but clearly also wants to paint his eponymous hero in a positive light — indeed, in his preface he defends the real Cortés against the criticisms of anticolonialists among his contemporaries (*FC*, préface, p. 209). Any mention in the play of executing enemies would clearly compromise the contrast Piron is setting up between the two nations as well as his depiction of Cortès as a paragon of virtue, but, worse, an indication that the method of execution was burning, a favourite of the Inquisition, would provide a ready reminder that the Central Americans had no monopoly on the commission of violence in the name of religion.

Nevertheless, it is not only Cortès who is being presented in the best possible light here; so is Montézume, whom the plot of the play requires to be a viable suitor for Elvire. So not only did he have no role in the conspiracy against the Spanish, his bravery too is stressed by the fact that it takes a whole army to make him submit to the humiliation of being put in chains. In Gómara's version, there is no such struggle: Montezuma is made to submit to house arrest entirely by diplomatic means (G, pp. 102a–103b). Piron's character is shown to be a much harder man to bully than his historical counterpart.

These are not the only details to emerge in this first scene that aid the favourable characterization of these characters; we also discover that Montézume has converted to Christianity. Stressing the missionary aspect of Cortès's invasion takes our attention away from the lust for gold, and, as for Montézume, not only is this Westernization essential for him to be a suitable husband for the daughter of a Spanish nobleman, it also shows his espousal of the best of the attributes of the invaders; it is the best explanation that Piron can provide for behaviour that could, otherwise, look like treachery towards his own people, and Piron's insistence on the fact that, in abandoning his religion, he is rejecting human sacrifice makes it difficult to feel that his change is not for the better. The religion of his people, Montézume tells the High Priest, is not only false, it is cruel (*FC*, I. i). Piron has learnt a useful lesson from Gómara, for he too makes much of Cortès's success in converting the natives or, at least, dissuading them from making human sacrifices, but his character's treatment of Montézume and the rest of his people differs from Gómara's narrative; this passage describes events that occur during the house arrest of Montezuma, but before the execution of the insurgents and his chaining:

> Pendant la prison de Moteczuma[,] Cortés par vne belle, & longue harangue lui feit entendre, & aux principaux de sa court, & aux plus grãds prestres de ses tẽples, ce qui ils deuoient tous croire du vrai Dieu tout puissant, createur du ciel & de la terre, & de tout ce qui est en iceux: & feit tãt par ces remõstrãces qu'ils promirẽt de ne tuer personne en leur sacrifices, & de mettre entre leurs idoles vn crucifix, & vne image de la vierge Marie: ce qui fut tost executé au grãd Tẽple. (G, p. 104a)

Clearly this compromise, in which all the Mexicans have abandoned human sacrifice and agreed to worship Christian images without actually abandoning their own religion, is undramatic. Hence the dramatist chooses to represent a situation of extremes — Montézume converted fully to Christianity and the High Priest rejecting it entirely — which provides him with the conflict required by his drama. It is also, as we have noted, essential for Montézume to have converted for him to play his part convincingly as rival in love to Cortès; but it is likely that there is an additional motive for change at work here, which takes us back to Piron's decision to make Callisthène a Spartan, though his historical counterpart was from Olynthus, a city that was an enemy of the Spartans.

Stereotypically the Spartans are renowned for their austerity, and in the world of eighteenth-century tragedy this implies extreme virtue and a refusal to betray one's principles. Hence Callisthène's uncompromising and self-destructive behaviour is explained: he has been brought up according to a code of conduct which teaches that sincerity is more important than life itself. The historical Callisthenes has no such motivation, and so risks looking simply foolish. Indeed, Plutarch even quotes a remark made by Alexander himself commenting on his foolishness: 'I can't stand a clever man who doesn't apply his intelligence to himself.'[22] Tragedy seeks a more noble cause for its hero's suffering than simple stupidity, a defect more suited to comedy.

Montezuma's behaviour in relation to the Spaniards risks similar accusations of foolishness. Gómara relates how he sends a message to the advancing Spaniards trying to prevent them coming to the city of Mexico, telling them (falsely) that the route is too arduous (G, p. 73a), and then offering to provide Cortés with all he might need for the return journey if he turns back (G, p. 74a). Nevertheless, although Cortés has caused many of his subjects to rise up against him (G, p. 77b), Montezuma still meets him in ceremony at the gates of his city and allows him to enter in peace (G, pp. 88b–90a). As well as providing a palace for the Spaniards (G, p. 90b), he treats them as privileged members of his society, spends much time with them, and even begins sometimes to dress like them:

> [Il][23] tenoit vne maiesté si grãde qu'il ne permettoit qu'aucun fut assis en sa presence, ou [portast][24] souliers, ou le regardast en face, exceptez quelques grands Seigneurs au ranc desquels il tenoit les Espagnols, ou pource qu'il les estimoit beaucoup, ou pour le plaisir qu'il prenoit de cõuerser souuẽt auec eux. Et de faict son plaisir y estoit si grãd que bien souuent il [changeoit][25] ses habillemens aux leurs. (G, p. 91b)

And yet, shortly afterwards, as we have already seen, he is found to be involved in a plot against them, allows himself to be placed under arrest, and is put in irons.

It is not our task here to explain the psychology behind this behaviour, which was clearly extremely complex, although perhaps more straightforward in Gómara's version than in most accounts, since he makes no mention of the Central Americans mistaking the Spaniards on horseback for centaurs, or Cortés exploiting the fact that the natives mistook them for gods;[26] what is important is to consider the effect this behaviour would have in a French classical tragedy, where the willingness to welcome these foreigners into his city and treat them as privileged guests, despite his earlier fears about them and evidence that they have conquered the cities of his compatriots, would almost certainly appear to be an act of rash stupidity, even a betrayal of the needs of his people, and the use of underhand plotting rather than open action to defeat them would signally lack the nobility required of the tragic hero. Montézume's conversion to Christianity (coupled with the refusal of the single representative of his people to make any compromise over his religion and its human sacrifices) provides an explanation for his solidarity with the Spaniards that exonerates him from the charge of foolishness in precisely the same way as Callisthène's transformation into a Spartan, and his innocence of any charge of underhand practice completes his reinvention as a hero worthy of classical tragedy.

It is not until the end of *Fernand Cortès* that Piron next draws on Gómara to any significant extent. It concludes with Piron's version of the uprising that caused the death of Montezuma; this is Gómara's account of that death:

> Ces escarmouches sanglantes durerent si longuement qu'en fin les Espagnols furent contraincts de prier Moteczuma, lequel ils auoient retenu auecques eux, de commander à ses habitans qu'ils eussent à se retirer chez eux. Mais comme ce Roi estoit monté en vn haut estage de ce Palais pour leur faire ce commandement comme ces Indiens iettoient vne infinité de pierres, vne le frappa à la tempe si estroit, qu'au bout de trois iours il en mourut. (G, p. 114b)

The similarities are clear: in the play too, Montézume is killed by his own people, and the blow comes from the crowd, but here delivered by Piron's symbol of his subjects' opposition to Montézume's Christianity and support of the Spaniards, that is, the High Priest. The method of death is similar, but the weapon different: a rock lacks the nobility required for tragedy, but would also produce an injury which, if it were going to be fatal, would be obviously grave from the outset. The substitution of a poisoned arrow allows Piron his double *coup de théâtre* in which we first believe Montézume to have been killed, then discover he received only a flesh wound, only to be surprised again by the discovery that the arrow was poisoned, followed by his rapid decline and death. The poisoned arrow, or perhaps even more the poisoned dart, is a weapon with strong Central American associations, so its use does not seem at all far-fetched, even though it is a weapon that receives no mention in the section of Gómara's history dealing with Cortés's advance on and conquest of the city of Mexico. Piron increases its significance by giving it a symbolic role indicated in a speech for the High Priest earlier in the action:

> Mes cris sont descendus au centre de la terre;
> Ils en ont évoqué le démon de la guerre;
> Devant lui, vont s'ouvrir les portes de l'enfer;
> Et la flèche sacrée est prête à fendre l'air. (*FC*, III. iv)

The printed text even provides a footnote, suggesting the authenticity of this detail — 'Cérémonie qui donnoit le signal du combat chez les barbares' (*FC*, III. iv) — but if Piron has an authentic source, it is not Gómara. The importance of this arrow, and its final appearance as a poisoned weapon which kills despite initial indications, will also lead us to see it as yet another of Piron's symbols of the disparity between appearance and reality.

Other links between the play and the source text are more tenuous, and concern only points of detail. Pedro de Alvarado, one of the most famous of Cortés's soldiers, who was left as governor of the city of Mexico during his absence despite having caused earlier problems, has similarities to his namesake in the play, Dom Pèdre, to whom Cortès hands over power at the end; Piron preserves local colour by adopting a version of Pedro closer to the original than Fumée's total Gallicization, Pierre. Aguilar, the friend and confidant of Cortès and relative of Dom Pèdre, takes his name from Cortés's interpreter, Jerónimo de Aguilar, a survivor of an earlier voyage who had escaped death and become integrated into Mayan society (G, pp. 68a–b), despite having nothing else in common with him. The detail of the arrival during the battle of the Tlaxcalans at the top of the temple (*FC*, V. i) has links with another passage found shortly after the death of Montezuma in Gómara (G, pp. 115b–116a), but these are quite approximate: Piron is taking inspiration from his source, but not showing concern for historical accuracy.

But if the beginning and end of the play are the parts that owe the most to historical fact, what of the middle? Clearly the historical situation is never forgotten, but the bulk of the action is taken up with Piron's major invention, the love plot, and in this sense *Fernand Cortès* is largely comparable to both *Callisthène* and *Gustave Wasa*. In fact, Piron tells us via his prefaces that he deplored the insistence by audiences on the inclusion of a love plot in tragedy. In the preface to *Callisthène*, for instance, he argues that love is a subject more suited to comedy; that the only type of love noble enough for tragic treatment, married love, is derided by contemporary public taste. Hence, *Callisthène* will be a tragedy not of love, but of ambition (*Cal*, préface, pp. 173–76); nevertheless, this play does have an important love plot. The issue is also alluded to at the opening of the preface to *Gustave Wasa*:

> A l'amour près, qu'il a fallu faire entrer dans mon sujet, pour me conformer à l'usage bien ou mal établi sur nos théâtres; tout est ici très-exactement tiré de l'*Histoire des Révolutions de Suède*, publiée par M. l'Abbé de Vertot. (*GW*, préface, p. 180)

Piron returns at greater length and with more obvious reservations to the issue in the preface to *Fernand Cortès*:

> L'impitoyable usage, ce tyran devant qui tout raisonnement tombe, a statué qu'il y auroit de l'amour dans nos tragédies sur peine d'être renvoyées au collège. Est-ce bien ou mal statué? *Adhuc sub judice lis est.* Nos meilleures plumes, après s'être fort exercées sur le pour & le contre, ont laissé beaucoup à dire encore là-dessus. Je me garderai bien d'oser entrer en lice. Ce sont jeux de princes: A vous le dé nos maîtres. Je révère trop les chefs des deux partis, pour en oser prendre aucun. Je n'en prends donc point: car obéir n'est pas opiner, & j'obéis; l'humble soumission, tant que l'usage est en règne, étant le seul parti qui convienne à mes pareils. Seulement, pour prix de la mienne, je demanderois un peu d'indulgence, en faveur de ce qu'il m'en a dû coûter dans un cas où subir la loi, c'étoit la subir dans toute sa rigueur. (*FC*, préface, pp. 212–13)

He seems to be hedging his bets here: disapproval of the insistence on love plots in tragedy is coupled with a pragmatic realization that, for a play to have any chance of success, it must have one. Hence, he can take the moral high ground, suggesting that he has included a love theme not because he wanted to, but to satisfy public taste. Nevertheless, he then goes on to suggest that, in this play, he has achieved an ideal integration of the love plot into his subject:

> Comment [...], sans surcharger un plan si vaste & déjà si resserré; comment, sans dénaturer un sujet sauvage & tout martial, y pouvoir introduire & faire agir à l'aise une passion de la mollesse & pourtant de l'activité de celle-ci? Comment, sans détonner, fondre une couleur si tendre & douce avec d'autres si dures & si fières? Tout ce que j'y sus, pour conserver quelque harmonie dans l'ordonnance & dans le coloris du tableau, ce fut, en construisant ma fable avec toute la précision dont j'étois capable, de faire que l'amour, cet accessoire embarrassant, devînt la base même du sujet principal. Il est en effet le ressort primitif & continuel de l'action. (*FC*, préface, p. 213)

Is this true, and how does it relate to the practice in Piron's other tragedies?

Certainly it would be difficult to argue that the love plot of *Callisthène* was well integrated into the main action. It is almost independent from the central focus identified by the title, and even risks overwhelming it. The main plot centres on Alexandre's perceptions of Callisthène: will he continue to regard his outspoken frankness as proof of treachery, or will he come to understand that it is an expression of true loyalty? He reaches this understanding only after Callisthène has fatally stabbed himself. There are links between the love plot and this principal theme: Callisthène's friend and supporter Lysimaque, and his detractor Anaxarque are also the rivals for the love of Callisthène's sister Léonide, and, while Lysimaque's love is accepted by her and supported by Callisthène, Anaxarque's is rejected by both. There is even a degree of interaction between the two plots: there is a constant fear that, because she shares Callisthène's Spartan outspokenness, Léonide might also share his fate if Alexandre decides to execute him; Callisthène's refusal to support Anaxarque's suit is one of the main reasons for the latter's attempts to turn Alexandre against him; Lysimaque's killing of Anaxarque is ostensibly due to his opposition to Callisthène, but also brings to an end the rivalry of the two men over Léonide. Nevertheless, it is difficult to avoid the sense that the two are independent threads in the action, particularly since the role of the central character in the love plot is a tangential one. Furthermore, this action, which should be subsidiary, takes up so much stage time that, particularly in view of the public's fondness for love plots, it risks seeming like the main action, with the issue of Callisthène's fate being of subsidiary interest. If Piron does manage to keep the main focus on the fate of Callisthène — and I am not fully convinced that he does — it is because the love plot is relatively lacking in tension. Indeed, he came very close to writing the tragedy of married love which he later mentioned in his preface, for, by making Léonide a Spartan, Piron allows himself to create a female character completely lacking in the traditional coquettishness and indecision which cause tension in most love plots. Hence, although Lysimaque and Léonide are not actually married, both regard their promise to each other as so binding that there is never any doubt about their feelings. Consequently even Anaxarque's rivalry fails to be a serious romantic threat, and so tension arises not from love itself, but from dangers external to it: the fact that Léonide's life is at risk and then our belief that Lysimaque is dead, allowing Piron a *coup de théâtre* when we discover that he is alive after all; he will use a similar effect in *Fernand Cortès*, when the false report of Montézume's death is followed by the surprise revelation that he is alive, but there, as we have seen, he caps it with a further *coup de théâtre* when he reveals that he has been poisoned and really is dying.

The love plot of Piron's first tragedy, then, is very far from demonstrating the ideal integration he claimed to have achieved in his last. What of *Gustave Wasa*? Here too, much of the principal action centres on the invented love plot, but the sense of integration is significantly better, since all the principal characters are involved in it. Furthermore, it is fused with the political action, rather than simply being parallel to it, to the extent that the romantic tensions almost symbolize the political. Gustave is the true and legitimate lover of Adélaïde, just as he is the legitimate ruler of Sweden, but has to seize her back from Christierne whose lust is causing him to plan to take her by force, just as he has Sweden. Meanwhile, Frédéric is being strung along by Christierne over his love for and impending marriage to Adélaïde, just as he is about the throne; at the end, he will generously relinquish both to Gustave. Here the integration is superbly judged.

Fernand Cortès is somewhat different: rather than standing as a symbol of the political conflict of the play, the love plot seems almost to replace it, becoming the principal action, while the attendant political events largely take place in the wings. Perhaps Piron himself is showing some discomfort at this when he has Cortès chide Montézume for wasting time talking about his love for Elvire when the political events taking place off stage are threatening him with disaster (*FC*, IV. iv). Cortès, we are told, has undertaken his entire conquest of Central America to convince the disapproving father of his beloved Elvire that he is worthy of his daughter. While this absolves Piron's character completely from the charges which have been levelled at his historical counterpart of coveting the Aztec's gold and silver, it nevertheless risks trivializing the entire, bloody enterprise; as Pascale Verèb puts it: 'La Conquista [est] réduite à une affaire de cœur.'[27] Furthermore, to resolve this plot within the confines of the unities of time and place, Piron has to bring Cortès's beloved and her father to Central America. His solution to this problem — a shipwreck and their capture to be sacrificed by the High Priest — is described by Verèb as 'un coup de théâtre digne d'un opéra-comique',[28] so it is perhaps worth remarking that it has both tragic and historical precedent, being closely comparable both to the situation presented in *Iphigenia in Tauris* and to the fate from which the historical Jerónimo de Aguilar escaped. Nevertheless, it is true that Elvire's being disguised as a man — Piron's explanation of how Cortès fails to recognize her when he rescues her — does encourge the comparison with less noble theatrical genres.

As in *Callisthène*, the political conflict is separate from the romantic conflict: in the former Montézume and the Spaniards oppose the High Priest, in the latter the High Priest has no role other than to express condemnation of Montézume's intention to marry a Spaniard, and Montézume himself, the rival in love, simply exists on the sidelines as a complicating factor in a conflict between Cortès and Dom Pèdre. The tension we saw between Lysimaque and Anaxarque in *Callisthène* is absent, since, for most of the action, neither Cortès nor Montézume knows the other to be his rival, and when this is discovered, Cortès is convinced that Montézume will step aside for him. This conviction, however, is never put to the test, for the death of Montézume resolves all remaining complications. This death should represent the tragedy of open-mindedness destroyed by bigotry, but instead — despite the fact that he has not killed himself — it seems like the final act of self-sacrifice required to crown the happiness of the central couple.

Perhaps, then, the success of *Gustave Wasa* and the comparative failure of Piron's first and third tragedies is attributable to the success with which the love plot is integrated into the rest of the action, a particular irony given that it is in *Fernand Cortès* that he thought he had handled this most successfully.

One common feature of all these love plots is confusion about the identity of the beloved. This takes different forms in all three plays, and although *Gustave Wasa* and *Fernand Cortès*, in which a lover fails to recognize the beloved in the midst of a combat, are more obviously similar than *Callisthène*, where the lover falls in love with an unknown figure in a crowd, there are less obvious links and differences on both the psychological and dramatic levels.

Although *Gustave Wasa* contains a scene in which, at their first meeting during the course of the action, Gustave fails to identify himself to Adélaïde in order to test her love for him (*GW*, III. vi), it is Christierne's description of his first encounter with her and the fact that he only later came to love her that has interesting links with the other plays. This is how Christierne describes the first time he sees her:

Par un dernier assaut, cette ville emportée
Couvroit de ses débris la mer ensanglantée;
La vengeance y faisoit éclater sa fureur;
Et le droit de la guerre y répandoit l'horreur.
Ce palais renfermant de nombreuses cohortes,
Nous y courons. La hache en fait tomber les portes;
J'entre, on fuit devant nous, le sang coule, & nos cris
Font voler la terreur sous ces vastes lambris.
Mourante entre les bras d'une femme éperdue,
Adélaïde alors fut offerte à ma vue.
Sa pâleur, à mon œil de colère enflammé,
Déroba mille appas qui m'auroit désarmé.
D'un mortel ennemi je ne vis que la fille,
Que le reste d'un sang funeste à ma famille.
Les armes de son père ont fait périr mon fils;
Et cette image alors fut tout ce que je vis.
De peur de trahir même un courroux légitime,
Je détournois les yeux de dessus la victime,
Et ce courroux ainsi, libre dans son essor,
L'envoya dans la tour où je la tiens encor. (*GW*, I. i)

He goes on to recount how it was politically expedient to solve the problem of the people's love for her, and so he decided to marry her to his heir, Frédéric. It is only because after two years she has still not agreed to this match that he sets eyes on her for a second time:

Enfin, je m'accusai de trop de complaisance;
Et croyant qu'à mon ordre, il manquoit ma présence,
Je vis Adélaïde. Ah! Rodolphe, peins-toi
Tout ce qu'a la beauté de séduisant en soi!
Tout ce qu'ont d'engageant la jeunesse, & des grâces,
Où la tendre langueur fait remarquer ses traces!
Jamais, de deux beaux yeux, le charme en un moment
N'a, sans vouloir agir, agi si puissamment;
Ni jamais, dans un cœur, l'amour ne prit naissance,
Avec tant d'ascendant, & si peu d'espérance. (*GW*, I. i)

The emotions of warfare and his knowledge that she is his enemy, then, prevent him from seeing Adélaïde's beauty; when he meets her in a calmer state, those obstacles have disappeared, and he is overwhelmed with love. Already, we have a reasonable psychological explanation for his failure to recognize Adélaïde for what she was on his first encounter with her. But Piron suggests more subtle motivations at work here: in that description of their first meeting, he hints that Christierne had indeed already been struck by her beauty, but that his knowledge of her ancestry caused him to suppress those feelings, for he tells us that he had to turn his eyes away in order to avoid betraying his sense of how he should feel about her. The decision to marry her to Frédéric could be seen as another subconscious denial of his true feelings. These feelings remain suppressed for two years, until he sees her again, when they surface, this time irresistibly. So he has not failed to notice her charms at their first encounter but has simply resisted the temptation to succumb to them. And there is more, for when he first identifies the object of his love to his confidant, he responds to the latter's surprise by confirming her identity. If this speech is principally intended to inform the audience who the character is, that does not prevent the author also giving it psychological significance, and it suggests that, even if her connections were originally his reason for resisting her, they have become an important motivation for his desire: she is the last remaining conquest for a man who cannot resist taking what belongs to others:

RODOLPHE

Tout le monde en effet, Seigneur, en est encore
A connoître l'objet que votre flamme honore.

CHRISTIERNE

Que ta surprise augmente en apprenant son nom:
Adélaïde.

RODOLPHE

Elle!

CHRISTIERNE

Oui: la fille de Sténon,
Héritière du trône, attachée à Gustave,
Promise à Frédéric, détenue en esclave,
Reste unique & plaintif d'un sang que j'ai versé;
Voilà d'où part, ami, le trait qui m'a percé. (*GW*, I. i)

That neither his promise to Frédéric of marriage to Adélaïde, nor his belief that his love will not be reciprocated, prevents him from pressing ahead with his intention to wed her confirms the impression that his desire is motivated by the need to possess.

The failure of Cortès to recognize his beloved Elvire is also explained partly by the fact that they meet in the middle of a battle, but there is no subtle psychology here: Cortès is simply so busy dealing with the High Priest that he fails to look at her properly, and so does not physically recognize the woman he is already in love with. This is the more understandable, since her father has disguised her as a boy to protect her from the unwelcome attentions of men on their voyage — even her relative Aguilar, who takes care of her when she is rescued, fails to recognize her immediately. It is he who is telling the tale:

Cortès que rien n'arrête & qui semble voler,
Fond sur le scélérat prêt à vous immoler;
Tandis que non moins prompt, je relève & délie
L'Espagnole à vos pieds, pâle & presque sans vie.

Le nom de votre chef lui fait rouvrir les yeux.
Que deviens-je à mon tour, quand l'examinant mieux,
Dans ses traits délicats où la couleur expire,
Je démêle ... je vois ... Je reconnois ... Elvire! (*FC*, II. i)

There are clear similarities to *Gustave Wasa* in that Cortès, without having seen Elvire and, consequently, without knowing who she is, supports Montézume's desire to marry her. Piron explains this again by the pressure of the moment — they are still in the midst of the battle when Montézume communicates his love to Cortès, who tells Dom Pèdre (whom he has never seen before and so cannot recognize) about it immediately:

Dans le tumulte encor d'un premier mouvement,
Nous pouvons, vous & moi, respirer un moment.
Des sacrificateurs le zèle mercenaire
N'armera que trop tôt ce peuple sanguinaire;
Et d'ennemis sans nombre alors environnés,
Nous mourrons glorieux, ou vivrons couronnés,
Mais, Seigneur, qui l'eût cru, qu'une telle journée
Feroit naître en son cours des projets d'hyménée?
Le Roi met sa couronne aux pieds de la beauté
Que soumet la naissance à votre autorité.
Accablé d'autres soins, je n'ai pu voir encore
Ces charmes si puissans que Montézume adore. (*FC*, II. ii)

That they continue not to meet is explained by the father's determination to keep them apart until after the marriage; they do meet before this — although not entirely in time since the betrothal has already been agreed by Dom Pèdre — only because that meeting is engineered by Elvire herself. Having begun this plot-line with one coincidence, Cortès's beloved turning up in Central America, Piron is clearly anxious to avoid others, but the dramatic irony arising from the fact that it is Cortès himself who urges Montézume's suit, and the suspense over whether or not Cortès will meet and therefore recognize Elvire before it is too late, both make this into a supremely theatrical situation. It is true that the father's hatred for Cortès is the cause of the plotting that keeps Elvire's identity secret for so long, but generally this sequence of events depends too little on psychology and too much on chance to have enough sense of tragic inevitability. Not only are the similar events in *Gustave Wasa* better handled from this point of view, Piron also renders implausibilities less obvious in that play by confining them to the pre-play action, rather than making them the main subject of the play itself.

The events surrounding the unknown identity of the beloved in *Callisthène* do not share the similarities of those in the other two tragedies, but there are still points of comparison. Here, Anaxarque has fallen in love with an unknown beauty he has seen from a distance in Sparta and has still not identified her.[29] When Léonide, Callisthène's sister, betrothed to Lysimaque, arrives from Sparta, it transpires she is Anaxarque's unknown beauty. Piron takes some care to suggest that Anaxarque is attracted by the Spartan ideal, thereby suggesting hidden complexities and jealousies in his rivalry with Callisthène, and perhaps, in consequence, a certain inevitability that he should fall in love with his rival's female equivalent:

Le jour que je quittai cette ville orgueilleuse,
Que les loix de Lycurgue ont rendu si fameuse,
La jeunesse intrépide y célébroit des jeux,
Dont le prix disputé reste au plus courageux.
Je m'approchai du cirque; & j'y vis la vaillance,
Par la témérité s'annoncer dès l'enfance.
J'admirai quelque temps ces élèves de Mars;
Mais un autre spectacle attacha mes regards.
La plus tendre moitié de l'espoir des familles,
Tout ce que Sparte avoit de rare entre ses filles,
La couronne à la main, assistant au combat,
Y brilloit à l'envi du plus naïf éclat.
On veut être invincible aux yeux de ce qu'on aime;
Et de Lycurgue ainsi la sagesse suprême
Voulut que la beauté triomphante en ce jour,
Allumât le courage en inspirant l'amour.
D'inutiles atours ne brilloient point sur elles;
Ils auroient avili leurs grâces naturelles:
La simple modestie étoit leur vêtement,
Et l'austère pudeur leur unique ornement.
Quelle âme, à cet aspect, ne se fût pas émue!
Parmi ces beaux objets où s'égaroit ma vue,
J'en vis un qui bientôt fixa par ses attraits,
Mes yeux, pour un moment, & mon cœur pour jamais. (*Cal*, I. iii)

So far so good: what risks looking like pure coincidence is given some degree of psychological plausibility. But, in what follows, any inevitability results less from destiny and more from those theatrical conventions that require that any absent character — Anaxarque's beloved — eventually turn up, and that any character whose identity is mysterious — again, Anaxarque's beloved — turn out to be a character we already know; as the only female character in the play, let alone the only female Spartan, Léonide is the only possible candidate. Clearly both conventions operate in the case of Elvire too; the only real difference is that the mystery of the identity of the unknown Spanish woman is preserved longer for Cortès than for either the audience or the other characters, whereas Anaxarque and the audience discover the identity of his unknown beloved simultaneously. In avoiding such conventionality, *Gustave Wasa* again proves itself to be the superior play for technical reasons.

Another relevant feature common to Piron's first and last tragedies which we are spared in his second is the transformation, apotheosis even, undergone by the tragic victims as death approaches. Callisthène gains the gift of prophecy so that he can map out for the audience something of what happened to Alexander after the events depicted in the play — although previously a voice of reason for Alexandre, he has never been the voice of the gods:

Alexandre, écoutez les Dieux, qui, par ma voix,
Se font entendre à vous pour la dernière fois. (*Cal*, V. vii)

The transformation of Montézume is rather more a logical development from previous events, as the Christian convert himself becomes Christ-like: he first rounds off the historical plot by interceding for the very people who have killed him and urging Cortès to be a father to them, which, even if not coinciding with every historian's view of subsequent events, echoes the attitudes to Cortés expressed in Piron's preface; he then rounds off the love plot by giving his blessing to the union of Elvire with Cortès. This ending however fails to offer any logical explanation of why the Mexicans should respond any more positively to Cortès if he behaves like a father to them than they have to either him or their converted king throughout the rest of the action, and so seems to be using religious sentiment to disguise the fact that the outcome Montézume predicts does not arise from what has gone before:

Daignez m'entendre;
Et recueillir du fond de ce cœur paternel,
Quelques mots que doit suivre un silence éternel.
Oui, j'imite, en mourant, votre Dieu que j'adore.
Sacrifié par eux, pour eux je vous implore;
Pour eux je vous demande, en ce dernier moment,
Une pitié bien due à leur aveuglement.
Vous m'avez fait connoître & plaindre leur misère.
Vous fûtes mon ami; daignez être leur père.
Ils peuvent être heureux, vous m'en êtes garant;
Que ce flatteur espoir me suive en expirant.
(*A Elvire*)
Faites-en souvenir l'époux que je vous laisse,
O vous dont je n'ai pu mériter la tendresse!
Je n'en murmure plus, connoissant mon rival. (*FC*, V. v)

The tragedy of this ending is potentially undermined both by this prediction of a happy future, and because Montézume's death removes the final obstacle to the love of Cortès and Elvire. The message provided by this dénouement is an important one for our theme, for Montézume, whose identity is divided, is doomed to die, rejected by his own people but never fully integrated into the new society of the invaders either, for the poisoned arrow — symbolizing the legacy of his origins from which he cannot escape — prevents his marriage to Elvire. But that death risks being overshadowed by the positive outcome of the other main issue of identity, the question of whether Dom Pèdre will understand Cortès for what he is, for, while Alexandre's realization of the personal worth of Callisthène comes too late to save him, Dom Pèdre's error has caused not a death, but something less irrevocable, the betrothal of Elvire to Montézume. Dom Pèdre, jealous of his stereotypically Spanish honour, sees no way around the problem; Piron, via Cortès, demonstrates that a happy ending could be achieved through the generosity of Montézume —

Le Prince est équitable
Je saurai, sans m'y prendre en rival redoutable,
Et n'opposant qu'honneur, que raison, qu'amitié ... (*FC*, V. vi)

— before interrupting this demonstration with the alternative solution more appropriate to tragedy, the death of the noble rival. While Pascale Verèb is surely going too far in describing this as '[une] fin heureuse',[30] it is true that the fortunate outcome of the love plot means that the tragedy is not unmitigated:

Montézume, the Christ-like sacrificial victim, purges the evil, allowing a happier future.

Again, *Gustave Wasa*, where Piron manages to include similar indications of what the future holds without such transparent artifice and without compromising the tragedy of the ending, is more effective. Here there is no change in character: Gustave and Christierne end the play snarling at each other as they have done throughout; Christierne, judging Gustave by his own standards, tells him to cut short his moral homily and get on with killing him; Gustave shows clemency, but only after a fashion, for, as he spares Christierne's life, he curses him with a future of wandering unhappy and unwanted; he then turns his attention to rebuilding Sweden. The historical sequel to the action has been well filled in, but in a way that neither draws attention to the technique used for achieving it, nor does violence to the established identities of the characters, and although, in keeping with historical fact, no death concludes this play, the dénouement fully retains the serious nobility required by tragedy.

Pascale Verèb has suggested that *Fernand Cortès* shows the influence of *Le Cid*:

> L'intrigue s'inspire largement de certains épisodes du *Cid*, Don Pèdre accordant sa fille, Elvire-Chimène à Don Sanche. La rivalité des deux pères existe toujours. Entre les pères de Cortès et d'Elvire demeure 'la haine invétérée / Que de [ces] deux maisons les chefs se sont jurés' et Don Pèdre se sent insulté de 'voir [en la Cour d'Espagne] le triomphe insultant du père de Cortès'.[31]

Although there is no similarity in the titles here, as with *L'École des pères* and *L'École des femmes*, the name of the minor character referred to by Verèb provides evidence of a possible link. But, as in that other case, if there are similarities, there are also differences, suggesting that, if *Le Cid* was a direct inspiration, Piron has created an anti-*Cid*. As in the earlier play, the enmity of their parents creates a threat to the marriage of the romantic couple, but the precise circumstances of this are quite different. In Corneille's work, the marriage is already agreed, but is compromised by a dispute unforeseen at the beginning of the action.[32] In Piron's, Dom Pèdre's hatred of Cortès's family is long-standing even when Cortès and Elvire fall in love — part of the pre-play action — so he has not even been told about their feelings.

The key difference between the two plays is how each of the male protagonists reacts to the enmity of his beloved's father for his family. In Corneille's he kills him, in Piron's he sets out to prove he is a worthy match for his daughter. Corneille stresses the immediacy of the situation in which his principal characters are caught up and their obligation to follow the demands of family honour selflessly. Piron, stressing the duration of the enmity, emphasizes its futility, and shows how Dom Pèdre is led by it to ignoble acts; hence Cortès's nobility comes from rising above this negative situation and attempting to remedy it. Both plays show the destructiveness of a system in which hatred and vengeance become a family affair, but while Corneille depicts the heroic suffering of protagonists who accept the system and take on its responsibilities whatever the threat to their personal happiness, Piron, adopting a much more eighteenth-century view of morality, offers practical advice on how prejudice can be overcome to build a more positive society; it is a lesson that we also find at the end of his final comedy, *La Métromanie*.

Le Cid is not the only other tragedy to be present in the background of *Fernand Cortès*. Piron's was certainly not the first stage work to have been written on a subject inspired by the conquistadors, but the genre, success, and, not least, author of *Alzire*, Voltaire's Peruvian tragedy, must surely have made it, for Piron, the most significant predecessor; it is the only one he mentions in his preface of 1758.[33]

Voltaire presents a more rounded picture of both the invaders and the indigenous population of Peru than we find in Piron's depiction of the Spanish in Mexico. Don Alvarès and the father of Alzire, Montèze, recognize that kindness and understanding are in the best interests of all, but they are counterbalanced by Alvarès's son, Don Gusman, the Spaniard Alzire marries, whose cruelty towards those he has conquered make him an almost entirely negative character, and by Zamore, the lover Alzire believes is dead until after she has married, whose mistreatment at the hands of Gusman causes a hatred that results in him killing his rival. Even though the dénouement condemns all racial hatred and seems to redeem Gusman by giving him a speech in which he forgives Zamore and speaks of the superiority of Christianity, which preaches forgiveness, over religions that preach vengeance, during the course of the main action his cruelty is seen as the result of pure prejudice, and hence unforgivable, while Zamore's hatred is a response to mistreatment, so something we are invited to understand, even if we are not ultimately intended to condone it. This is very different from Piron's version, in which all the Spaniards are well disposed towards the Mexicans, who, for their part, divide into those who support the Spanish and are therefore characterized entirely positively, represented by Montézume, and those who are against the Spaniards and so are viewed entirely negatively, represented by the High Priest. Even if Piron is not so blinded by pro-European bias as to see all the conquistadors in an entirely favourable light (he does not attempt to excuse Pizarro (*FC*, préface, p. 209)), his characterization coincides with the positive view of Cortés expressed in his preface; and the fact that he not only describes Zamore there as '[le] furieux amant d'Alzire' (*FC*, préface, p. 209) but also equates him directly with his own High Priest suggests that he has not entirely got Voltaire's point that the Spaniards themselves may have been the direct cause of the hatred of the indigenous peoples. It seems likely that Voltaire is one target, if not the only target, of Piron's criticism of anticolonialists in his preface and it is consequently not impossible that *Fernand Cortès* was intended, at least in part, as a response to the negative depiction of the Spanish through Don Gusman in *Alzire*, hence a sort of anti-*Alzire* just as it may also be an anti-*Cid*. As in the treatment of *L'École des femmes* in *L'École des pères*, there is no systematic imitation of the plot of the earlier play, but a number of details are to be found inverted. Thus a proposed inter-racial marriage creates a love triangle in both plays, but while in Voltaire's a South American princess is to marry a Spanish nobleman, in Piron's a Spanish noblewoman is offered in marriage to the Mexican ruler; despite this inversion, however, in both cases the desired spouse is a man who belongs to the same race as the bride. In both suspense is created over whether or not the marriage will take place before the true beloved is identified, but whereas in Voltaire's play it is Alzire's ignorance — she thinks Zamore is dead — that causes the danger, in Piron's it is that of Cortès, who does not know the identity of the woman Montézume is to marry. In *Alzire* the unsuitable marriage takes place; in

Fernand Cortès it is averted. Although in both the desired marriage is eventually made possible by the death of the undesired spouse, there are differences: in *Alzire* the final violence proves necessary to purge the hatred by making both Gusman and Zamore see the error of their ways; in *Fernand Cortès* it is suggested that the situation could have been resolved by reason and so, as far as the love plot is concerned, the death is largely gratuitous.

What Montézume's death does achieve is both a sense of Christian sacrifice and the suggestion that, since the Mexicans have been deprived of their true leader, Cortès will be responsible for taking over, being like a father to them. The pro-colonialist notion of the white man's burden is strongly felt here, and the healing force of the Christian religion is a prominent aspect of this. Despite the fact that Voltaire has more even-handedly depicted in his play some of the evils of colonization, the message of his dénouement is essentially the same, for the dying Gusman's change of heart allows him, through his Christianity, to understand that the way to govern the native peoples is by paternalism, not oppression. With the same death-bed omniscience adopted by Piron for Callisthène and Montézume, Gusman gives instructions to the Peruvians:

> Instruisez l'Amérique, apprenez à ses rois,
> Que les chrétiens sont nés pour leur donner des lois.[34]

And, although he returns to Zamore responsibility for governing his people, implying that those Americans who have converted to Christianity are capable of self-government, he nevertheless gives his own father, Alvarès, parental responsibility for Zamore and Alzire.[35] We might feel that such a message is at least more convincing coming from the converted ruler Montézume than from an invader whose Christianity has, up to this point, so signally failed to regulate his behaviour, but the similarities between the two endings remain, suggesting that the main difference in the opinions of Piron and Voltaire about colonialism concern more how it was done than its legitimacy. For the most obvious sense in which *Fernand Cortès* is an anti-*Alzire* is in its entirely positive depiction of Cortès, his companions, and their mission in Mexico. Voltaire, in choosing Peru as his setting, situated his action in the area in which the outrages of the conquistadors were at their worst — as we have noted, even Piron condemns Pizarro — but his decision not to use historical names allows his message to have a more general application, encouraged by giving his Peruvian king, Montèze, a name that clearly recalls Montezuma.[36] So Piron's corrective to Voltaire is to depict the historical figure whom he believed to be an honourable exception to this generalization.

The transfigurations of Montézume and Voltaire's Gusman at the point of death, like that of Callisthène, provide the final catharsis. The Mexicans, the Incas, or Alexandre have come, as a result of the sacrifice and the revelation of the Christian religion or, in the classical play, the wishes of the gods, to an understanding that will ensure a better future. *Gustave Wasa* provides only a mitigated catharsis: the evil has been purged by Christierne's exile from Sweden, but it lives on, for he has undergone no change of personality, has learnt nothing from his experiences. This may be a less classically tragic ending, but its greater realism surely makes it more satisfying.

Notes to Chapter 4

1. The first public performance of this tragedy was on 18 February 1730, with a subsequent performance at Versailles on 2 March 1730 at which it was well received, but Pascale Verèb records an earlier unsuccessful performance at Versailles in 1729.
2. As the full title — *Epitoma historiarum philippicarum Pompei Trogi* (*Epitome of the Philippic History of Pompeius Trogus*) — tells us, this is an abridged version of a longer original, but since that is now lost, Justinus's work stands alone. In very recent years, translators have begun to take an interest in this text, but for a long time the only available English translation was that published in 1853 by the Reverend John Selby Watson (London: Bohn). The standard published French translation has long been that from 1936 by Émile Chambry and Lucienne Thély-Chambry (*Abrégé des histoires philippiques de Trogue Pompée*, 2 vols (Paris: Garnier, [1936])), and both because this version is useful in being a parallel text with the Latin original and because, after beginning with Piron's own French translation, it seems logical to continue in the same language, it is from there that subsequent quotations are taken. To facilitate consultation of the Latin original, I have used the referencing system traditional for this text of Book, Chapter, Section; references will be found in the text. It is generally Books XI and XII, where the life of Alexander the Great is recounted, that are of most interest to us, although the specific text claimed by Piron as his source is an isolated retrospective reference from Book XV, Chapter iii.
3. As we shall see, he includes incidents not found in Justinus, proving a wider knowledge of Greek history of the period, as we would expect of someone who had had the benefit of an eighteenth-century classical education. It is perhaps most probable that he was familiar with the *Historiae Alexandri Magni Macedonis* of Quintus Curtius.
4. Plutarch, for instance, says that accounts note either that he was hanged, or that he died of disease in prison, and depicts Lysimachus as an opponent not a supporter (*Alexander*, §55, in *Greek Lives: A Selection of Nine Greek Lives*, trans. by Robin Waterfield, introduction and notes by Philip A. Stadter (Oxford: Oxford University Press, 1998)); of battles with lions he makes no mention.
5. Plutarch confirms the historical accuracy of this part of Justinus's narrative (*Alexander*, §§50–52).
6. 'Alexandre, désireux de s'attribuer une origine divine [...], se fit précéder d'émissaires chargés de suborner les prêtres et de leur dicter les réponses qu'il désirait. Dès son entrée dans le temple, les prêtres le saluent comme fils de Jupiter Hammon' (XI. xi. 6–7).
7. Although we will also note below some minor details in the case of *Fernand Cortès*.
8. See Plutarch, *Alexander*, §52.
9. See Plutarch, *Alexander*, §16.
10. See Plutarch, *Alexander*, §55.
11. Léonide's name, which would appear to be a feminization of Leonidas, is related to this issue of nationality. The most famous bearer of this name was the king of Sparta who died at the battle of Thermopylæ in 480 BC many years before the birth of Alexander in 356 BC, and so could well be Piron's source. However, another candidate is Alexander's first tutor. This Leonidas, although not Spartan by nationality — he was a relative of Olympias, Alexander's mother, and from Epirus — has been described as Spartan in his attitudes, and, in his moral severity and refusal to flatter his pupil, has much in common with Callisthenes (see Plutarch, *Alexander*, §§5, 22, 25).
12. I have found a reference to a 1552 edition, but this appears to contain only the first part of the text.
13. Identified in the earlier editions as Sieur de Marly le Chastel and in the fifth as Sieur de Genillé.
14. *Histoire generalle des Indes Occidentales, et terres neuues, qui iusques à present ont esté descouuertes. Augmentee en ceste cinquiesme edition de la description de la nouuelle Espagne, & de la grande ville de Mexicque, autrement nommee, Tenuctilan*, trans. by Martin Fumée, 5th edn (Paris: Michel Sonnius, 1584; repr. 1605, 1606). After 1606, the work would not be reprinted again until 1787. The Bibliothèque Nationale's Gallica website reproduces both the original 1584 impression and the generally less reliable version of 1605, although both have problems of legibility; the 1584 edition has been tightly bound and the reproduction consequently loses the beginnings or ends of lines,

the 1605 has poor printing on many pages even resulting on occasion in blank patches. This means that neither text can be used entirely independently, but, because the problems with the 1605 text are more intermittent, I have used that for quotations, adopting the reading of 1584 when it seems faulty, and also correcting some dubious punctuation. References appear in the text identified by the abbreviation G (only right-hand pages are paginated in the 1605 edition; as in the index of the volume itself, I have used a and b to indicate, respectively, recto and verso).

15. Of the two forms available in modern English, Montezuma and Moctezuma, I have preferred the former to refer to the historical figure in what follows, since, as well as being the more common, it is also closer to Piron's version; Spanish uses the latter form.
16. Piron appears to be conflating two classical examples here: the Roman emperor Julian burnt his fleet after crossing the Tigris into Persia; the African connection is found more clearly in the story of Agathocles of Syracuse, who burnt his fleet while on campaign in Africa against Carthage, although he was not a Roman but a Greek, albeit a Greek from Sicily.
17. Of course, it is possible, whatever the method he used to destroy his ships, that Cortés was himself inspired by classical precedent and also, if Gómara's version of events is true, that the more popular version has been influenced by the tales from classical history.
18. Fumée's Tenuctilan, although, unsurprisingly, both he and Piron prefer to call it simply Mexique. For this reason I too have used Mexico and Mexicans to refer to the city and its inhabitants, and have preferred Central America for the region in general, although the distinction between Central and South American is not one that would have been particularly meaningful for Piron and his contemporaries: T. E. D. Braun gives in the introduction to his edition of Voltaire's *Alzire* a number of examples of writers of the period confusing Peru and the Incas, as featured in that play, with Mexico and the Aztecs (*Œuvres complètes*, XIV (1989), 19, n. 25).
19. Fumée gives the spelling Xicotencatl (G, pp. 80b–82a), but this is Gallicized quite radically by Piron to Sicotenfal.
20. 1584 reading; the 1605 edition has 'sçavoit'.
21. 1584 reading; the 1605 edition has Moctezuma, one of a few hesitations over the spelling of the name in this text.
22. *Alexander*, §53.
23. 1584 reading; the 1605 edition has 'Ils'.
24. 1584 reading; the 1605 edition has 'portassent'.
25. 1584 reading; the 1605 edition has 'changoit'.
26. Piron mentions the Spaniards being mistaken for centaurs in his preface (*FC*, préface, p. 206), but is slightly less explicit about their being mistaken for gods and their exploitation of this mistake, saying only: 'L'Européen, sa foudre à la main, étoit une espèce de divinité dont la présence suffisoit pour glacer les plus fermes courages' (*FC*, préface, p. 207). The closest Gómara gets to mentioning anything of the sort is this brief parenthesis referring to the Spaniards: 'lesquels ces Indiens admiroient comme Dieux' (G, p. 87b); his Cortés is a plain dealer who openly promotes the claims of the king of Spain and the Christian religion.
27. *Alexis Piron, poète*, p. 573.
28. *Alexis Piron, poète*, p. 570.
29. In the parody *Colombine-Nitétis* (1723), Piron had mocked Danchet for using the topos of love at first sight in his tragedy *Nitétis*:

    En un moment, de pareils feux
    L'âme peut-elle être saisie?
    Cambyse devient amoureux,
    Comme on tombe en apoplexie. (*CN*, v)

    The clichés of classical tragedy are easy to laugh at, but harder to avoid.
30. *Alexis Piron, poète*, p. 574.
31. *Alexis Piron, poète*, pp. 573–74.
32. Chimène expresses fears of 'un grand revers' (I. i), but there is no indication of what this might be, and certainly no sign of parental enmity.
33. See *FC*, préface, p. 209, where there is a problematic reference to '[le] furieux amant d'Alzire', to which we shall return, and p. 216 where Voltaire is identified in a periphrasis as 'le célèbre

auteur de *Zaïre* & d'*Alzire*'. T. E. D. Braun's introduction to his edition of *Alzire* gives details of works on New World subjects that preceded *Alzire* (*Œuvres complètes*, XIV, 13–14). On a subject closer to Piron's was Ferrier's *Montézume*, performed in 1702, but never published and now lost; Montezuma was also the subject of Dryden's *The Indian Emperour* (1665) (see Henry Carrington Lancaster, *Sunset: A History of Parisian Drama in the Last Years of Louis XIV, 1701–1715* (Baltimore: Johns Hopkins Press, 1945), pp. 55–56).

34. *Alzire*, V. vii.
35. *Alzire*, V. vii.
36. See Braun in the introduction to his edition of *Alzire* (*Œuvres complètes*, XIV, 19, n. 25). He also points out that this similarity led d'Argenson to refer to the character as Montezuma (p. 5, n. 3).

CHAPTER 5

A Double Bill

L'Amant mystérieux and *Les Courses de Tempé*

The three-act comedy *L'Amant mystérieux*[1] and the one-act pastorale *Les Courses de Tempé*, the better known and better of Piron's two plays in this genre,[2] were first performed together at the Théâtre Français on 30 August 1734. *Les Courses de Tempé*, performed second, was much appreciated; *L'Amant mystérieux* failed. Piron tells how the latter was originally written for private performance, but was so successful that he was encouraged to put it on in a public theatre. He continues:

> Je sentis assez la différence des lieux pour retoucher l'ouvrage; mais non pas, comme j'aurois dû, pour le brûler. Mes yeux ne s'ouvrirent que deux ou trois jours avant la première représentation: mais il étoit trop tard. Ma vanité se satisfit à prédire ma honte; & le public remplit parfaitement la prophétie. La pièce fut bien sifflée, comme elle le méritoit; & disparut du jour au lendemain. (*AM*, avertissement, p. 5)

This was the last performance of the comedy. The difference in the responses to the two works led Piron to comment to those congratulating him afterwards, as a famous anecdote recounts, that they should kiss him on one cheek but slap him on the other (*AM*, avertissement, p. 5).

Despite the radically different fortunes of these two plays, an interesting feature of the double bill is that they do, in fact, have a number of thematic features in common. Of these, the one most obviously related to our theme is that both feature odd or unexpected behaviour. While, as we have seen, Piron often in his tragedies reveals mysteries concerning the characters' identity to the audience and even to other characters quite quickly, here the plots frequently rely on the conservation of the mystery as a device for retaining interest.[3]

The central mystery of *L'Amant mystérieux* is announced by the title: why does the lover Valère behave so oddly? He is clearly besotted with his beloved Isabelle, yet is determined to keep her identity secret. His love is indicated in the first scene by conventional means: he has had a portrait of himself painted for her with verses to accompany it, and is asking his valet, Pasquin, about the progress of *couplets* he is having written for a serenade; he also demonstrates the conventional abstraction of a lover, being unable to concentrate on the matter in hand and instead becoming lost in his own thoughts. Yet there are unexpected and apparently unromantic aspects to his behaviour too: he complains about Pasquin identifying him and his beloved by name; he has ordered *couplets* that give no clue about the identity of the person for whom they are intended; the serenade will not be performed under her window; he has not given the portrait to her because it would make their love public if she were seen with it; when he sees her at her window, he runs away, afraid she may come down and they will be seen together in the street in daylight.

We will get no more explanation from Isabelle for this bizarre behaviour than from Valère. Her first line reveals her to be as puzzled by it as we are: 'Comment! quand je descends, ton maître se retire?' (*AM*, I. iii). By the time we hear the explanation, we will have seen evidence of Isabelle's love and the suffering it causes her in an interview with Lisette and a conversation with Valère himself, in which, despite trying to reassure her, he still refuses to explain himself:

VALÈRE

Mais si j'ai des raisons qui me ferment la bouche?

ISABELLE

Quelles raisons, Valère?

VALÈRE

On ne vous les dit pas;
Vous les saurez un jour & vous en ferez cas.

ISABELLE

Quoi donc! avec moi-même employer le mystère? (*AM*, I. vi)

Isabelle's distress has brought her to the point where she is trying to take Lisette's advice to end her relationship with Valère; Philinte, Lisette says, would be glad to take his place. After all this, it is easy to agree with Valère when he announces, at the beginning of the monologue that provides the explanation for his behaviour, that he finds himself 'tant soit peu ridicule' (*AM*, I. viii). What then is the mystery behind his perverse treatment of Isabelle? He is in love with her and is convinced that marriage brings love to an end, so, by keeping their relationship secret, he wishes to delay marriage as long as possible (*AM*, I. viii).

This is an ingenious commentary on two comic conventions, one of which sees marriage as the fitting happy ending for all comedies of young love, while the other shows married couples to be invariably *mal mariés*. These conventions usually belong to different comic genres, Italianate comedy on the one hand, and French farce on the other, but even when combined, as they had most famously been in certain comedies of Molière,[4] the young lovers are not usually cynical enough to predict that they will share the marital fate of the parents. This cynicism is just one aspect of Valère's attitude which, despite its avowed romantic intentions, makes it problematic, the others being that his behaviour is causing distress to Isabelle, and that we have already had indications, in Lisette's attempts to persuade Isabelle to change her affections, that it is not sustainable. Given the presence of both a Philinte and a Célimène in the play, it may not be too far-fetched to see Valère as an anti-Alceste, believing in the value of secrecy just as his predecessor claims to value openness. Indeed, at one point Piron even gives Valère a phrase directly from *Le Misanthrope*: 'Je ne dis pas cela',[5] a particularly clever quotation, since it is entirely characteristic of Valère's habitual evasiveness, but in the case of Alceste provides proof of his inability to live up to the agenda of frankness he has set himself, and so gives us a clue that, in the long term, Valère's agenda cannot succeed either.

Once we know the reason for Valère's behaviour, and we are still a little way from the end of Act I, the nature of the dramatic interest changes, and, instead of keeping us guessing about Valère's identity, Piron shows how his eccentricity is ultimately self-destructive. Hence he has other characters point out to us in advance the flaws inherent in Valère's behaviour. A problem for the writer of *comédie de caractère* is that the line between eccentricity and madness or stupidity is a very fine one. However, staying on the right side of that line is perhaps less important when the eccentric at the centre of the action is, as so often, the father-figure or even an unsuccessful suitor than when he is, as here, a suitor who will succeed at the dénouement. Perhaps, then, a significant reason for the failure of *L'Amant mystérieux* is that Piron has not managed to stay on the right side of this fine line; that Valère appears too foolish ever to engage our sympathies fully; no matter how sincere his love for Isabelle — and Piron is constantly at pains to make it clear that it is — her acceptance of a man capable of such bizarre behaviour is itself supremely foolish. And, far from attempting to make us forget Valère's eccentricity in the rejoicing of the happy ending, Piron reminds us of it in Pasquin's witty, but perhaps ill-advised, curtain line:

Son chagrin,
C'est de n'avoir pu faire un hymen clandestin. (*AM*, III. viii)

Much of what follows centres on Lisette's attempt to promote Philinte as a rival suitor, an enterprise in which she is significantly helped by Valère's foolishness. Not until III. ii, in an exchange between Lisette and Pasquin, do we receive a clue that we should perhaps not take her efforts at face value. She advises him to tell Valère that Philinte will marry Isabelle the following day. Why should she do this if she is acting against Valère as she has suggested? Pasquin has doubts about whether this is true or not, alerting the audience that, if they are not already suspicious, they should be, and Lisette, while refusing to clarify matters, hints that this is part of a bigger plan that will provide the dénouement; the use of theatrical vocabulary foreshadows similar techniques in *La Métromanie*.

LISETTE

Dis tout bas à ton Maître,
Que Philinte, sans faute, est demain son époux [i.e. d'Isabelle];
Et des trente louis voilà la marchandise.

PASQUIN

Il s'évanouira.

LISETTE

Tant mieux! cours sans délai.

PASQUIN

Mais ce que je dirai sera-t-il faux ou vrai?
Ne me fais pas mentir innocemment.

LISETTE

Qu'importe?

PASQUIN

Je n'ai point de plaisir à mentir de la sorte.

LISETTE

Ce petit coin obscur t'en prépare un plus grand:
Viens y voir à ton aise un joli différend.

> Viens! j'ai besoin de toi, tu les verras aux prises;
> Et quand tu jugeras les choses à leurs crises,
> Montre-toi; ta présence importe au dénouement. (*AM*, III. ii)

She follows this up by telling Géronte, Isabelle's father, who now agrees to her choice of Philinte for Isabelle after earlier support of Valère, that she has already passed his refusal on to Philinte — again, a surprising action in view of her determination to marry Isabelle to Philinte to save her from Valère (*AM*, III. iii).

The dénouement takes place in two stages, and we at last understand Lisette's plan; Valère arrives infuriated by Lisette's message that Isabelle is to marry Philinte, and promises to see Géronte immediately to seek Isabelle's hand in marriage, provoking the retort from Lisette that he is too late: the notary and Isabelle's intended have both already arrived. Of course, while Valère and Isabelle both think that by 'le futur' she means Philinte, the audience should by now have worked out, since she has said she has already dismissed Philinte, that she means Valère himself. The final confirmation of what has been going on comes with the arrival of Géronte, whose mission to tell Philinte that he may marry Isabelle after all has resulted in the discovery that he is to marry Célimène and was never in love with his daughter. Lisette reveals that everything to do with Philinte, and so, by implication, all her other actions, have simply been a stratagem to force Valère to make up his mind:

> Je ne sais seulement si Philinte est au monde.
> Ce n'étoit qu'un fantôme aposté de ma main,
> Pour engager Monsieur à faire son chemin. (*AM*, III. viii)

Hence, Lisette, whom we have taken at face value during the course of the first and second acts, in the third gradually reveals that she has been playing a role throughout.

This also sheds new light on the very obvious symbol presented to us in Act II. The symbols we have identified in the plays already studied have all related to the theme of appearance and reality. At first sight, the symbol in this play seems more straightforward: a tearful Lisette tells Isabelle that Valère has kicked her dog because it showed affection to him in public:

ISABELLE

> Pour qui donc ces sanglots?

LISETTE

> Pour Quinquin.

ISABELLE

> Pour ma chienne?

LISETTE

> Nous avons elle & moi belle affaire vraiment,
> Au ridicule outré de votre sot amant!
> Nous l'avons par malheur rencontré dans la rue;
> Il a bien affecté de ne m'avoir pas vue:
> Je le lui rendois bien. Quand la chienne a couru
> Battre queue, & sauter aux jambes du bourru;
> Maudissant dans son cœur cette queue indiscrète,
> Et craignant qu'elle n'eût quelque habile interprète,

> Votre vilain Monsieur, moins homme que cheval,
> Vous sangle une ruade à ce pauvre animal,
> L'estropie, & pour prix de sa flatteuse joie,
> Perçant l'air de ses cris, sur trois pieds le renvoie. (*AM*, I. i)

There is a straightforward analogy to be drawn here: Isabelle's dog, punished for a public show of affection, is like Isabelle herself, who is expected to keep her love secret and suffers as a result. The explanation of Lisette's actions at the end of the play, however, retrospectively implies — even if it is not stated outright — that this tale was a fiction, part of Lisette's campaign to turn Isabelle against Valère and hence provoke a confrontation. And if we had been attentive in the first place, we might have noticed that there is rather too much of the omniscient first-person narrator present here in Lisette's interpretations of Valère's internal reflections and motivations, giving us from the outset the clue that the anecdote is not to be believed. It presents an untrue portrait of a Valère whose cruelty is malicious and knowing, rather than foolish and inadvertent. Hence, through its false symbolism, this tale too is related to the theme of appearance and reality, seeming to encapsulate Valère's nature, but turning out to be emblematic of Lisette's double dealing.

While the title of *L'Amant mystérieux* simply tells us there will be a mystery, that of *Les Courses de Tempé* provides a mystery of its own. Piron's audience would perhaps have known the Vale of Tempe as the place where Apollo pursued Daphne, who was turned into a laurel tree to allow her to evade his attentions. They might also have made an association with the Pythian games, created by Apollo at Delphi as a celebration of his killing of the Python, and at which the victors, in memory of Daphne, received a laurel crown. But this only partly explains the full significance of Piron's title.

It is the actions of Thémire which, apart from the puzzle of the title, provide the mystery that dominates the first half of *Les Courses de Tempé*. However, Piron develops her behaviour rather more interestingly than that of Valère in *L'Amant mystérieux*, whose ideas are strange to the point of irrationality from the outset. Initially, she seems merely playful, but Piron builds on this to intrigue us more and more. Hence, in the first scene, her oddity is limited to her being polite to the irritating Hylas, despite the obvious annoyance this is causing her lover Sylvandre. His impatience is quite understandable: Hylas, despite his advanced age, is clearly setting himself up as a rival suitor. At his stage she seems simply to be teasing Sylvandre, but her odd behaviour continues as its implications become increasingly serious. She will then surprise us by suggesting that she has done Sylvandre a favour by choosing to advantage a man over sixty, rather than a younger suitor; we are led to believe that the reason is the traditional one we might expect to find in more cynical comic genres but not in pastorale: old men die more quickly than young ones (*CdT*, iv). Only subsequently will we be given the true explanation (and with it the explanation of the title): in memory of Apollo's pursuit of Daphne, any young woman in the Vale of Tempe who does not approve of her father's choice of spouse is allowed to challenge him to a race; if the man wins he has full power over the woman ('Il a tout droit sur elle' (*CdT*, vi) — the phraseology will prove important), but if she wins she gains a year's grace before her father chooses again. Since Thémire's father is unlikely to approve her choice of Sylvandre, it is clear now why she should have preferred her father to choose the sixty-year-old Hylas rather than an unsuitable man her own age.

With these explanations we reach a similar point in the structure to that created by Valère's confessional monologue in *L'Amant mystérieux*: although the whole business of sustaining the mystery has been better handled than in the comedy, it is now solved. At this point in *L'Amant mystérieux* the tension sags: we have not yet reached the end of Act I of a three-act structure, and it is only in Act III that we will begin to become aware of the additional mystery created by Lisette's plotting. In *Les Courses de Tempé*, Piron allows no such relaxation: the first mystery is replaced by a second of a similar type, a second threat to the happiness of the central couple, but this time not from within the couple itself, but from Sylvandre's best friend. This mystery will dominate the rest of the action.

We have not previously met Célémante, but know him to be the suitor of Thémire's sister Doris as well as the friend of Sylvandre, and have been given three other details about him that seem straightforward, but will soon need to be interpreted: Hylas has told Sylvandre that Célémante has sworn to play a trick on Sylvandre before the day is out (*CdT*, i); despite their friendship, Sylvandre has annoyed him for showing jealousy over his relationship with Thémire, although she assures us that any attention he paid to her was entirely aimed at helping Sylvandre (*CdT*, ii); he has visited Doris's father, and she has drawn the obvious conclusion that he has asked permission to marry her (*CdT*, v).

Célémante duly arrives, and with him the next mystery, which relates to his unexpected behaviour, just as the first did to that of Thémire. He announces that their similarity of temperament makes him and Thémire perfectly suited and that he has asked her father for his permission to marry her — hence, the visit did not concern her sister Doris — and has been accepted in preference to Hylas (*CdT*, ix). Cue incomprehension followed by distress for all the other characters, in the midst of which Célémante maintains a curious matter-of-fact serenity. These contrasting attitudes are sustained until Célémante wins the race and provides the explanation, which hinges on the phrase we have noted in the explanation of the local custom. Clearly we are intended to assume, as the characters do, that the man who catches the woman in the race will inevitably marry her, but this is not exactly what was said: 'Il a tout droit sur elle' (*CdT*, vi). Had Thémire raced Hylas and won, she would simply have given herself a year's grace before her father made his next choice of a spouse for her; by catching her, Célémante has not just won the power to marry her himself, he has also put himself in a position to give her to Sylvandre immediately, which he now does, having also won permission to wed Doris himself. Piron does, however, need to explain why the character should have caused such upset, even potential violence, by not explaining his motives at the outset — although for him to have done so would clearly have deprived the second half of the play of all its interest. It was, we are told, a lesson to Sylvandre not to be jealous of Thémire, whose sincere love has been proved by her reactions to the danger of losing him, and to Thémire not to tease Sylvandre, because she now knows what it feels like herself. Whether or not we find this convincing, it does owe something to the idea that theatre should teach a lesson. And so, with a final divertissement, 'tout finit par des chansons'.

Hence both plays create confusion by having characters behave in a way which is open to misinterpretation. Valère claims to be deeply in love, and yet behaves as if he has no regard for, is even ashamed of, his beloved; Thémire and Célémante both act in a way that seems to be detrimental to their friends while claiming to be serving their best interests; Lisette too seems to be working against Valère, but turns out to have been supporting his interests, although in her case, initially at least, she says nothing to make us question our assumption. So we are faced with a conflict between the appearance of their actions and the reality of their intentions, and, until the problem is resolved, we are uncertain about how we should judge the characters concerned.

Interestingly, these issues of the ambiguity of identity and actions are backed up in both plays by questions of the ambiguity of language. *L'Amant mystérieux* even begins with a lesson in linguistic ambiguity as Valère encourages Pasquin in the art of deliberate imprecision, beginning with a demonstration of how to use 'on' in order to avoid naming names (*AM*, I. i). When Valère goes on to ask Pasquin if he expressed himself properly ('Et t'es bien exprimé?' (*AM*, I. i)) when ordering his *couplets*, the phrase will turn out to mean 'with the utmost lack of precision'.

Valère will continue to exploit such vagueness in order to conceal his love for Isabelle. However, not only is he not the only one to use language in this way, he is also far from being the best at it. When Lisette asks Valère if Isabelle knows whom he is in love with, this is how he responds:

> Mais comme ce n'est qu'une, elle & celle que j'aime,
> Qu'adorer celle ci, c'est l'aimer elle même;
> Sa médiation s'est offerte entre nous,
> Et par elle on m'annonce un destin assez doux. (*AM*, I. ix)

What he means by this contorted reply is, of course, that it is Isabelle he is in love with, but Lisette, who has decided to tease him by pretending he is in love with Célimène, is able to exploit its ambiguities to pretend that this is what she has understood him to be saying. Valère rejects this misidentification, but, thinking it proof that Lisette does not know his secret, later amuses himself by using imprecise vocabulary to refer to Lisette herself without, as he believes, her understanding:

> La suivante de celle à qui je songe à plaire,
> De notre liaison n'a pas le moindre vent. (*AM*, I. ix)

Since both Lisette and the audience know precisely what he is up to, Valère is the only dupe, and Lisette will continue exploiting her superior knowledge in the rest of the scene while apparently being taken in. This vagueness seems to become an end in itself, so that Valère later proves unable to express himself unambiguously even when it would be in his interest to do so: towards the end of his interview with Géronte, he manages to persuade his interlocutor that he is in love with Célimène, without having intended to do so. Despite realizing his gaffe, his denials are themselves so ambiguous that they fail to disabuse Géronte, who has clearly begun to expect nothing but ambiguity from Valère (*AM*, II. ix). It is hardly surprising, given this debacle, that Valère begins the monologue of the next scene by concluding: 'Il faut, bon gré, mal gré, que bientôt je la nomme' (*AM*, II. x). So unsuccessfully has he handled things, Isabelle still believes he loves Célimène as late as III. vi.

Lisette, however, as one would expect from a soubrette, is rather better at intrigue, and consequently better too at the use of linguistic ambiguity. So she is able to speak openly of Valère's love for Isabelle in front of him without his realizing that she knows his secret, for, when she comments to Isabelle: 'Monsieur veut me cacher l'objet de son amour' (*AM*, II. ii), Isabelle and the audience know that the phrase refers to Isabelle herself, whereas Valère thinks she still believes he is in love with Célimène. The audience similarly understands when she teases her victims in the same way as the play nears its end, so that when she speaks to Géronte of his 'gendre' he thinks she means Philinte, but we know she is talking of Valère (*AM*, III. iii), and, as we have noted, when she tells Valère and Isabelle that his open declaration of love has come too late, because the notary and 'le futur' have both arrived, they assume she means Philinte, while we know she is teasing and means Valère. Even an earlier ambiguity, which at first looks like a simple misunderstanding, turns out to be significant: an offended Isabelle thinks Lisette's comment 'la pauvre bête' (*AM*, II. i), which in fact refers to her dog, is intended to mean her; our subsequent discovery that the story is an invention suggests that the ambiguity, which strengthens the symbolic link between the mistreated Isabelle and her abused pet, was deliberate.

A slightly different type of verbal ambiguity pervades the plot of *Les Courses de Tempé*, and while the examples we have just examined rely largely on the effect of dramatic irony that depends on the audience understanding what most of the characters do not, here the audience's ignorance is an important part of the impact. The first instance occurs when Thémire claims to have been acting in the best interests of Sylvandre despite having just, as she admits, quite deliberately encouraged Hylas to ask her father for her hand in marriage.

> C'est l'unique moyen d'unir
> Votre destinée à la mienne. (*CdT*, iv)

The claim seems contradictory, impossible even, but it is by deliberately puzzling not just the other characters, but the audience too, that Piron retains the interest in much of this play. Thémire will make similar claims in the following scene, where Doris is added to the company of those who fail to understand, but it takes only a very partial explanation from Thémire — an explanation that leaves Sylvandre and the audience none the wiser — for her to exclaim, 'Ah! J'entends' (*CdT*, v). The vagueness of the language is being used in the same way as jargon or slang to create an in-crowd from which outsiders are excluded. Doris, as a local, understands the implications of what Thémire is saying; the rest of us need the fuller explanation that we will not be given until the following scene.

Célémante uses similar ambiguities concerning his plan. His first ambiguous statement comes into the same category as those of Lisette in *L'Amant mystérieux*, although here the audience is taken in just like the other characters, and so shares their surprise when the truth is revealed. When Doris asks him how his meeting with her father went, his reply —

Mon air satisfait dit assez
Qu'apparemment j'ai ce que je désire. (*CdT*, ix)

— is clearly intended to suggest that he has been granted Doris's hand in marriage, and so provokes surprise, shock even, when he reveals that it is Thémire he has obtained. Thémire, who is clearly not used to being an outsider, tries to explain the remark as a joke intended to exclude Hylas (*CdT*, x), but she is wrong; this time the mystery is understood only by Célémante. His subsequent remarks are more like those of Thémire when she was teasing Sylvandre, for he claims that, despite appearances, his intentions are honest and he is acting in the best interests of Sylvandre — claims that are not understood by the other characters and will clearly not be understood by the audience either (*CdT*, x, xii, and xvii). The most explicit of these sounds almost like a riddle:

Et croyez [...]
Que le sort peut livrer Thémire à Célémante,
Sans ôter pour cela Célémante à Doris. (*CdT*, xiii)

However, since this predicts the outcome without explaining how it is to be achieved, it is of little more help to us than Célémante's other ambiguous remarks. Like the characters, we have to wait until all is revealed at the end.

A further feature of linguistic ambiguity may be found in the way a remark not intended as ambiguous by the speaker may, nevertheless, have more than one meaning for the person who hears it. The most obvious example is found in Doris's monologue in scene xiv of *Les Courses de Tempé*, a scene that makes use of the same device as IV. ii of *L'École des femmes*, as Piron was clearly aware, given the fondness he shows for this play elsewhere. In both, one character delivers a monologue, unaware of the presence of a second character, who not only overhears, but responds to the various ideas of the monologue in such a way as to create a conversation that makes sense in its own right, but also reinterprets the original ideas according to the agenda of the second character — in Piron's version Doris is musing on the riddle that Célémante has posed for her, while Hylas thinks she is talking to him about her father's decision to give Thémire to Célémante:

DORIS *bas & à part*[6]
Que le sort peut livrer Thémire à Célémante,
Sans ôter pour cela Célémante à Doris.
(*Haut*)
Ceci, tout de nouveau, commence à m'interdire.

HYLAS
Votre père jamais n'a voulu s'en dédire.

DORIS *à part*
Et je ne sais plus qu'en penser.

HYLAS
Ni moi, sinon qu'au jeu l'on veut m'intéresser;
Mais je prends le parti d'en rire.

DORIS *à part*
Ma flamme ingénieuse à prendre de l'espoir,
S'est laissée, à coup sûr, follement décevoir
Sur une apparence frivole.

HYLAS

L'espérance n'étoit point folle:
Il étoit permis d'en avoir.
Un homme est honnête homme, & n'a que sa parole. (*CdT*, xiv)

This continues for another fifteen lines before Hylas pronounces the sentence that is finally heard by Doris. Clearly neither of these scenes, Molière's nor Piron's, is even remotely plausible, mainly because both the double meaning and the failure of the monologist to notice the other character are sustained far longer than any analogous real-life situation could be. Indeed, that is the whole point, since it is the source of the comedy. However, if it is stage convention that allows us to laugh at these situations, rather than simply rejecting them as unrealistic, the humour also depends on the fact that they do have recognizable real-life parallels — people do turn things over in their minds, sometimes even speaking out loud to themselves, even if it is never as sustained as a theatrical monologue; people wrapped up in their own thoughts do sometimes fail to notice or hear another person; people do sometimes talk at cross-purposes.

Another overheard monologue occurs in *L'Amant mystérieux*, although the issue it raises is slightly different. Here the overheard phrase is incomplete, and so has the potential to be completed by Lisette in a way that is clearly not intended by Valère. He has been discussing his theory that marriage destroys love, which is why he wishes to delay it as long as possible:

VALÈRE *seul*

D'un cœur vraiment touché tels sont les doux caprices;
Il met dans les désirs ses plus chères délices;
Et même il seroit bon, s'en tenant aux souhaits,
Pour s'aimer toujours, de ...

LISETTE *à part*

De ne se voir jamais. (*AM*, I. viii–ix)

The comedy of Lisette's completion derives from the fact that, although clearly ridiculous, it is only a slight exaggeration of what Valère was going to say. But how do we know what he was going to say, since he never actually says it? Because it is a logical development of the argument that has led up to it, making it clear that he was going to say 'de ne se marier jamais'. In other words, coherent linguistic expression is not the only thing needed for communication, and consequently an incomplete thought might be clear from the logic of what has gone before. In order to make the point clearly, Piron provides a further variation on the effect in the following scene. Pasquin arrives to give Valère an update on the progress of his serenade, but tries to do so in front of Lisette, causing Valère to interrupt him three times, cutting him off not only mid-sentence, but mid-word. The very fact that he interrupts proves that Valère knows what Pasquin is about to say, and the audience too, having heard the earlier conversation on the subject, is in no doubt that the incomplete words are 'couplets', 'sérénade' and 'Crotambule',[7] but the uninformed Lisette, despite her usual quick-wittedness, is completely in the dark:

PASQUIN

Monsieur, voici vos coupl ...

VALÈRE

Ah! tête de linotte!

PASQUIN

Pour la sérén ...

VALÈRE

Encore!

PASQUIN

Et la Muse de Crotte ...

(*Valère lui arrache impatiemment le papier des mains, lui en donne par le nez, & s'en va.*)

LISETTE

Quel diantre de jargon! Explique-nous un peu
Tes couples, ta sirène, & la crotte. (*AM*, I. x–xi)

By the use of 'nous' — Valère has by now left — Lisette seems to include the audience in her call for clarification, but, as we have remarked, we do not need it, for here our superior knowledge makes us part of the in-crowd.

Both plays begin with passages designed to mislead the audience by a false style or tone. Hence, Valère's opening remark in *L'Amant mystérieux* gives a favourable impression because of his politeness to his servant; Pasquin knows he is polite only when angry:

VALÈRE

Monsieur Pasquin, de grâce?

PASQUIN

Eh! Monsieur! sans façon;
Ces politesses-là ne sentent rien de bon. (*AM*, I. i)

At the opening of *Les Courses de Tempé*, we find ourselves, as we might expect, in the conventional world of the pastorale, but this will soon be undercut, as we find that the lines are a parody of the traditional language of the genre, which is eschewed in the rest of the play. The hesitation in the last line of Hylas's opening speech may give a clue that this is not natural communication (characters in plays written in rhymed verse do not normally need to search for their rhymes, hence he must be improvising a poem), but it will then be condemned outright by Sylvandre, and recognized by Thémire as conventionally poetic in terms that what follows will make clear to be ironic:

HYLAS

O le délicieux asile!
Qu'au gré d'un cœur passionné,
Zéphyre y souffle un air amoureux & tranquille!
Et qu'un amant heureux y seroit ... fortuné!

SYLVANDRE *à part*

Le pesant personnage!

THÉMIRE *à Hylas*

A ce langage orné
Des grâces de l'éclogue, & des fleurs de l'idylle,
On reconnoît le tendre & le galant Hylas. (*CdT*, i)

Not only is Piron making the extra-dramatic point that he is rejecting the conventional language of pastorale, he is also condemning the character by the way he speaks, for Hylas is that most ludicrous figure in romantic comedy, the old man who dares to love a young woman, typified by the fact that he is the only character to think such old-fashioned poeticism appropriate in the language of love. Lisette in *L'Amant mystérieux* so mistrusts conventionally romantic language that Pasquin succeeds with her only when he adopts a more down-to-earth approach:

PASQUIN

Cruelle, arrête, écoute un pauvre diable;
Qui brûle ...

LISETTE

Brûle, soit; je suis impitoyable. (*AM*, I. xi)

PASQUIN

Je suis homme à t'aimer, comme à ne t'aimer pas;
A chacun là-dessus liberté tout entière.
Et quand je me suis plaint de te trouver trop fière,
Quand je te retenois, crois que de mes besoins,
L'amour étoit celui qui me pressoit le moins.

LISETTE

Ce petit ton brutal a pour moi plus de charmes,
Qu'une fadeur bien tendre & que le don des larmes. (*AM*, I. xi)

Such changes of tone can cause a shift of attitude that, at its most extreme, becomes a change of meaning. When Valère in *L'Amant mystérieux* decides that he is 'ridicule', and then baulks at the extreme term, arriving via 'singulier' at 'un peu trop délicat' (*AM*, I. viii), the softening of the vocabulary has surely resulted in a complete distortion of the point. Similarly, when Géronte asks Lisette what Pasquin has said to her and she replies: 'Il me parle d'affaire' (*AM*, II. vi), we will be amused by the way that, although the reply is literally accurate, its tone suggests something more respectable than the insults proffered by Pasquin because Lisette has refused money on a point of principle:

Refuser de l'argent pour garder un secret!
Lâche! & tu ne meurs pas de honte & de regret. (*AM*, II. vi)

There is a similar progression in the way Valère's paradox about the relationship between love and marriage, which provides the main reason for his behaviour, is distorted until it becomes a burlesque inversion of itself. We first hear it in Valère's monologue:

Je ne me presse pas de me voir son époux?
Non, parce qu'elle m'aime, & que rien n'est plus doux
Que de jouir d'un feu que l'hymen peut éteindre;
Que d'aller à pas lents, où l'on est sûr d'atteindre. (*AM*, I. viii)

When Pasquin explains this to Lisette, the language is down-to-earth, but the sense is accurate enough:

On estime sa femme: on aime sa maîtresse;
Et, sachant qu'il aura tout le temps d'estimer,
Il veut, tout à son aise, auparavant aimer. (*AM*, I. xi)

When Lisette decides to use it against Valère, however, not only has the language changed, so that 'estime' degenerates into 'indifférence', so has the logic which, in order to suit her ends, Lisette makes reversible in a way that was never intended:

> L'hymen, sans qu'on y pense,
> De l'amour très-souvent mène à l'indifférence:
> L'hymen aussi parfois prend un tout autre tour;
> Et de l'indifférence il nous mène à l'amour. (*AM*, II. vi)

When the paradox is applied not to the ruling classes, but to the servants, it achieves its least idealistic but also its most practical form. The lack of seriousness typical of servant love affairs is apparent, with the 'indifférence' of the previous version being pessimistically debased even further, but the conclusion is reversed: if the inevitable is going to happen, why postpone it? The sentiment is much the same, but the tone renders it almost unrecognizable:

> En effet, à quoi bon tourner autour du pot?
> Six mois, un an, deux ans, un couple se chicane;
> On s'approuve aujourd'hui, demain on se condamne,
> On fuit, on se rapproche; on rompt, on se rejoint;
> Elle est sotte, il est fou, j'en veux, je n'en veux point.
> A la fin on s'épouse, & puis l'on se méprise:
> Combien de temps perdu pour faire une sottise! (*AM*, III. vii)

But, of course, the ability of language to mislead does not depend only on ambiguity. While the characters of *Les Courses de Tempé* amuse themselves by the use of enigmatic language that will only later become clear, those of *L'Amant mystérieux* are not above lying. At its most subtle, this may take the form of lying to ourselves in an effort to avoid confronting the truth about our personality, behaviour or feelings — Valère's conclusion that he is not 'ridicule' but merely 'délicat' is one example of this — but we also find Isabelle doing something similar when, in her anger at Valère, she tries to convince herself that she is capable of leaving him, even though Lisette is aware that this does not represent her true feelings:

LISETTE

> Le plaisant caractère,
> Et le joli mignon que ce Monsieur Valère,
> Madame, pour vouloir que l'on courre après lui,
> Et vous faire descendre aux façons d'aujourd'hui!
> Oh! vous vous déferez d'une bonté si grande!
> Votre gloire le veut; & je vous le commande;
> Obéissez.

ISABELLE

> J'y tâche: & c'est tout mon espoir.

LISETTE

> Et vous le cherchiez?

ISABELLE

> Oui: pour ne plus le revoir.

LISETTE

> Vous?

ISABELLE

> Après ce que vient de dire Célimène?

LISETTE

Il n'a qu'à vous écrire: & sa grâce est certaine.

ISABELLE

Non.

LISETTE

(*Elle lui met la main sur le cœur.*)

Quoi! non? Mettez là votre main, sentez-y
La vérité du fait que vous niez ici.
Que vous dit ce cœur? (*AM*, I. iv)

The comments of Célimène mentioned here are an example of a more straightforward form of lying, since we will later find out that what Isabelle is referring to is an incident in which Célimène proffered false insults about Isabelle in order to test Valère:

Elle affecta, sur moi, de tenir des propos
Qui mettoient à bas prix tout le peu que je vaux.
L'on vous examinoit: vous fûtes si paisible,
Qu'elle vous croit pour moi tout à fait insensible. (*AM*, I. vi)

Célimène is not the only liar here, for Valère shows (and not only on this occasion) that it is not only words that can lie, but actions too. Nevertheless, ultimately it is Lisette who is the most successful liar in this play, creating a whole alternative reality that takes in even the audience for most of the action.

A final incident, found in both plays, shows that it is not only the speaker who can indulge in deliberate linguistic misrepresentation. Thémire and Lisette both deliberately misunderstand a request, in both cases to remain silent, by wilfully taking the speaker over-literally and behaving in a way they know not to have been intended. Lisette accepts money from Valère not to gossip about what she knows, and then includes Valère himself in the prohibition, even refusing the offer of additional money to make an exception (*AM*, II. iii). Thémire, who knows that Sylvandre has asked her to be silent in the presence of Hylas in order not to encourage his advances, persists in her silence even when Hylas chooses to assume it means the opposite (*CdT*, iii).

Hence, linguistic ambiguity and its capacity to replace reality with appearance are used in both plays, but, although both initially exploit a detective-story structure, in which a mystery is to be solved, this is sustained to the end only by *Les Courses de Tempé*, with Piron preferring in *L'Amant mystérieux* situations of dramatic irony, where the comedy arises from the audience knowing more than the characters, combined with the *coup de théâtre* provided by the final revelation that Lisette was in control of events, a revelation that causes us to reinterpret our understanding of what has gone before.

In a final paradox, one of these plays became the subject of a scandal, which, although minor, was seen by Piron to be important enough for him to tackle it both in his preface of 1758, and his dedicatory epistle. For this scandal was itself based on the issue of linguistic ambiguity: someone characterized by Piron as a foolish *bel esprit*, but unfortunately not identified more specifically, claimed to have identified in *Les Courses de Tempé* obscene double meanings (*CdT*, préface, pp. 107–13). A hint in the dedicatory epistle[8] allows us to identify the passage: Hylas, realizing that Célémante has taken Thémire from him, decides to turn his attentions to the apparently abandoned Doris. There is no doubt that his wooing is intended to be linguistically playful, for it is another passage where Piron characterizes and mocks Hylas with parodically old-fashioned language, but the matter of obscenity is a different matter. This is the passage in question:

Comme un jeune & sot écolier,
Je ne me tiendrai pas à la simple fleurette.
Tous les matins, au chant de l'alouette,
Mon amour vif & régulier
Vous promet une chansonnette,
Quelqu'air de vielle, ou de musette,
Des fleurs plein le petit panier,
De beaux rubans à la houlette,
Dedans la cage une fauvette,
Nouvelle devise au collier
Du levron & de la levrette ...
Le petit cœur fût-il plus dur que les cailloux,
Je lui peindrai si bien l'amour & tous ses charmes,
Vous me verrez si tendre à vos genoux;
Et j'y serai si doux, si doux,
Qu'il faudra bien rendre les armes ... (*CdT*, xiv)

It is easy to see why the man dogged by his authorship of the *Ode à Priape* would have been upset by new accusations of obscenity, but that is not in itself proof that the passage is innocent in its intentions. It is also true that Piron is not generally in the habit of including obscene double meanings, which would have been an infringement of the *bienséances*, in his plays for the Théâtre Français, although *L'Amant mystérieux* does include both the vague scatology of the abbreviation of Crotambule's name to 'Crotte' (*AM*, I. x–xi) and Pasquin's slightly risqué admission to Lisette that love (clearly 'amour' in the spiritual sense) is not the most important reason for his interest in her (*AM*, I. xi). But it is perfectly possible that Piron could have written something he thought playfully and acceptably naughty and been shocked when the reaction it received was more than he bargained for. The standard defence at the period would have been precisely what we find here, to claim innocence in satellite texts like dedications and prefaces.

Does the passage in question then bear out the accusation? There is no doubt that it contains a number of terms that are traditionally open to double meanings, since, largely by virtue of their shape, birds, any long-necked and round-bodied musical instrument, like the lute, the guitar, or, as here, the hurdy-gurdy, the bagpipe with its pipe and sack, the shepherd's crook have all been seen as male sexual symbols, while the cage and the basket are equally obvious symbols of female sexuality,[9] so if the passage really were intended entirely innocently, Piron has no one but himself to blame for providing so many opportunities for misreading. Nevertheless, it must be said that the image of copulation, which Piron's accuser obviously found in the line about the bird in the cage, is not so easily identifiable in all other cases: the hurdy-gurdy and bagpipes, for instance, are not associated with any corresponding female image. The accusation also rests on the word 'amour' being understood in a physical rather than a spiritual sense, and surely a line like 'mon amour vif & régulier' might have been better avoided if the sense were intended to be innocent. And yet, while on balance it is difficult to feel that such a concentration of potentially sexual symbols is unlikely to be accidental, it is also true that, in the logic of the speech, all these images are intended to depict for the beloved the charms of love — surely 'amour' on that later occurrence more readily invites a spiritual interpretation — and will, Hylas tells us, eventually result in her surrender, something which clearly, in a figuratively sexual reading, has already happened many times over. It is that final detail, which, if the speech is read in such terms, makes little sense, and so is perhaps the only remotely convincing proof of the sincerity of Piron's denials. Perhaps he intended simply a general sense of eroticism, rather than the explicit obscenity of which he was accused. But in a double bill that spends so much time stressing the ambiguity of language, who knows?

Notes to Chapter 5

1. As the extract from Piron's *avertissement* quoted below indicates, the version performed in 1734 was a reworking of an earlier original in one act. Pascale Verèb gives no explanation for her decision to designate this work 'pastorale' despite its urban and contemporary setting (see *Alexis Piron, poète*, p. 559).
2. His other pastorale, *La Fausse Alarme*, also has a plot relevant to our concerns, but treats its theme too straightforwardly to warrant extended discussion. The inconstant shepherd Hylas persuades the faithful shepherd Lysis to play the part in a divertissement of an inconstant shepherd. The latter's beloved Sylvie spies on him and takes his rehearsal of a monologue expressing impatience with fidelity as a true expression of his feelings. She rejects him, but the confusion is quickly sorted out and all ends happily. This plot is juxtaposed with one of Piron's characteristic symbols: at the outset it is thought that a sheep precious to Sylvie because it was given to her by Lysis has been killed by a wolf. Towards the end it is found unharmed, and, although the first reaction of Sylvie, who at this point thinks Lysis faithless, is to tell him to give it to whoever wants it, once she understands the truth, she accepts it back. The allegorical *opéra-comique La Rose* also draws on the conventions of pastoral literature.
3. One of the reasons the effect of *La Fausse Alarme* is so anodyne is that the audience is never in any doubt over the reasons for the behaviour of the shepherd that is misinterpreted by the shepherdess.
4. For instance, *Le Bourgeois Gentilhomme*, *Les Femmes savantes*, or *Le Malade imaginaire*, where the marriages of the fathers show varying degrees of strain. Beaumarchais would later combine them even more strikingly in *Le Mariage de Figaro*.
5. *AM*, II. ix; see *Le Misanthrope*, I. ii.
6. *A part* here indicates the lines that belong to Doris's monologue, rather than an aside in the conventional sense. The initial couplet, marked *bas*, is spoken too quietly to be heard by Hylas; *haut* tells us that he hears the rest.
7. We will realize at this point, of course, that this particular witticism is the only reason the poet has been given this grotesque name, which, by making it rather forced, weakens the joke somewhat.
8. The poem affects regret for the peaceful mythic time in which the pastorale is set when double meanings were unknown and,

   Chaque terme à l'esprit ne portoit qu'une image;
   Un oiseau, vouloit dire un oiseau; rien de plus;
   Et cage vouloit dire cage.
   La basse allusion, de son impureté,
   N'avoit rien encore infecté. (*CdT*, 'épitre')

9. Piron had already used such an image with fairly transparently sexual connotations in the ridiculous wedding masque in *L'Âne d'or* (1725), where the character Le Cocuage turns to the bride-to-be and sings:

> Prête-moi, jeunette bergère,
> Prête-moi ton panier. (*AdO*, II. iv)

Similarly, in the allegorical *opéra-comique La Rose*, the blooming of the rose represents the arrival of the girl's sexual maturity, and the flower itself, which blooms in the girl's garden and which her mother tells her must not be plucked or even damaged before she is married, is clearly her virginity; when she eventually decides which shepherd to give it to, he presents her in return with his crook, and the scene ends with the sound of bagpipes. Even though this allegory has a general feeling of pastoral innocence about it, its meaning was felt scandalous enough to delay the first performance of the work, written in 1726, until 1744. Bearing this in mind, it would seem ill-advised of Piron to have deliberately made use of similarly allegorical images in a play written for the Théâtre Français, where the *bienséances* were much more of an issue than at the Fairs, but that is far from being proof that he did not do so.

CHAPTER 6

❖

A Theatrical Debut

Arlequin-Deucalion

From 1722 to 1726, before turning his attention to the Théâtre Français, Piron wrote or collaborated on some twenty-two plays, mostly for the Fair theatres, although three were destined for the Italians.[1] He subsequently returned to the Fairs only in 1734, when he was involved in the production of four works of which only one, now lost, appears to have been entirely his own work.[2] The recent revival of critical interest in popular culture has led to serious study of the repertoire of the Fairs,[3] and Piron's first play, *Arlequin-Deucalion*, has been singled out as one of its masterpieces, receiving significantly more attention than any of Piron's other works for the Fairs; it is the only play to be included in all three of the modern collections to re-edit works from that tradition, despite also being the only Fair play in two of them not to come from the *Théâtre de la Foire* of Lesage and D'Orneval.[4] Yet, despite being one of the finest plays written for the Fair theatres, it is far from being typical, being the only Fair play in any of these editions not in *opéra-comique* form. All of Piron's subsequent works for the Fairs conform to the *opéra-comique* model which had become conventional there, and he even makes use of the form in works he wrote for the Italians, as we shall see. However, the uniqueness of this work has been seen as a great strength, and justifies its study here independently of Piron's other works for the Fair troupes and the Italians. But if it is so different from other works of the heyday of the Fair theatres, how does it fit into the Fair tradition? We need to begin by looking at the general development of the Fair theatres and the characteristics of the Fair repertoire when Piron wrote this first play for a Fair company.

The early history of the Fair theatres is most obviously characterized by the ingenuity of the efforts of the troupes to circumvent the measures taken by the established theatres to limit their dramatic activities.[5] Marionette shows had long been part of the accepted entertainment at the Fairs, but no sooner had the rope-dancers and other acrobats of the Foires Saint-Germain and Saint-Laurent decided to fill the void created by the banning of the old Italian troupe in 1697 by incorporating a major dramatic element into their acrobatic entertainments, than the Théâtre Français began to use legal means to protect its monopoly. The entrepreneurs of the Fair theatres sought ways of avoiding the bans imposed on them, but the penalty for failure could be severe: fines were imposed, theatres demolished. They tried ignoring the edicts, relying on the brevity of the Fair seasons and the slow progress of the law to allow them to continue their activities, but this was a short-term measure of limited effectiveness. An attempt to profit from different laws governing the Swiss in Paris by appointing Swiss citizens as figurehead owners of one troupe was equally ill-fated. But it is their artistic inventiveness that is of most interest to us.

Initially they adopted literal interpretations of the law: if they could not perform plays, they would perform isolated scenes, although the dénouement would generally reveal that these had indeed been linked; if they could not perform dialogue, they would deliver monologue, although this included rapidly alternating monologues for different characters, and scenes where the speaking character would repeat aloud what others had apparently whispered. The 'commissaire' in charge of overseeing their compliance was not convinced; more radical alternatives had to be found.

Plays in nonsense languages were one solution, mime plays another. The problems of enacting even basic plots in mime led to the use of explanatory captions written on scrolls which the actor would remove from one pocket, display, and return to the other. These prose captions developed into verse captions dropped from the flies on placards, to be sung by the audience to well-known tunes, or vaudevilles. These 'pièces à écriteaux', as they were known, marked the beginning of *opéra-comique*, which found its definitive form as a result of financial negotiations with the Académie Royale de Musique, or Opéra, leading to the actors being allowed to sing themselves. From the outset the scripts included tiny fragments of spoken dialogue, but this rapidly became more developed as the rules were bent further and further.

With this new form the Fair companies had found a niche, a product with which audiences, writers, and actors were all happy. Artistically the Fair had found itself, but practically its troubles were far from over. The opposition of the Théâtre Français continued, joined in 1716 by the new Italian troupe. The Opéra was capricious over the arrangement allowing the Fair players to perform *opéra-comique*, and there were other complications too: although plays performed at the Fair theatres that depict the relations between the Fair and the established theatre companies tend to show the Fair as a unified entity, this was far from being the case — disputes arose between the various entrepreneurs, and the nature of their relations with the authorities differed. These problems came to a head when an act of the Parlement suppressed the Fair theatres completely at the end of the 1718 season. After a tentative reopening in 1720, the Fair players were back in business in 1721, but further attacks in 1722 forced them to seek alternative ways of getting round the law.

The events of 1720 and 1722 hold a particular interest. *Opéra-comique* began as an ingenious way of avoiding the laws preventing the Fairs from performing straight dialogue, but gradually established itself as the standard medium of the Fair theatres. While the balance of power among the troupes changed too frequently for any one to dominate, the preferred authors remained the same; Lesage, D'Orneval, Fuzelier, and their collaborators formed an authorial establishment, whose preferred form was *opéra-comique* in vaudevilles. So in 1720, when the Fairs were forced, on their tentative reopening of their theatres, to perform plays in prose, their impatience to return to *opéra-comique* was such that they began performing it again even before permission to do so had been obtained, and in 1722 the three principal authors preferred to abandon live actors and go back to the old Fair staple of the puppet play in order to continue performing *opéra-comique*. Their fidelity to this form is proved by the fact that with puppets they could legally have performed in any form they liked. In other words, *opéra-comique*, invented as an ingenious way of circumventing the law, had become so established that the authors still wrote it when there was no legal requirement to do so (as when performing with marionettes), or even when it was against the law (as in 1720). Ingenuity had been replaced by self-imposed conformity.

The actor Francisque, who arrived at the Fairs halfway through the 1718 season, perhaps represented something of the old-style values of the Fair. Like the first actors of the Fair theatres he was an acrobat who had only recently turned to acting, and his first years at the Fair were far from trouble-free. He arrived at a difficult time, but then made his own contribution to the tensions: in 1721 he obtained the right to perform *opéra-comique*, unusually taking it away from Lalauze in the middle of his term.

On the suppression of the *opéra-comique* in 1722, Francisque broke ranks and refused to take the easy way out. The decision of the Fair establishment to use marionettes was, after all, devoid of confrontation: marionettes had always been a legitimate entertainment of the Fairs, not a way of avoiding suppression. Francisque, on the other hand, resorted to one of those tested devices for resisting the authorities by commissioning a monologue from Piron, at once an act of defiance in the traditional style of the Fair, and a refusal to comply with the commitment of the Fair establishment represented by Lesage, D'Orneval, and Fuzelier to *opéra-comique* at all costs. Piron, who would later describe himself as being '[du] parti des indifférents [...] celui qui se f... des deux autres',[6] was an ideal partner in this venture.

This sense of being in opposition to all sides, including the Fair, is emphasized within the play itself. The dramatization of artistic conflict in the context of the Fair theatres is a very regular feature of the works in Lesage and D'Orneval's *Théâtre de la Foire* and reappears in some of Piron's subsequent *opéras-comiques*, but certain elements of his treatment here are uncharacteristic. The Théâtre Français and the Théâtre Italien, mocked in the figures of Melpomène (I. iii) and Thalie (I. iv) and the satirical references to contemporary plays that pepper the text, were the traditional enemies, and therefore fair game. The Opéra appears as Apollo, god of Music, who has designs on Arlequin's wife and is ultimately pursued from the stage by him, a depiction which is unusual, but understandable: the Opéra's agreement with the Fairs allowing them to perform *opéra-comique* usually led to a more affectionate portrayal as their ally, but this negative view is only to be expected at a period when the concession had been withdrawn and the Opéra therefore seemed to be attacking what the Fairs saw as their own. It is the negative portrayal of the Fairs and of *opéra-comique* which is more surprising, and it is a satire that appears to be approached with even more relish than the more conventional attacks, since it takes so many forms. Individual authors are attacked: two of those members of the Fair establishment who had taken the easy way out and abandoned live theatre are named and shamed: 'Que d'ici à la fin des temps on n'entende plus parler de pistolets, de fusils, ni de Fuzelier' (*AD*, III. iii); 'Pourquoi le fou, de temps en temps, ne diroit-il pas de bonnes choses, puisque le Sage, de temps en temps, en dit de si mauvaises?' (*AD*, III. iv). Other points are more general: Apollo is chased from the stage for the last time because his efforts to express himself through the medium of vaudeville prove incomprehensible (*AD*, III. ii), a clear attack on the most fundamental technique of *opéra-comique*; Momus, the presiding deity of the Fairs,[7] played by Polichinelle, star of the productions being mounted by Lesage and his colleagues in the marionette theatre,[8] asks to be thrown into the sea by Arlequin, because, as he says, 'Je deviens honteux & las de mon baragouin' (*AD*, III. iv). A note in the first published edition[9] tells us, 'C'étoit y jeter Le Sage & Fuzelier', but we may feel that the symbolism of the gesture is potentially broader, referring to the theatre of the Fairs in general.[10]

In certain respects, this mockery and rejection of the Fair of 1722 can be seen to coincide with the espousal of elements associated with the older Fair that preceded the invention of *opéra-comique*, the Fair in a more combative and inventive phase, and most obvious among these elements is the use of monologue.

Such is Piron's skill that this is far from being one of those composite monologues described in Parfaict (P, I, 63), which avoid the problems of sustained writing for a single speaker by alternating monologues for different characters with such speed that they form a sort of dialogue. It may not be true monologue in the literal sense that the character is always alone, but it is monologue in the sense that the plot uses a single speaking character who carries the whole action, or, at least, virtually the whole action.[11]

On the other hand, it does make use of certain techniques of the earlier Fair monologues, for it is also very far from being one of those monologues in which the author limits the action to a single speaker as a piece of self-conscious virtuosity. Here monologue has been adopted to keep on the right side of the law, and so the virtuosity and ingenuity lie as much in testing the boundaries between what is and is not legal as in sustaining the dramatic action with a single speaker.

The dramatization of its conflicts with its rivals and the authorities is a frequent device of Fair theatre, and the feeling of sharing in something illicit must have been a significant part of the pleasure of attending the Fair theatres, but Piron emphasizes this more than ever in this play through a reference to the real presence of the 'commissaire' in the audience (*AD*, I. iv), transforming him almost into a participant in the action. He is the enemy in the midst of an audience which is on the same side as the actors. The close relationship between stage and audience is intensified by considerable use of communication across the footlights, generally avoided in higher forms of comedy, but characteristic of farce and the popular comedy given at the Fairs. It is, however, more than usually present in *Arlequin-Deucalion*, whether in the proliferation of references to a common culture or in the way that Arlequin speaks as much to the audience as to himself in scenes where he is alone on stage.

To an extent, this is simply a logical feature of the fact that the play is a monologue — it is in monologues and asides that such direct address would most frequently be found in other popular forms too — but its use is intensified here by the inclusion of references to the actual situation in the auditorium: for instance, Arlequin's remarks in the first scene about his solitary state refer as much to the small audiences at the work's first performances as to his position within the action of the play. Significantly, it is in the very scene in which the 'commissaire' is mentioned that this sense of community and of breaking down the barriers between stage and auditorium, illusion and reality, is at its most pronounced, for Arlequin's silencing of Thalie has absolutely no motivation or justification within the plot, but refers entirely to the real situation in which, if the actress speaks, the troupe will be fined by the 'commissaire'.

Consequently, we are impressed by Piron's ingenuity in finding loopholes in the law. Melpomène's entrance speech, consisting of nothing but conventional tragic exclamations (*AD*, I. iii), and Apollo's singing of vaudevilles, with at least some of the words, and then speaking the refrains (*AD*, III. ii)[12] are examples of him sailing close to the wind, but most ingenious are the actual dialogues with partners not covered by the ban: a puppet (*AD*, III. iv), and that other staple Fair act, a performing animal, in this case a parrot (*AD*, I. ii),[13] although neither is extended for long enough to jeopardize the virtuosity of the monologue. Perhaps for similar reasons, Piron never resorts to anything quite so obvious as the trick described in the account in Parfaict of the early monologue *Scaramouche pédant scrupuleux* (1707): 'L'Acteur répétoit tout haut ce que son Camarade lui avoit dit tout bas' (P, I, 63–64), but the device of making sure that the audience understands the more obscure parts of Pyrrha's dialogue in sign language, or that they are following the sense implied by Apollo's performance on the flute of 'Le Sommeil d'Issé',[14] by incorporating the explanations into Arlequin's monologue, is a related technique.

Another aspect of *Arlequin-Deucalion* which links it more obviously with the early days of the Fairs than with the period of *opéra-comique* derives from the skill of Francisque himself. The early Fair performers were acrobats, who began by incorporating dramatic elements into their acrobatic displays. Over the years, as the dramatic aspect of the performances increased, more actual actors joined the troupes,[15] and the acrobatic element decreased. The Fair players retained a reputation for physical acting, but during the period of *opéra-comique* the scripts tend to suggest that this physicality was little different from that of the Italian actors, whose archetypal characters the Fair players had adopted. *Le Monde renversé* (1718) contains a ballet of dancers dancing on their hands (xvi), and in *Les Comédiens corsaires* (1726) the Fair is still singing its own praises in this matter:

> On voyait du plus haut du mât
> Un Arlequin sauter en bas,
> Accompagné d'une cohorte
> De Pierrots & de Mezzetins:
> Et pour voltiger de la sorte,
> Je ne connais que les forains. (iii)

Significantly, however, the action described here is not witnessed by the audience. If the Fair actors continued to pride themselves on their gymnastic legacy, the scripts of the *opéra-comique* suggest that the early acrobatics had generally changed into more conventional song-and-dance routines. Francisque, though, was a more recent arrival on the Fair scene who, before turning to acting, had, pursued a career as a 'sauteur'. Piron makes full use of his talents and those of his troupe, something of a family affair which shared his skills. The description of the divertissement that ends the first act as 'Exercices des sauteurs' makes it sound more like a gymnastic display than a dance routine, and 'sauts périlleux', the mid-air somersaults so popular with the acrobats and rope-dancers of the early Fair entertainments, are specified on three different occasions (*AD*, I. i, I. v, II. iv), the text even pointing out on the third that they were a particular speciality of Francisque. This is the vocabulary of the script for *Les Forces de l'amour et de la magie* (1678), given in Parfaict (P, 1, pp. lvi–lxxix) as an example of those early entertainments that introduced a plot as a way of adding interest to acrobatics, rather than that of the texts of Lesage and D'Orneval's anthology.

The personal attacks on Lesage and Fuzelier, then, alongside the more general criticisms of *opéra-comique* and even the Fair theatres as a whole, coupled with the espousal of techniques characteristic of the Fair before the advent of *opéra-comique*, seem to constitute a rejection of the Fair of 1722, typified by the work of Lesage, D'Orneval, and Fuzelier, for lacking the old spirit of invention and being too compliant in the face of opposition, and with it an advocacy of the old attitudes and techniques.

Nevertheless, other aspects are more obviously conventional: the use of the Italian archetype Arlequin as central character had been characteristic of the Fairs since they stepped into the gap left by the Italians in 1697, and neither is there anything unusual about his transformation into a mythological character, or the burlesque treatment of the tale. Piron's character has the traits we associate with the archetype: he is greedy (whether for food, drink, or money) and sexually predatory, and has a healthy lack of respect for authority, which here extends even to his attitude to the divinities. More unusual are the force of his social comment in the final act, which seems to be much more overtly political than the character's habitual subversiveness,[16] and his critical awareness of contemporary French drama: references to the productions of other theatres are very common at the Fairs, but they are generally presented either allegorically or as parody, rather than as the more direct references found here.[17] Yet even here, although Piron goes much further than other dramatists for the Fairs, it would be difficult to say that he was making a significant departure from the aspirations of the more established Fair writers. Lesage and D'Orneval were as ready in the preface to their anthology as writers of other types of drama to argue their own version of the 'plaire et instruire' formula, saying that the plays they present would satisfy 'les personnes qui veulent de la morale' and that vaudeville was, among other things, 'l'espèce de poésie [...] la plus propre de toutes à [...] corriger les mœurs'. In Parfaict too we find the suggestion that the 'forains' had taken Italian archetypes onto a higher plane of seriousness than the Italians themselves: the text quotes an address to the audience delivered at the opening of a Fair theatre in 1715, containing the comment, 'Quoique vous aimiez les Personnages Italiens, vous n'aimez pas qu'ils grimacent en Tabarins grossiers' (P, 1, 171). A superior image of the Fair is also implied when a play premièred in 1718 is discussed in the following terms: 'LA REINE DU MONOMOTAPA [...] tomba, & merita bien son sort, puisque ce n'étoit qu'une farce grossiere & mal digérée, plus propre pour une parade, que pour le Théatre de l'Opera Comique' (P, I, 203). And the dramatic criticism is a feature of the parodic strain found in the majority of Fair plays. Nevertheless, it must be admitted that both the range and the tone of Piron's satire are more extreme than we will find in any other writer for the Fairs.

So we have a play which, as well as rejecting the *opéra-comique* form which had become conventional in the Fair theatres by 1722, launches an attack on it and its purveyors. On the other hand, it also adopts many of the techniques of the Fair both old and new, often pushing them further than had been done before, or indeed was to be done subsequently. It appears to be both anti-Fair play and Fair play par excellence.

How seriously then should we take Piron's condemnation of *opéra-comique*? Not very, by all accounts, for he went on to write a significant number of them for the Fairs himself, the first of which, *L'Antre de Trophonius*, was, if Pascale Verèb is correct, performed less than a month after *Arlequin-Deucalion*.[18] What is more, at least one of the two that followed *L'Antre de Trophonius* in the same year was performed by marionettes just as were the other *opéras-comiques* of 1722.[19] This might lead us to believe that, as with some of his Voltaire-baiting, no matter how satisfying the result of Piron's anti-Fair propaganda in *Arlequin-Deucalion*, ultimately, like the Duchess's baby in *Alice*, 'He only does it to annoy, because he knows it teases'. Nevertheless, the evidence suggests that, unlike Voltaire in the case of *La Métromanie*, Lesage, D'Orneval, and Fuzelier took this in good part. Although it is presented anonymously,[20] Piron's *Le Caprice* is one of only two plays to appear in the later volumes of *Le Théâtre de la Foire* that is not by Lesage, Fuzelier, or D'Orneval.[21] Furthermore, in 1723 he collaborated with Lesage and D'Orneval on *Les Trois Commères*, which appears as the final play in their final volume of the collection, although admittedly with the indication 'Par M^{rs} Le S★★. & D'Or★★'. It is, as his relations with Voltaire show, quite characteristic of Piron not to care about whom he upset,[22] but is there not also a significant artistic justification for the stance Piron takes in *Arlequin-Deucalion*, which suggests that setting out to upset his rivals was probably not his aim? The Fair theatres had, after all, frequently used their disputes with the authorities as a subject for their plays in such a way that the audience was drawn into a sense of collusion with the performers. A major part of the aesthetic pleasure is consequently derived from the audience's sense of participating in something that is both defiant and illicit. By encouraging his audience to feel that even the rest of the Fair artists had become staid, conventional, and cowardly, had sold out to the authorities, this sense is intensified, and it is no longer the Fairs as a whole, but just Francisque-Arlequin and his troupe who are standing boldly alone when all others have given in. Piron does not have to have believed what his characters tell us about the other Fair artists any more than any other dramatist needs to believe what he puts into the mouths of his characters, for the dialogue is at the service of an overall artistic aim. The sense of defiance, subversion, getting one over on the opposition — personified by the 'commissaire' — and doing it when all others have given in, was and remains a significant element in the impact of this play, but is also a guiding characteristic of the ethos of the Fairs as a whole. It identifies this work as one that puts into action the underlying characteristics of the Fairs, even though it is completely untypical of the *opéra-comique* form that had become their stock in trade by the time Piron began writing for them.

Notes to Chapter 6

1. A version of this chapter appeared as 'Piron's *Arlequin-Deucalion*: Fair Play or Anti-Fair Play?', in *Essays on French Comic Drama from the 1640s to the 1780s*, ed. by Derek Connon and George Evans, French Studies of the Eighteenth and Nineteenth Centuries, 7 (Berne: Peter Lang, 2000), pp. 127–38, and is re-used here with the kind permission of the publisher. Some issues have also been tackled in the introduction to the edition of the play included in *Anthologie de pièces du 'Théâtre de la Foire'*, ed. by Derek Connon and George Evans (Egham: Runnymede, 1996), pp. 115–17.
2. Information based on Pascale Verèb's chronology of Piron's Fair plays in *Alexis Piron, poète*, pp. 635–39. Some of the plays listed by Verèb are lost, and some are collaborations. Dufay, who does not include the collaborative projects, reprints nineteen surviving texts, of which none dates from 1734.
3. Three publications that had a significant influence date from the 1980s: Dominique Lurcel's anthology *Le Théâtre de la foire au XVIIIe siècle* (1983), and the studies by Michèle Venard, *La Foire entre en scène* (Paris: Librairie Théâtrale, 1985), and Robert M. Isherwood, *Farce and Fantasy* (Oxford: Oxford University Press, 1986), although Jacques Truchet had already included four plays from the repertoire in the first volume of his *Théâtre du XVIIIe siècle* in 1972.
4. Lesage and D'Orneval's collection *Le Théâtre de la Foire; ou, l'opéra-comique* appeared in ten volumes (Paris: Étienne Ganeau, Pierre Gandouin, Prault fils, 1721–37; repr. in facsimile, Geneva: Slatkine, 1968), although the last of these, designated not volume x but volume IX, part 2, was the work of Carolet; the collection includes only one of Piron's plays for the Fairs. Connon and Evans include alongside *Arlequin-Deucalion* eight plays from the Lesage and D'Orneval anthology; in Dominique Lurcel's anthology it appears with ten plays from Lesage and D'Orneval and two others by Piron, *Tirésias* and *L'Endriague*; Jacques Truchet represents the Fair repertoire with *Arlequin-Deucalion* and three works from *Le Théâtre de la Foire*.
5. The following historical details derive mainly from [Parfaict *frères*], *Mémoires pour servir à l'histoire des spectacles de la foire, par un acteur forain*, 2 vols (Paris: Briasson, 1743). This is most easily accessible in the electronic edition by the late Barry Russell on his website *Le Théâtre de la Foire à Paris: textes et documents*, <http://foires.net/>: all quotations are from that edition and are identified in the text by the abbreviation P. Venard, *La Foire entre en scène*, is a further useful and concise source.
6. Quoted by Pascale Verèb in 'Alexis Piron défenseur des modernes ou un épisode inédit de la Querelle des Anciens et des Modernes', *Revue d'Histoire Littéraire de la France*, 95 (1995), 282–93 (p. 290, Verèb's ellipsis), where the source is given as 'Dijon, B.M. ms. Breuil 41, lettre XV autographe du 1er mai 1755 à Dumay'.
7. See Chapter 7 for a fuller consideration of the significance of the figure of Momus.
8. While Italian characters who appear in plays for live actors may also have roles in those destined for marionettes, the Fairs tend to use Polichinelle only in marionette plays, where he often has the leading role generally given to Arlequin in plays for live actors (but see Chapter 7 for an exception and additional details).
9. In the third volume of *Œuvres complètes d'Alexis Piron*, ed. by Rigoley de Juvigny, 7 vols (Paris: Lambert, 1776).
10. Walter Rex offers a further interpretation of this action, seeing it as the end of the comic strand of the play (*The Attraction of the Contrary: Essays on the Literature of the French Enlightenment* (Cambridge: Cambridge University Press, 1987), p. 69).
11. See on this subject Pierre Gobin, '*L'Arlequin-Deucalion* de Piron: pertinence de l'impertinence', in *Transactions of the Fifth International Congress on the Enlightenment*, III, Studies on Voltaire and the Eighteenth Century, 192 (Oxford: Voltaire Foundation, 1980), 1478–86 (p. 1480).

12. The refrains apart, the stage directions do not make it clear whether he sang the words to the first two vaudevilles or simply 'la-la'ed the tunes, although the latter solution would have been safer and in keeping with the use of melody to imply words found in the performance of 'Le Sommeil d'Issé' on the flute. In the case of the third vaudeville, where he clearly does sing the words, Arlequin allows him to get no further than the end of the first line before chasing him from the stage.
13. As I have suggested elsewhere (see *Anthologie de pièces du 'Théâtre de la Foire'*, ed. by Connon and Evans, p. 117), it seems unlikely that an actual parrot provided the dialogue in this scene — one cannot imagine such an animal being particularly reliable at providing the right lines at the right time — but who knows? In any case, could the 'commissaire' have proved it?
14. A popular number from *Issé* (1697), a *pastorale héroïque* by André Cardinal Destouches to a libretto by Houdar de La Motte, which had been revived in 1720 and 1721.
15. Parfaict lists the new arrivals for each season and describes their skills.
16. See Rex, *The Attraction of the Contrary*, pp. 68–70, on this aspect. Sainte-Beuve seems anxious to downplay any suggestion of serious political thought in this passage: 'Malgré ces boutades d'un bon sens bariolé d'humeur, il ne faut voir en toutes ces pages que de la gaieté gauloise, narquoise, des hardiesses comme du temps du bon roi Louis XII, et non des révoltes comme au lendemain de J.-J. Rousseau. Piron est, en politique comme en religion, un railleur du vieux temps, non un novateur à aucun degré' (notice to *Œuvres choisies*, pp. 14–15).
17. Parallels will, however, be found in the scene with Mercure Galant in Piron's next work for the Fairs, *L'Antre de Trophonius* (*AT*, xi).
18. Verèb suggests that *L'Antre de Trophonius* was probably premièred on 24 March 1722; *Arlequin-Deucalion* had its first performance on 25 February 1722. See *Alexis Piron, poète*, p. 636.
19. *Tirésias* and *Le Mariage de Momus; ou, la Gigantomachie* were both premièred in September 1722. According to Verèb, both were performed by Francisque's marionettes (see *Alexis Piron, poète*, p. 636), coinciding with the account in Parfaict, which adds that permission was later given to use live actors, although this account is made suspect by the fact that it conflates the two works into a single play called *La Vengeance de Tirésias; ou, Le Mariage de Momus* (P, II, 8–9). The *avertissement* in Rigoley de Juvigny's edition, quoting letters from Piron and Francisque, suggests that *Tirésias* was performed with live actors, resulting in the arrest of the troupe and causing them to use puppets for their next production, *Le Mariage de Momus* (*T*, avertissement, pp. 97–104). Piron's *avertissement* to *L'Antre de Trophonius* tells us that the fact that it was performed during Lent, when other theatres were closed, allowed it to be performed by live actors.
20. 'Par M**' (*Le Théâtre de la Foire*, VIII, 184).
21. Although, apart from Carolet's additional volume, Lesage, D'Orneval, and Fuzelier dominate the whole collection, in the first three volumes other authors are credited; thereafter, the only play apart from Piron's attributed to another hand is *L'Impromptu du Pont-Neuf* by 'Monsieur P**' (Charles-François Pannard) in volume VII. *Le Caprice* appears (with cuts) as *Le Mariage du Caprice et de la Folie* in *Le Théâtre de la Foire*, VIII, 184–238. Because of the modified title and anonymous presentation, I had not recognized this play as Piron's when I wrote the first version of this text, although the conclusions remain largely unchanged. *Arlequin-Deucalion*, as a monologue, was not, of course, in the right genre to have appeared in a collection subtitled *L'Opéra-Comique*.
22. Although he is also quite capable of flattering Voltaire when the need arises.

CHAPTER 7

A Comedy for the Italians

Les Enfants de la Joie

During the first phase of his dramatic career, when he was writing mainly for the Fairs, Piron also completed three works for the Italians. Interestingly, two of these, both designated 'parodie', are written in the *opéra-comique* form that we associate with the Fairs, and the first of them, *Philomèle* (1723), as a parody of an opera, is even more strongly affiliated with the Fair repertoire — generally, and quite logically, the Fairs used *opéra-comique* to parody the repertoire of the Opéra, while the Italians used their usual spoken comedy to send up the tragic repertoire of the Théâtre Français.[1] Bearing this in mind, the choice of *opéra-comique* for Piron's other parody for the Italians, *Les Huit Mariannes* (1725), is more unusual, since its principal object of satire (amongst others) is not an opera, but Voltaire's tragedy *Mariamne*. Hence, of these three works for the Italians, only one, *Les Enfants de la Joie* (1725),[2] 'comédie en un acte avec des agrémens', is in the form we usually associate with the Théâtre Italien.

We can only speculate on why Piron chose *opéra-comique* form for the two parodies. Perhaps the choice for *Philomèle* was made because it is logical to parody one sung form in another; a possible clue for *Les Huit Mariannes* is found in a note in the text suggesting that Piron might have conceived the work in *opéra-comique* form for performance at the Fairs before adapting it for the Italians: 'Fuzelier venoit de faire jouer les *Quatre Mariannes* [...] à la Foire; & comme il m'en avoit dérobé l'idée, je donnai les huit aux Italiens, pour m'en venger' (*HM*, xv); perhaps Piron had the same loyalty to the genre as we have seen in other writers for the Fairs in our study of *Arlequin-Deucalion*; or perhaps the Italians themselves had asked him to write *opéras-comiques*: complaints by the Fair theatres that their rivals imitated their material are frequent in plays dramatizing their relationships with the other theatrical troupes. Whatever the explanation, there is every sign here that, even though he was writing for the Italians, in the two parodies Piron simply wrote in the same way that he would have written for a Fair troupe. For that reason, I intend to deal with them at the same time as his parodies for the Fairs. *Les Enfants de la Joie*, because it is not written in *opéra-comique* form, conforms more obviously to what we expect from the Italian repertoire. And yet, the crucial matter of the absence of sung vaudevilles apart, this play does not give the impression of being significantly different from the works Piron wrote for the Fairs in the way that his plays for the Théâtre Français clearly do.[3] Can this play be seen as an example of imitation of the Fairs by the Italians?

For three reasons, it is impossible to come to definitive conclusions over the question of the influence of the Fairs on the Italians. First, the genre of *opéra-comique* was already established at the Fairs before the arrival of the new Italian troupe in 1716, so any influence could have begun immediately; hence, we have no plays from the repertoire of this troupe dating from before their contact with the Fair repertoire. Secondly, like the old Italian troupe, they were forced to supplement the Italian repertoire with plays by French authors. Their first French play, Autreau's *Le Port-à-l'Anglais; ou, les Nouvelles Débarquées*, dates from as early as April 1718,[4] and the collaboration today regarded as the most significant began with Marivaux's *Arlequin poli par l'amour* in 1720. Since neither author wrote for the Fairs, this means that the Italians were subject to Gallicizing influences independent of the Fairs well before Piron first wrote for them. Thirdly, but perhaps most obviously and most importantly, the Fairs had themselves borrowed extensively from the Italian repertoire, filling the gap left in the market by the suppression of the old Italian troupe.

Nevertheless, a comparison of *Les Enfants de la Joie* with the plays of the Fair repertoire may give us some insights into its meaning. Although we must remember that both the actors and the authors of the new Italian theatre were different from those of the old, and that almost twenty years had passed between the suppression of the old troupe in 1697 and the arrival of the new in 1716, the French repertoire of the old Italian troupe is of interest, since this was the material which the 'forains' originally adopted and adapted into the repertoire they were performing by the time of the arrival of the new troupe.

Let us begin with the title: *Les Enfants de la Joie*. The capitalization of the initial letter of the final word is significant, since, as we discover during the course of the action, the reference is not to the emotion, but to its allegorical personification, and the cast also includes the allegorical figure of la Morale and a singing and dancing company of Ris, Jeux, Caprices, Grâces, Quintes, and Fantaisies. These personifications of abstractions exist, somewhat illogically, alongside figures of gods and goddesses, whose relationship to the abstractions, qualities or functions they represent is of a different order. Here we find Momus,[5] god of mockery and fault-finding and jester to the gods, to whom we will have cause to return, and the more obscure figures of Até,[6] goddess of infatuation, rash foolishness, and strife, who wanders the earth causing mischief after banishment from Olympus, and Lucine, here a simple midwife to the gods, although her name is more properly the epithet of Juno in her role as goddess presiding over childbirth. The latter is accompanied by Esculape, here the divine doctor and more properly god of the healing arts. Presumably also belonging to this second group are the three Graces, who appear in addition to the less numerically specific group of Grâces already mentioned; the situation is further complicated by the fact that they appear dressed as Scaramouchette, Arlequine, and Pierrette. This brings us to the third group of characters, the male counterparts for whom the Graces are intended as spouses, Scaramouche, Arlequin, and Pierrot, principal archetypes of the *commedia dell'arte*, and central not only to the Italian repertoire, but also to that of the Fairs, who made them their own and continued to regard them as their personal property even after the return of the Italians. To complete the cast list, apart from an anonymous 'suivant', we have Mathurine and Gros-Jean — characters whose names and cod peasant accents come straight from the world of French farce.

The nature of the rivalries between the various theatres and their tendency to steal ideas from each other mean that none of these groups of characters is unique either to the Fairs or to the Italians; even though the Fair repertoire grew from that of the old Italian theatre, the Italians had already made their own borrowings from their French contemporaries, so that even the most obviously French characters in the line-up of this play, the dialect-speaking peasants, were already a feature of the old Italian theatre. True, we will search Evariste Gherardi's collection of French plays from the old Italian repertoire in vain for a name as characteristically French as Gros-Jean, male peasants usually being played by the *commedia dell'arte* figure Pierrot, but that is not to say that there are no examples of French male stage-peasant names,[7] and the more frequent female names include a Mathurine in *Les Aventures des Champs Élysées* (1693).[8] Such characters had also already begun to appear in the repertoire of the new Italian theatre before Piron wrote for them: most famously, Marivaux begins his second play for the company, *La Surprise de l'amour* (1722), with a dialect scene for Pierre and Jacqueline. Perhaps the typical farcical prefix to peasant names, 'Gros', is slightly more likely to be found at the Fairs than in the Italian repertoire (there is even a Gros-Jean in *La Forêt de Dodône* (1721)),[9] but this is far from conclusive enough to point to any strong affiliation of *Les Enfants de la Joie* to the Fair repertoire.

The use of mythological characters is also a feature common to both traditions, and they appear in various ways. They are an inevitable feature of parodies, since they are the stock in trade of both the tragedies and the operas that are the targets of such works, but both theatres also make free use of burlesque versions of mythological subjects in works that are not targeting specific contemporary adaptations; mythology was, after all, part of the common cultural currency in the age of the classical education. We also find comic imitations of the sort of mythological prologues typical of contemporary opera, as in *Les Chinois* (1692) from the old Italian repertoire or Piron's own Fair play *Le Claperman* (1724), or plays which simply use mythology as a starting point for the magical element in a more contemporary tale, such as the Fair's *La Ceinture de Vénus* (1715). It is common to find interaction between mythological characters and other types of character in all these types of play. In parodic works — and others too — the mythological characters will often be 'played' by *commedia* archetypes: hence, the cast list indicates that a mythological character is to be represented by a particular Italianate figure, and frontispieces show that the characteristic costume and other attributes (such as mask and slapstick) were visible beneath the classical costume; the mythological character might also share some of the personality traits of the archetypal figure, but there is no sense within the plot in which the Italianate figure is disguised as the classical character. It is also a characteristic of both theatres, mainly in those plays with a classical subject that are not direct parodies, to introduce into the mythological context figures from that stock repertoire of contemporary French objects of satire found in so many comedies — fops, poets, philosophers, doctors, lawyers — often also 'played' by *commedia* archetypes. Sometimes the archetypes even appear, as it were, as themselves in such contexts, as they do in *Les Enfants de la Joie*, where their interaction with the mythological characters has an allegorical significance. So there is nothing here to put Piron's play definitively into either the Italian or the Fair camp.

The use of characters identified simply by the attribute they personify is rather more a feature of the Fairs than of the old Italian theatre. In the fifty-five complete plays or collections of scenes that make up Gherardi's anthology, we find such personifications only in *Les Aventures des Champs Élysées* (1693), where the cast of otherwise conventionally named gods and goddesses includes La Discorde, and *Pasquin et Marforio, médecins des mœurs* (1697), which includes La Vérité and La Médisance. A related, but slightly different, procedure is found in *L'Union des deux opéras* (1692), where the two opera companies of the title are personified as characters. In the fifty-two plays from Lesage and D'Orneval's *Théâtre de la Foire* that were performed up to and including 1725, thirteen include abstract personifications in more or less major roles, and a further five have characters that personify theatres or their attributes.[10] Piron's own eleven complete productions for the Fairs written up to 1725 include two that are centred on an allegorical figure, *Le Caprice* (1724) and *Les Chimères* (1725),[11] as well as an appearance of the figure of Le Cocuage in a divertissement in *L'Âne d'or* (1724) and the silent, but vital, role of La Foire as the bride in *Le Mariage de Momus* (1722). In addition, the prologue to *Les Chimères* has a character representing the first version of Voltaire's *Mariamne* alongside another who represents La Motte's *Inès de Castro*, and in *L'Antre de Trophonius* (1722) the character of Mercure Galant manages to represent the periodical of that name as well as the god. It would appear that such allegorical or symbolic subjects were to Piron's taste, for his subsequent five extant works for the Fairs include two with subjects of this sort, *Crédit est mort* (1726) and *La Rose* (1726). In this case, then, techniques are being used in *Les Enfants de la Joie* that are more typical of the Fairs than the Italians, but can still not be said to provide proof positive of a particular affiliation to one or the other tradition, particularly since Piron had already made use of allegorical characters himself in an earlier play for the Italians, *Les Huit Mariannes* (1725), so that the appearance of such characters in *Les Enfants de la Joie* is not even a unique case in Piron's own œuvre.

When we arrive at the archetypal Italian characters, we are clearly dealing with a common property: even if the Fairs did inherit them from the old Italian theatre, their constant use had firmly established them as their own before the arrival of the new Italian troupe in 1716. There are, however, perhaps one or two observations to be made.

The role of Pierrot, although one of the regulars of the old Italian theatre, appears largely to have been developed by the actor Giuseppe Giaratoni in France.[12] As Virginia Scott shows, with Arlequin and Mezzetin, he played an important role in the French repertoire of the troupe, while other Italianate characters from the company do not appear in Gherardi's collection of French repertoire at all.[13] His very name is clearly idiomatically French in a way that those of the other archetypal characters are not, and not only does he frequently appear in Gherardi's repertoire with a French peasant accent, he is also the only archetypal character ever to do so; Giaratoni, who came from Italy only in 1661,[14] must have been a gifted linguist.[15] In the Fair repertoire Pierrot remains one of the most regular of the Italian archetypes to appear, and although in these plays he appears only twice with a peasant accent in the period up to 1725, the only other example of an archetype using such an accent, or, indeed, any non-standard accent apart from Italian,[16] is Gille — a character said to have derived from Pierrot — in the role of La Fausse Foire.[17] Hence, although, as in the Italian repertoire old and new, Arlequin is most likely to take centre stage, Pierrot is nevertheless the most French of the Italian archetypes, and consequently the character who most typifies the French adoption of the Italian theatre found in the Fair repertoire.

With this in mind, it is interesting to see how the characters' affiliations are shown in the plays from the Fair repertoire that deal with the relationships between the various theatrical companies. *La Querelle des théâtres* (1718) in fact sets a trend by having the Fair 'played' by Pierrot and its associate the Opéra by Arlequin.[18] Neither the Comédie-Française nor the Comédie-Italienne is 'played' by a particular figure, but when they are allotted supporters, while clearly the Théâtre Français has no right to any of the Italianate characters, the Fair claims Mezzetin, Polichinelle,[19] and a Gille, whereas the Théâtre Italien is allotted only a Pantalon and a Scapin, characters who never found a secure foothold in the Fair repertoire and who, like the Gille, are de-individualized by the use of the indefinite article. *Les Funérailles de la Foire* (1718) again finds Pierrot as the Fair and Arlequin as the Opéra with Scaramouche and Mezzetin as the Fair's chief followers, a situation repeated in *Le Rappel de la Foire à la vie* (1721). In *La Fausse Foire* Pierrot represents the genuine Fair, and he is supported by Arlequin, le Docteur, Mezzetin, Scaramouche, Colombine, and Arlequine, a character who usually appears only when, as in *Les Enfants de la Joie*, a precise female equivalent for Arlequin is required. *Le Régiment de la Calotte* (1721) has no representation of the Fair, but has that rare character in either the Fairs or the French repertoire of the Italians, Pantalon, as the representative of the Théâtre Italien, and in *L'Ombre du Cocher Poète* (1722) the troupe of marionettes who arrive in Paris to claim their inheritance of the Fair consists of Polichinelle, the usual main character in puppet plays at the Fairs, Pierrot, Arlequin, and Colombine. Nevertheless, we note a slight change of affiliation in the untitled *Prologue* performed in 1722, for this is one of those plays from *Le Théâtre de la Foire* that was written to be performed at the Fair by the Italians, and here their theatre is represented not only by Pantalon, but also by Arlequin. Although performed the year after *Les Enfants de la Joie* in 1726, *Les Comédiens corsaires* is also close enough to that work to be of interest, particularly with regard to the figure of Scaramouche, for in this play, which represents all three rival troupes, while Pierrot is, as usual, a representative of the Fairs (the only one to appear on stage), Scaramouche is not only, with Pantalon and le Docteur, a representative of the Italians, he also speaks with an obvious Italian accent. As for Arlequin, although 'un Arlequin' — the article shows a telling refusal to individualize him — is spotted off stage on the *forains*' ship, he does not appear on stage at all.

So what does all this prove? The Frenchness of Pierrot, already apparent in the repertoire of the old Italian theatre, where he was invented, encourages the Fair writers to claim him as their own, even to the extent of using him as the personification of the Fairs.

However, they recognize that Arlequin, despite being the dominant Italian archetype of their own theatre, is also the undisputed property of the Italians. Consequently, he appears as a supporter of the Fair where representatives of the other theatres do not appear, but in plays that personify the different companies, he is always the Opéra, a friend to the Fair, but not the Fair and not one of the Fair's followers either; in *Les Comédiens corsaires*, where he would have to be assigned to either the Fair troupe or the Italians, he is simply left in the wings. The same writers, however, are happy to show him as a representative of the Italian theatre in a play written by them for that company.

Scaramouche, although a regular character in many Fair plays, normally speaking perfect French, is left out of *La Querelle des théâtres*, and then, despite appearing as a follower of the Fair in plays devoted more to the fate of the Fair companies than to rivalries between the troupes, becomes a representative of the Italians, complete with accent to prove it, in *Les Comédiens corsaires*. He is a stalwart of the Fairs, but this last play recognizes an underlying Italianate quality also suggested in two other plays from the Fair repertoire, for in both *La Forêt de Dodône* (1721) from Lesage and D'Orneval's collection and the prologue to Piron's own *Tirésias* (1722) he similarly has an Italian accent. In other words, the Fairs have adopted him as their own, but the recognition that he is above all an Italian archetype remains.

We will return to this issue of the distinctions between the treatment of the different archetypes by the troupes when we consider the issue of the meaning of Piron's play, but it may be useful to pause here and consider what we have learnt about the differences between the two types of play, the Fair play and the Italian play. And, of course, the answer is that, in truth, there is very little difference at all. The peasant characters with their traditional stage-accents may look more French than Italian, but they were already a feature of Italian theatre before the development of the Fair repertoire, and, while the mixture of conventional mythological characters and figures that personify qualities, found in *Les Enfants de la Joie*, is more characteristic of the Fairs than the old Italian theatre, there are examples of it in Gherardi, showing it not to be a significant enough difference to prove a particular classification. Perhaps the tiny role given to Pierrot in this play for the Italians is a reflection of his inherent Frenchness, but even he cannot be seen as a character unique to the Fairs, since he was developed by the old Italian theatre. Ultimately, the similarities derive from the fact that the Fairs had so thoroughly assimilated the Italian tradition that, when the new Italian troupe arrived in France, it was impossible for them to develop a French repertoire based on the traditions and archetypes of the *commedia dell'arte* without appearing like a copy of their rivals. The only significant feature of *Les Enfants de la Joie* setting it apart from the Fair repertoire as an unambiguously Italianate comedy is that it is not an *opéra-comique*, so that, when a writer provides the Italians with plays in that form, as in the two parodies Piron wrote for them, the two traditions appear to have merged. It is paradoxical that it was not until 1762 that the two companies themselves merged, since, by then, their repertoires had drifted further apart than at this earlier period, and equally paradoxical that, if the plays of that greatest of writers for the Italians, Marivaux, feel so different from the productions of the Fairs, it is largely due to the gradual process of Gallicization he and others worked on the Italian repertoire.[20] But then, if Piron accepted, even emphasized, the similarities between the Fair and the Italian repertoires in his plays for the Italians, rather than give them a more individual stamp, perhaps that was part of his point.

This leads to the consideration of Momus, another figure who features in the repertoire of both the Fairs and the old Italian theatre, although not particularly frequently in either case. He appears in four plays in the Italian anthology of Gherardi, and twice in Lesage and D'Orneval's *Théâtre de la Foire*. To these relatively infrequent appearances, Piron, in his comparatively small number of plays for the two theatres, adds two in plays for the Fairs and a major role in the present play for the Italians.

Dominique Quéro, referring to the Frères Parfaict's selective response to his role in Alexandre Hardy's *La Gigantomachie; ou, Combat des dieux avec les géants* (1626), an earlier version of a theme dealt with by Piron, suggests that his function as entertainer to the gods at feasts was principally what was associated with him by the time they wrote their *Histoire du théâtre français* between 1745 and 1749.[21] This is certainly how he is depicted on two of those four appearances in Gherardi's collection, *Les Adieux des officiers* and *Les Aventures des Champs Élysées* (both 1693),[22] where he is only a contributor to the closing divertissements, and consequently not given individualized characteristics. The same is not true of his other two appearances, which both depict a very similar character, notable in particular for his cynicism. In the second, *Les Souhaits* (1693), where he appears in three out of ten French scenes,[23] Jupiter comments of him: 'Hé, quel diantre de cinique est-ce que ce dieu-là? Je crois parbleu qu'on ne te sert que du fiel & de la moutarde au lieu de nectar & d'ambroisie.'[24] The same cynical disposition and an even more unpleasant personality is found in the earlier *Arlequin Phaéton* (1692), where he is a more major character, the villain of the piece who deliberately leads Phaéton to his death.[25]

The Momus found in *Le Théâtre de la Foire* engages in a less unpleasant form of mockery. Admittedly his first appearance is similar to, indeed briefer than, those from the Italian repertoire where he features only at the end, for in *Le Temple de l'Ennui* (1716) he appears as a *deus ex machina* descending to banish boredom from the world in a single quatrain, but more interesting is the way he is characterized: he is 'dieu de la joie' in anticipation of the association we find in Piron's play, a character who turns the Temple of Boredom into 'un lieu agréable' and could make even the most unfortunate individuals laugh. Perhaps most important, he is the patron of the Fair and its actors. He is a similar character in the other play from Lesage and D'Orneval's anthology to feature him, *Le Régiment de la Calotte* (1721). A central figure here, he has lost his immediate connection with the Fairs; he is the patron of the Calotins, the spoof regiment founded at court in 1702, which recruited as its members all who were seen to be ridiculous. This society was close to Piron's heart; he was orator of the organization, which met for soirées at the château of the Comte de Livry.[26] Nevertheless, the character, although 'played' by that representative of both companies, Arlequin, finally comes down on the side of the Fairs by recruiting the Italian troupe into the regiment for having set up a theatre at the Fair, spent a lot of money on an unsuccessful play, and put on a ball during a heatwave. The mockery of the Italians on their admission to the regiment in a ritual modelled on the medical ceremony in *Le Malade imaginaire* forms the grand finale.[27] The character's close association with the Fair is re-established the following year in Piron's own *Arlequin-Deucalion* (1722), where, 'played' by the puppet Polichinelle, he actually represents the Fair, and a different bond is established with the Fair in *Le Mariage de Momus*, when he chooses La Foire for his bride (*MdM*, III. iv).

A play for the Italians demands a different wife, so in *Les Enfants de la Joie* his spouse is La Joie herself, and, in keeping with such an alliance, he is '[le] Dieu des fous' (*EdJ*, ii) and remains the congenial character depicted in the Fair repertoire, not the vile cynic of the old Italian theatre. The play deals with the birth of his first male children,[28] Scaramouche, Pierrot, and Arlequin. These are not mythological characters represented by these archetypes, but the archetypes themselves, hence the play is an allegory of the birth of the Italian theatre itself, the offspring of Momus and La Joie, at first glance a fitting parentage for the comic vivacity of the Italian troupe, as Lucine comments: 'Momus & la Joie. Hem? Ce n'est pas là pour engendrer mélancholie, du moins' (*EdJ*, ii). However, even if it is of his association with the Régiment de la Calotte that Momus speaks in the play (*EdJ*, vi), his connection with the Fairs cannot be ignored.[29]

Furthermore, the three children, representatives of the *commedia dell'arte* and hence also of the Théâtre Italien, turn out to be significant disappointments to Momus, for Até, goddess of misfortune and sworn enemy of Momus, La Joie, and everything connected to them (*EdJ*, xv), like the traditional wicked fairy, curses them. While much of the comedy of the Italian archetypes generally derives from their vices, which we laugh at but usually also sympathize with, Piron seems quite deliberately to underplay the comedy here: Scaramouche, perhaps the eldest because the most Italian, turns out to be a bully, rants and raves for four short speeches, and then disappears; Pierrot, who has possibly been given the smallest role because he is the most French, does nothing but burst into tears before he too leaves;[30] Arlequin, meanwhile, the only one allowed to remain on stage for any significant time, demonstrates an extreme form of his usual vices, turning out to be a kleptomaniac with his hand constantly in his father's pocket, who can be distracted from his thieving only by the smell of food.

A happy and a moral ending is achieved when La Morale brings on the three Graces transformed into Scaramouchette, Pierrette, and Arlequine, promising that they will reform their spouses. Hence the dénouement stresses the moral worth of theatre, which corrects vice, a clear reworking of the old 'plaire et instruire' formula. So theatre in general and the Théâtre Italien in particular are given a moral justification.

The Italian troupe must have been satisfied with this conclusion, but it is difficult not to suspect that there is another hidden message that would have pleased them less: the new Italian theatre, as the child of Momus, does not descend directly from the Italian tradition, but comes more immediately from the Fairs; hence, as the play shows, the products of the two traditions are virtually indistinguishable. Of course, playwrights of the period were quite happy to work for any company that paid them — Fuzelier, one of the most active writers for the Fairs, wrote for a wide range of other companies too — so it is unlikely that Piron's hidden message was an expression of antagonism to the Italians born of loyalty to the Fairs,[31] but it is certainly characteristic of the author who in his first play for the Fairs criticized the Fair tradition as a whole that he should conceal a sideswipe at the Italians in a play written for them.

Notes to Chapter 7

1. Although another exception, proving that this is not a hard and fast rule, is Piron's first parody for the Fairs, *Colombine-Nitétis*, which uses *opéra-comique* to parody a tragedy by Antoine Danchet.
2. Following the conventions of his edition, Dufay spells the title *Les Enfans de la Joie*. Since it is the only title to feature an archaic spelling, I have preferred to modernize it.
3. Oddly, after noting that they do not belong to the genre, Pascale Verèb, in the section of her study devoted to the plays, deals with both *Arlequin-Deucalion* and *Les Enfants de la Joie* under the general heading of *opéra-comique*, and includes the plays for the Italians in a bibliographical entry headed 'Répertoire des pièces foraines' (*Alexis Piron, poète*, pp. 422–509 and 635–39).
4. For more information on this collaboration, see Richard Waller, 'The Theatrical Writings of Jacques Autreau and the Problems of Experimentation', in *Essays on French Comic Drama from the 1640s to the 1780s*, ed. by Derek Connon and George Evans, French Studies of the Eighteenth and Nineteenth Centuries, 7 (Berne: Peter Lang, 2000), pp. 99–115.
5. The Latin form of the Greek Momos, although Momus is also used in Greek contexts in some sources. Momus is the form preferred by the majority of French writers, although Mome will be found in some older sources.
6. She is an obscure enough figure for Piron to have her explain herself to the audience: she is 'la terrible Até', 'la divinité puissante & funeste à qui le sort a commis le soin de faire ici-bas des malheureux' (*EdJ*, i).
7. *L'Opéra de campagne* (1692) has a Jeannot (although apparently without a peasant accent), *L'Union des deux opéras* (1692) a Mathurin, and *Arlequin misanthrope* (1696) a Jaquet. In contrast to the careful notation of stage-dialect forms found in the plays of eighteenth-century authors, including Piron, indications that a character is expected to adopt an accent are often very slight in Gherardi's anthology (*Le Théâtre italien; ou, le recueil général de toutes le comédies et scènes françaises jouées par les comédiens italiens du roi*, 6 vols (Paris: Briasson, 1741; repr. in facsimile, Geneva: Slatkine, 1969)), suggesting both that it was mainly left to the actors to improvise accents, and that there may be instances where the text gives no indication that an accent was used.
8. And (see previous note) the male equivalent of the name crops up in *L'Union des deux opéras* (1692).
9. There is, however, only one other example — a Gros-Colas in *Les Arrêts de l'Amour* (1716) — in the plays in Lesage and D'Orneval's *Théâtre de la Foire* for the years up to and including 1725; this is the only appearance of such a name in Piron's plays.
10. Such as the Démon des couplets in *L'Enchanteur Mirliton* (1725).
11. *Le Caprice*, as the single play by Piron to appear in *Le Théâtre de la Foire*, is double-counted here. *Les Chimères* is centred on the figure of La Vérité, although, this being a comedy and a Fair play, she hands her job over to Arlequin for the duration of most of the action.
12. See Virginia Scott, *The 'Commedia dell'Arte' in Paris, 1644–1697* (Charlottesville: University Press of Virginia, 1990), pp 190–91.
13. *The 'Commedia dell'Arte' in Paris*, pp. 250–51.
14. See Scott, *The 'Commedia dell'Arte' in Paris*, pp 340–41.
15. The only other example of an archetypal character speaking with a non-standard French accent

in Gherardi's collection is when Colombine adopts a Gascon accent in *Colombine avocat pour et contre* (1685), but this is part of a disguise, rather than the accent of the role as a whole, as it tends to be in the case of Pierrot. Foreign accents (apart from Italian) are also very rare in Gherardi's repertoire.

16. And even in the case of Italian, there are only, as we shall see below, two examples before 1725, one in *Le Théâtre de la Foire* and the other in a work by Piron.
17. Pierrot's appearances, both in the character of a Garde-Moulin, are in *Le Tombeau de Nostradamus* (1714) and *Les Enragés* (1725); *La Fausse Foire* dates from 1721. Virginia Scott comments that 'the French adopted [Pierrot] as their own and rechristened [him] Gilles' (*The 'Commedia dell'Arte' in Paris*, p 190), but this is not the pattern we find in the Fairs. Pierrot remains an important character, whereas Gille tends to be used alongside as a generic term, usually in the plural and requiring an article even in the singular (Lesage and D'Orneval spell it with a final 's' only in the plural). The appearance without an article in *La Fausse Foire* is the first such use in *Le Théâtre de la Foire* as well as the character's first major role, but it is also the last time the name features in the anthology. Interestingly, the role given to the character here portrays him as a sort of upstart rival to Pierrot, since Pierrot it is who plays the shade of the true Fair. Pierrot makes regular appearances in Piron's plays for the Fairs, but he never uses the term Gille.
18. The Fairs, as we have seen, owed the right for their actors to sing to a financial arrangement with the Opéra.
19. Presumably, since live actors and marionettes were not usually mixed, played by a live actor here as in the old Italian troupe (see Scott, *The 'Commedia dell'Arte' in Paris*, pp. 266–71); but, as we have noted, at the Fairs Polichinelle was generally found only in puppet plays.
20. See 'The Servant as Master: Disguise, Role-Reversal and Social Comment in Three Plays of Marivaux', in *Studies in the 'Commedia dell'arte'*, ed. by David J. George and Christopher J. Gossip (Cardiff: University of Wales Press, 1993), pp. 121–37, for my discussion of one aspect of this development in Marivaux's works.
21. See *Momus philosophe: recherches sur une figure littéraire du XVIIIe siècle* (Paris: Champion, 1995), pp. 39–40.
22. In the latter he is named Mome, not Momus.
23. This is a late example in Gherardi's collection of a play only partly in French, for which he publishes only the French scenes.
24. The source text is the edition of 1741, reprinted in facsimile by Slatkine.
25. These four plays are by different authors, but the fact that the remaining three all date from the year after *Arlequin Phaéton* suggests that it sparked off a short-lived vogue for the character.
26. For further information on the regiment, see Jean Aymon and others, *Mémoires pour servir à l'histoire de la Calotte* (Basle: chez les héritiers de Brandmyller, 1725). For information on Piron's role in the regiment, see Verèb, *Alexis Piron, poète*, pp. 198–203, and, for a record of the Comte de Livry's soirées and more on Piron's contribution to them, *Histoire et recueil des Lazzis*, ed. by Judith Curtis and David Trott, Studies on Voltaire and the Eighteenth Century, 338 (Oxford: Voltaire Foundation, 1996). I have written briefly on both the regiment and the play in Jane Clark and Derek Connon, *'The Mirror of Human Life': Reflections on François Couperin's 'Pièces de Clavecin'* (Huntingdon: King's Music for Janiculum, 2002), pp. 44–45.
27. He is found again in his role of patron of the Calotins in a passing mention in the prologue of Piron's parody *Atis* (1726), written only shortly after *Les Enfants de la Joie*, ridiculing the Italians again, this time for unsuccessfully putting on a play from the French repertoire (*A*, prologue, vi).
28. The reason Momus has had his fill of daughters is made clear near the beginning of the play: 'La Joie n'a-t-elle pas je ne sais combien de filles qui courent le monde? Tout Paris en est pavé' (*EdJ*, ii).
29. Pascale Verèb also associates Momus with the Fairs, but, in failing to differentiate *Les Enfants de la Joie* from the Fair repertoire, also fails to note the incongruity of that association in a play for the Italians (*Alexis Piron, poète*, pp. 501–02).
30. Perhaps the fact that he is no more than a crybaby is an early indication of the sentimental character he would later become.
31. After all, the Fairs (and specifically Fuzelier) are one of the targets of satire in another play for the Italians, *Les Huit Mariannes*.

CHAPTER 8

❖

Four Parodies

Colombine-Nitétis, *Philomèle*, *Les Huit Mariannes*, and *Atis*

Of the four stage works by Piron designated *parodie*, two were written for the Fairs and two for the Italians, but all share *opéra-comique* form. *Colombine-Nitétis*, first performed at the Foire Saint-Germain on 7 March 1723, parodies Antoine Danchet's tragedy *Nitétis*, first seen just under a month earlier on 11 February;[1] *Philomèle*, premièred by the Italians in 1723, parodies the recently revived opera *Philomele* by the librettist Pierre-Charles Roy and composer Louis de La Coste, originally created in 1705; *Les Huit Mariannes* (1725), again written for the Italians, has as its principal object of satire Voltaire's *Mariamne*, first performed in its revised version on 10 April 1725, but also includes references to three other tragedies on the subject, one anonymous and the others by Tristan L'Hermite and the Abbé Nadal, as well as the earlier parody for the Fairs by Fuzelier, *Les Quatre Mariamnes*;[2] *Atis* (1726), a work for the Fairs, parodies the famous opera *Atys* by Quinault and Lully, which had been revived at the end of 1725.[3]

Parody is, in itself, of course a form of transformation, but since *Les Huit Mariannes* is also one of a small number of works from this period that additionally transforms our expectations in relation to what a parody actually is, we should begin by looking at the term itself, which is far from straightforward.

Writers on the terminology surrounding the forms loosely grouped together under the heading 'parody' complain, quite rightly, about the lack of precision in the use of the term, carefully differentiating parody, in which the style of a noble or serious genre is used to tell a trivial story to comic but not necessarily mocking effect, from travesty, in which a noble or serious subject is mocked by being presented in low style.[4] The idea of the travesty was certainly familiar during the period we are concerned with: Scarron's *Virgile travesti* (1648–53) was well known, Marivaux had published his *L'Homère travesti* in 1716 and his *Le Télémaque travesti*, written at about the same time,[5] would be published in 1736.

Nevertheless, it is not *travesti* but rather *parodie* that is invariably used by playwrights, even though the most common form of mockery used is that in which noble subject matter is debased by being expressed in language that falls short of the tragic ideal, or by being played out by lower-class characters or archetypes of the Italian *commedia dell'arte*, all with a more pragmatic outlook on life than the tragic heroes they are imitating. It is true that occasionally comic effect may be produced in the popular theatre by characters speaking in mock heroic style, parody in the strictest sense of the word, but the dominant device in these works designated *parodie* is that more strictly termed travesty.

So far it may look simply as if our eighteenth-century authors are guilty of precisely the same looseness of usage found today, in which 'parody' is used for any work which mocks another by distorted imitation, but its use in the theatre is more specific. Piron was not the only writer for the popular theatres to draw on classical mythology for comedies: comedy on mythological subjects was not unknown at the Théâtre Français, but was much more popular in the repertoires of the Italians and the Fairs. Nevertheless, although such plays were usually examples of travesty, they were not generally identified either as travesties or as parodies. The term *parodie* was reserved for works which lampooned recent theatrical productions, usually tragedies of the Théâtre Français or *tragédies lyriques* performed at the Académie Royale de Musique. Hence, a work designated *parodie* that dealt with a classical myth would be not just a send-up of that myth in general, but a spoof of a specific recent treatment of it. And a vital aspect of the mockery would be the inclusion of specific references to dramatic weaknesses in the work targeted. This aspect of the work was much more important than simple mockery of the myth on which the original was based. Without this specific thread of drama criticism, a play was not a *parodie*. For the Fairs in particular, parodies were one of the weapons in the war they waged with the established theatres, showing their superiority by pointing out the weaknesses of their rivals.[6] This is perhaps one of the things Piron has in mind when he mounts a justification of parody in *L'Antre de Trophonius*, his second play, first performed in 1722, hence before any of his own parodies (although we should not forget that in his first play, *Arlequin-Deucalion*, Piron was already including elements that mocked contemporary theatre). So, Mercure criticizes the genre of parody:

> Parodie; laboratoire ouvert aux petits esprits malins qui n'ont d'autres talens que celui de savoir gâter & défigurer les belles choses. (*AdT*, xi)

But Marinette defends it, as follows:

> J'y entendrois quelque finesse. Ne seroit-ce pas une satire contre les grands, dont la vanité semble être tympanisée dans ces folles métamorphoses? [...] Je goûte fort ces parodies, & le secret de changer les larmes en éclats de rire. (*AdT*, xi)

The 'grands' certainly include the authors of the Théâtre Français and the Opéra.

In Piron's own output for the Fairs and the Italians, we find a characteristically inventive but far-from-serious version of the myth of Tiresias as well as adaptations of non-dramatic works from various periods, but it is only the four plays devoted entirely to lampooning specific tragedies or operas from the French repertoire which had recently been premièred or revived that qualify for the designation *parodie*. Furthermore, the most inventive of these works, *Les Huit Mariannes*, is very far from being either a conventional travesty or parody, since, despite making use of both techniques, it makes no attempt to present a thoroughgoing adaptation of the plot of the object (or, in this case, objects) of its satire, being instead an allegory of the proliferation of dramatizations of the same subject.[7] This example invites us to conclude that it is the criticism of contemporary theatre that was a much more important reason for the appellation *parodie* for playwrights of this period than the actual dramatic or poetic techniques on display,[8] so 'parody' is the term used to describe these plays in what follows. It is also worth noting that the urge to mock the other theatrical troupes was so strong that examples of parody are dotted here and there in many other of Piron's and other authors' works for the Fairs too, but only those works devoted entirely to a parodic end were designated parodies.

Parody, then, involves an act of transformation: the original must remain recognizable through the distortions, or the act of comparison of that original with the distorted version which is the parody could not occur. And it is from that comparison that both the comedy and the literary criticism derive. Nevertheless, it is perhaps not coincidental that the works Piron chose as the objects of mockery in his three more conventional parodies, *Colombine-Nitétis*, *Philomèle*, and *Atis*, are all related to his own preoccupation with the instability of identity: the first makes copious use of the conventional devices of concealed identity and recognition, and the others are based on transformation myths. We will return to *Les Huit Mariannes* after considering these three works.

There was a common currency of devices used by writers of parody at this period (indeed, at any period), so the techniques used by Piron are not in themselves original, but it is of interest to examine how he makes use of them. All three parodies have a prologue that sets the work in its theatrical context, making some reference to the issue of adaptation. So in the prologue to the puppet play *Colombine-Nitétis* Pierrot is mocked for his tragic costume and his pretensions in thinking he can play a prince in the tragedy *Nitétis*. And not only is Pierrot an inappropriate actor, this is the wrong theatre for such a play. Nevertheless, Pierrot's response is significant:

LE DOCTEUR

> Mais encore, où vas-tu, avec cette guenille héroïque?

PIERROT

> Jouer le rôle de Psammenite dans *Nitétis*.

LE DOCTEUR

> Dans *Nitétis*! est-ce qu'on joue ici cette tragédie! Voici un plaisant théâtre pour cela!

PIERROT

> Oui, Docteur, on l'y joue; non pas tout à fait mot pour mot; mais dans son vrai sens au moins. (*CN*, prologue, i)

'Dans son vrai sens': this will not be an exact rendition of the original, but it will be true to the meaning, perhaps truer than that original. And if Pierrot is capable of playing this role, it is because of the ineptitude of authors who make their tragic heroes such poor representations of the originals on whom they are based:

LE DOCTEUR

> En bonne foi, je n'aurois jamais cru que tu fusses du bois dont on fait les héros.

PIERROT

> Oh que si. Depuis que nos auteurs dramatiques s'avisent d'en faire à leur tête, on trouve qu'ils me ressemblent tous, plus qu'à ceux dont ils portent le nom. (*CN*, prologue, i)

Hence, tragic authors deserve their fate at the hands of the parodists, since it results from their own ineptitude. In revealing the faults of the plays or operas they are mocking, the parodies set out to justify this claim.

Perhaps because the serious productions of the period were such easy game,[9] authors were almost queuing up to parody the same works, a fact underlined in the prologues of both *Philomèle* and *Atis*; the former features authors Sans-Rime and Sans-Raison deploring the fact that the parody they are about to see has appeared just as they were finishing their own,[10] the latter shows La Foire worrying that her parody of *Atys* will suffer by having been preceded by another at the Théâtre Italien.[11]

All these prologues approach the issue from a different perspective: in that to *Colombine-Nitétis* the puppet actors discuss the play and their roles (or lack of roles) in it, in the case of *Philomèle* representatives of the audience try to get into the theatre without paying, and the prologue to *Atis* begins with the allegorical figure La Foire worrying about the lack of both a play and a cast and ends with La Folie providing the parody we are about to see. Nevertheless, all insist on the fact that a play is about to be performed, and so stress the artificiality of what we are about to see. We are not to forget that we are watching a play and be drawn into the action, for that would destroy the self-consciousness inherent in parody — although, in truth, the drama is such that it would be difficult to imagine any spectator responding to it as an illusionistic piece of theatre even without this warning.

In addition, all draw attention to the notion of parody and its prevalence in the popular theatre of the time. We have noted the references in *Philomèle* and *Atis* to the existence of other parodies of the same works, and Pierrot draws attention in *Colombine-Nitétis* to his roles in other parodies: 'N'étois-je pas, l'an passé, prince romain? Me voilà prince d'Égypte; & la Foire prochaine, j'espère être prince portugais' (*CN*, prologue, i).[12] The prologue to *Philomèle* goes a step further, by including an extended close parody of two scenes in Quinault and Lully's *Alceste* (*P*, prologue, viii), an inclusion all the more unusual given the lack of topicality (the work had not been revived since 1716): generally Piron's parodies and his other literary references refer to the current artistic scene, hence to new works or recent revivals.[13] Perhaps, by providing a reminder of the work of the greatest French librettist of the seventeenth and eighteenth centuries directly before embarking on his parody of Roy's libretto for *Philomele*, he hopes to hammer home the latter's inferiority. And, although operatic parodies were generally more about the libretto than the music, a similar parody in the main text (*P*, III. vi) gives us a chance to compare the relative merits not only of the libretti but of the music too, when a parody of both words and music of another Lully opera, *Bellérophon*, this time with the illustrious trio of Thomas Corneille, Boileau, and Fontenelle as librettists, is immediately followed by a passage that parodies both Roy's words and La Coste's music.

Pierrot's versatility in the range of tragic heroes he can parody brings us to another aspect of parodic technique used by Piron. For dramatic parody commonly undermines the heroes of tragedy by having them played by recognizable comic actors who retain their usual stage personas for their role in the parody, and the parodists of the period with which we are concerned here had the additional advantage of being able to call not just on recognizable actors, but on recognizable comic types, the archetypes of the *commedia dell'arte*, figures whose characteristics remained reasonably constant even when played by different actors. Hence, the actor plays the archetype, and the archetype plays the character in the parody, giving the characters a double, even a triple identity. Furthermore, the usual associations of the archetype are often echoed in the parody, and its visible attributes would also carry significant comic weight. This is at its most obvious in *Colombine-Nitétis*, where the actors are marionettes, but it is, nevertheless, something by which Piron apparently sets less store than other parodists of the period, since, *Les Huit Mariannes* apart, the texts lack much specific indication of which archetype is to play which role. We discover from the title of *Colombine-Nitétis* who is to play the heroine, and the prologue tells us that Pierrot is to be her lover, but the *dramatis personae* gives us no additional details and, although it is fair to suspect that *Philomèle* also made use of the device, the text is entirely silent on the issue. Nevertheless, the *dramatis personae* of *Atis* confirms its use in that play by casting Pierrot as Atis, Le Docteur as the other male lead, and, using another stock device guaranteed to undermine the credibility of an originally serious character, the male archetype Arlequin in the female role of Cybèle.[14]

Atis also contains the most obvious example of a tragic character being given in the parody the singularly untragic attributes of the archetypal figure playing him, for Atis shares with Pierrot, and indeed all the *zanni* of the *commedia*, a fondness for drink. It seems most likely, since there is no obvious noble parallel to the character's drunkenness in the original, that Piron introduced this as a down-to-earth explanation for behaviour provoked in the tragic Atys by divinely induced madness. Nevertheless, he sustains the theme throughout the action, beginning with Sangaride claiming that Atis's declaration of love for her is merely the drink talking — a rather more rational explanation than we will find in the original text for why the character should have kept silent about his feelings until his beloved's wedding day — and ending with him metamorphosing not into a pine tree, but into something made from wood: a wine barrel. This is not the only appearance of this theme in these parodies. Although anxious to consummate her love for Cambyse, Nitétis would rather not do so in the evening, because he always smells of wine then, and drink is bad for the performance:

> Le soir vous sentez trop le vin,
> Mon cher Cambyse,
> Remettez à demain matin;
> Car, pour être à ma guise,
> Il faut aller droit en chemin;
> Ce qui n'est pas quand on se grise. (*CN*, xviii)

If the Bacchantes of Roy's *Philomele* (IV. v) are merely inspired by Bacchus, those of Piron's parody are positively drunk:

> Ma commère & moi j'ons couru des premières,
> Aussi j'en ons pris à tirelarigot!
> C'étoit, ma foi, de bon piot,

J'en ai bu, pour mon écot,
Un pot, deux pots, trois pots. (*P*, III. v)

And the villain Térée[15] responds to the destruction of his city and the murder of his son not by killing himself in despair, as in the original, but by deciding to drown his sorrows in drink, going off to join the Bacchantes' party. The murder of the son by the mother is an unusually violent act to remain in a parody, where such actions are usually replaced by something more characteristic of everyday life; Atis, for example, instead of killing his beloved, as in the opera,. merely gives her a drunken beating. Nevertheless, even this turns out to be related to the theme of drink: Progné drinks in order to summon up the courage to murder her son, but then gets lachrymose after the event, causing her sister to remark that this is typical of her when drunk.

This is not the only example of the heightened emotional world of tragedy being viewed through the filter of more down-to-earth attitudes: the Progné of the parody points out to La Jalousie that the murder of her son as revenge on her husband fails to take account of the possibility that he may not be the father (*P*, III. iii); Térée takes consolation for the loss of his son and his city in the fact that at least his wife has left him (*P*, III. ix); Psammenite comments that he is wetting himself with fear (*CN*, xiv); Atis complains that the nightmare sent by Cybèle was so frightening it nearly made him wet the bed (*A*, xii); Cambyse fends off Nitétis's suggestion that they marry, commenting that, like his ancestors, he prefers to take concubines (*CN*, xviii).

Another comic technique commonly used in parodies is compression. While the device of giving to the characters more down-to-earth attitudes than their tragic models mocks tragedy in general by showing how far removed its attitudes are from those of real life, particularly the physical appetites and urge for self-preservation that determine the behaviour of the characters of low comedy, compression is often used to more specific critical ends, by showing the lack of logic in characters' behaviour that is masked by the wordy deliberations of the tragic originals.

The most obvious examples in our three parodies occur in *Colombine-Nitétis*, since the other two are parodies of opera libretti which, by their very nature, are more compressed than spoken tragedy, as music drama takes longer to deliver its text. A corollary of this is, of course, that, in the hands of a good composer, text which seems perfunctory on the page may work perfectly well when set to music. Nevertheless, even bearing this in mind, although it is a trap that the great Quinault tends not to fall into, there are occasions when the less gifted Roy seems almost to have done the parodist's work for him. Take, for instance, the tiny chorus for the people fleeing the burning city, which is interrupted after only two short lines by a complete change of mood, as a group of spirits appear dressed as sailors:

Ah! nous perissons-tous!
Dieux! sauvez-nous.
(*On entend une Symphonie.*)
Qu'entens-je! quels concerts! quelle aimable harmonie!
Est-ce sa douceur infinie,
Ou ma foiblesse, helas! qui calme mes transports?
Je vois des Matelots paroître sur ces bords.[16]

No matter how elaborate the musical setting, these seem to be rather few words to express the necessary mood of despair before moving on to something else. And then the unexpected move from the emotional to the practical in the space of a single couplet, as the arrival of the sailors is announced, is dangerously bathetic. Piron too seems to have been struck by the problem of this chorus, for it is here that he parodies not just the words of the original, with the inclusion of comically untragic vocabulary, but also the music. He underlines the excessive contrast in the change of emotion by his use of a particularly trivial tune for the second phase of the scene, which he gives to Philomèle, and further comedy is added by another change of emotion to fear, still to the same trivial tune, before the arrival of the sailors, although surely he has missed a trick in stressing the supernatural aspect of the arrival rather than preserving the banal word 'matelot' from the original:

CHŒUR DE PEUPLE
Air: *Parodie de l'Opéra de Philomèle*, Act. V. Sc. II.
Ah! nous rôtissons tous!
Dieux, mouillez-nous!
(*L'orchestre joue un petit air de flûtes.*)
PHILOMÈLE
Air: *Tique, tique, tin.*
Quels sons me charment l'ouïe?
Aurois-je le tintouin?
Tique, tique, tique, tin;
L'agréable harmonie,
Qui se mêle au tocsin!
Tique, tique, tique, tin.
Ah! ah! ah! j'ai l'âme atteinte
D'une mortelle crainte;
J'apperçois un lutin. (*P*, III. vi)

Even more inept is the brief scene which ends the third act of Roy's libretto. Terée has had a surprisingly brief vision of monsters emerging from the Temple of Hymen when Progné appears in their stead:

PROGNÉ *sortant du fond du Temple un poignard à la main pour frapper Terée*
Des Monstres que tu vois, connoy le plus funeste.
Helas! ma haine expire, & l'amour seul me reste ...
Elle tombe sur Elise.
TERÉE
Ah! qu'est-ce que je voy!
Quelle main s'arme contre moy!
En dépit du Ciel qui m'outrage,
Allons sur mon Rival faire éclater ma rage.[17]

There is inadvisable potential comedy in having a wife who could, from a certain point of view, be described as shrewish,[18] call herself a monster, an opportunity not missed by Piron, but most problematic is her complete change of heart in a single couplet. The scant attention given to this by Terée before turning to a completely different issue is another incongruity that could easily be parodied, but, spoilt for choice, Piron wisely decides to concentrate his attentions on the issues raised by Progné's couplet. Nevertheless, so compressed is the original, that even a parodist needs longer to create his effects than is taken by Roy; note too that, even in a parody, Piron feels the need to add the detail of Térée staying Progné's hand to help motivate her change of heart:

PROGNÉ *sortant, un poignard à la main*

[...]

Traître, dans ton sang odieux
Mon courroux va s'éteindre!
De tous les monstres à tes yeux,
Je suis le plus à craindre.

TÉRÉE

Madame, vous avez raison,
La faridondaine, la faridondon.

PROGNÉ

Ah! tu veux donc être un mari,
Biribi,
A la façon de Barbari,
Mon ami?

[...]

Il faut chien que je te poignarde.

TÉRÉE *lui arrêtant le bras*

Ah! tout doucement, prenez garde!

PROGNÉ *se pâmant*

Soutenez-moi, Dame Alison!
Toute ma fureur se rétracte.

TÉRÉE

Ma foi, sans cette pâmoison,
Nous mourions tous au second acte. (*P*, II. ix)

The end of that quotation provides an example of another technique used as part of the literary criticism in these works, that is, an allusion to a specifically theatrical concern. Not only is this a play that we are watching, but its function is to signal the dramatic weaknesses of the play it is parodying. Not all such allusions need use specifically theatrical vocabulary, but they do all point to an awareness on the part of the characters that they are in a play, and that, furthermore, that play is either a poor reflection of reality, or is structurally defective, or both.

Hence, when in *Colombine-Nitétis* the habitual overdressing of tragic actors, regardless of the part they are playing, is mocked, it is done with no use of theatrical terminology, but the audience would still have recognized the remark as a reference to the actor's garb and appearance in the original production as well as in the parody: the indication that Thiamis's wig should be well powdered (*CN*, i) tells us the original actor's precise crime, while the reference to him looking as if he has just been taken out of his box takes its humour from the fact that, in the parody, he is being played by a puppet:

THIAMIS

Deux ans sont écoulés, depuis le jour funeste,
Que mes yeux sont privés de la clarté céleste.

PHANÈS

On diroit, te voyant si frais & si dispos,
Que tu sors d'une boîte, & non pas des cachots. (*CN*, i)

Piron would have personal experience of the insensitivity of tragic actors to matters of costume when, ten years later, the actress playing Adélaïde in *Gustave Wasa* appeared immaculately dressed and groomed in Act V, wearing the same costume as in Act IV, despite having supposedly been rescued from drowning in the icy sea in the interval. The wryly unconvincing defence mounted in his preface for the 1758 edition shows apparent solidarity with the actors, but actually makes his real feelings on the issue quite clear (*GW*, préface, p. 207).

Again in *Colombine-Nitétis*, the implausibility of the queen's disappearance without trace for fifteen years is similarly underlined without the use of theatrical vocabulary, although a conventional stereotypical joke allows Piron to draw out the issue of her failure to tell anyone who she is for long enough to be sure the audience gets the point:

LA REINE

[...]

Or écoutez petits & grands,
L'histoire d'un grand accident:
Sous une épaisse & noire voûte,
Depuis quinze ans, je ne vois goutte,
Et tout ce temps s'est écoulé,
Sans qu'à personne j'aie parlé.

PHANÈS

Diable, voilà le pis cela, pour une femme [...].

CAMBYSE

[...]

Je vous promets mon assistance.
Parlez; mais n'allez pas sur moi
Vous venger de ce long silence. (*CN*, vii)

And, similarly, he draws attention to the transparency of the plot device that makes Atys keep silent about his love for Sangaride until the day of her wedding by having his Sangaride comment on his bad timing; needless to say, there is no equivalent remark in Quinault's text:

J'aurois, en d'autres instans,
Trouvé l'offre honnête;
Mais, c'est bien prendre son temps,
Quand la noce est prête!
Et viens-t'en voir la fête,
Jean!
Viens-t'en voir la fête! (*A*, i)

The most developed of these jokes is the running commentary on the sequence of recognition scenes that runs through Danchet's *Nitétis*. Piron uses a number of techniques to make his point, one of the most important being the compression of the plot: in a short play the recognitions come thicker and faster than in a five-act tragedy, and their perfunctory treatment is also comic. But Piron also introduces here the standard theatrical term for such scenes, although, since the word 'reconnaissance' is not unambiguously theatrical, it inhabits a middle ground between vocabulary that is realistic in the mouths of the characters, and terminology that shatters the theatrical illusion. Further comedy comes from the characters' own awareness of the plot they find themselves in, which puts the word 'reconnaissance' constantly in their mouths. The play begins with two scenes that contain an element of recognition. The first is underlined by the use of inappropriate vocabulary:

PHANÈS
[...]
C'est Phanès qui s'offre à ta vue:
Ne connois-tu plus ton ami?
THIAMIS
Hélas! c'est que j'ai la berlue!
Et je ne vois plus qu'à demi. (*CN*, i)

The next presents an example of extreme compression:

CAMBYSE *à Phanès*
[...]
Eh bien, retrouves-tu ce cher ami qui t'aime?
Tout triomphant; j'en suis, au milieu de ma cour,
Dans une peine extrême;
PHANÈS
Il voit encor le jour ...
CAMBYSE *montrant Thiamis*
L'est-ce là?
PHANÈS
C'est lui-même!
CAMBYSE *à Thiamis* [...]
Bonjour! (*CN*, ii)

Neither of these, however, contains the element of surprise or discovery of a previously unsuspected identity, so it is only in the third scene that the key word is deployed, with Cambyse commenting: 'Voici déjà | Une reconnoissance' (*CN*, iii). The 'déjà' is interesting, for it refers to the time-scale of the play, not the time of the character, and so breaks the illusion by drawing attention to the artificiality of the performance in the same way as the comparison with the original text that is also contained in the remark. Later in the same scene, Cambyse finds himself in another recognition scene and, realizing that a pattern is emerging, comments: 'Autre reconnoissance' (*CN*, iii). It is a phrase he will use twice more (*CN*, vii and xiii); he is the only character to use this catchphrase, but not the only one to show awareness of what is going on: Psammenite, announcing the scene in which he reveals to Nitétis that she is not his sister, comments: 'Messieurs, vous allez voir encor | Une reconnoissance' (*CN*, ix), and, in so doing, breaks the illusion even further by acknowledging his awareness of the audience, to whom 'Messieurs' clearly refers. Piron satirizes the lengthy delay before characters realize what is glaringly obvious to the audience by having Nitétis suggest, in her recognition scene with the queen, that it is the characters, rather than the author, who milk such scenes for maximum effect:

Je ne saurois plus, sans rigueur,
Tirer davantage en longueur,
Cette reconnoissance.

[...]
Maman, je suis votre fille,
Apriès est mon papa. (*CN*, xii)

And similar self-consciousness is shown later when the two characters comment, presumably in a reference to the effectiveness of the equivalent scene in the original, on the poor effect it has had on the audience — although, rather as an author might, they blame the hard-heartedness of the spectators, not their own skill:

LA REINE

Une seule chose m'offense;
C'est que le monde est sans pitié;
On n'a ressenti qu'à moitié
Notre reconnoissance.

NITÉTIS
[...]

Quand je vis le spectateur humain,
Qui mettoit le mouchoir à la main,
Je crus que, sensible à mes alarmes,
Jusques aux pleurs j'avois su le toucher:
Mais au lieu d'en essuyer des larmes,
On ne s'en servit que pour se moucher. (*CN*, xvi)

It is difficult not to be struck by the similarity between the sequence of recognition scenes that Piron mocks here and the similar structure of *Gustave Wasa* performed ten years later. Is this an indication that Piron learnt nothing from his apprenticeship in the popular theatres that he could exploit in his work for the Théâtre Français, that it is easier to criticize than to avoid pitfalls oneself? Perhaps not, for we have noted that Piron is careful in his tragedy to avoid using his recognition scenes as constant sources of surprise or pathos, instead underplaying their impact, suggesting that he did indeed learn a lesson from the mistakes made by Danchet, which taught him how best to handle such a plot.

The most extreme form of this internal commentary on the original is the use of explicitly theatrical vocabulary. We have seen an example in *Philomèle*, where Progné's change of heart was necessary to prevent the play ending with the second act. Other comments on the progress of the action are found when Minerve predicts to Athamas that he will be lucky to make it to the middle of the play (*P*, I. viii), or when Nitétis announces the dénouement of a play in which she is a character, showing awareness not only of its structure, but also of its genre, criticizing the use of happy endings in tragedy — a charge of which *Gustave Wasa* will not, perhaps, be entirely innocent:

Voici Cambyse, & voila
La fin de la tragédie.
Croyez-moi, finissons-la,
Ainsi qu'une comédie. (*CN*, xviii)

We find explicit statements of literary criticism in other contexts too, for instance, Athamas's reaction when Térée tries to force him to mistreat his beloved Philomèle to convince her he is no longer in love with her:

> Eh fi! c'est une vieille finesse d'auteurs de romans & de tragédies, qui n'a jamais servi de rien; tout le monde sait cela. (*P*, II. iv)

Another transparent plot device is laid bare when Progné's confidante points out a lack of logic in the behaviour of the goddess Minerva:

PROGNÉ

J'ai trahi ma pauvre sœur:
Elle est! elle est perdue!

ÉLISE

Ah! ne vous embarrassez pas; Minerve en prend soin. Je ne sais pourquoi elle n'en prend pas également de vous, il ne lui en auroit pas plus coûté. (*P*, II. iii)

And some excessively transparent expository plot-narration is criticized:

PROGNÉ

Quoi, ma chère confidente; depuis le temps que tu es à moi, je ne t'ai pas encore appris que le Roi est amoureux de ma sœur, & qu'il l'empêchera de partir?

ÉLISE

Non, Madame; en voilà la première nouvelle.

PROGNÉ

Je ne sais donc comment cela s'est fait.

ÉLISE

Bon! & n'est-ce pas la coutume de vous autres reines de tragédies, de ne nous confier vos secrets, que lorsque vous voulez que tout le monde les sache? Nos oreilles sont comme une sarbacanne, à travers laquelle vous les annoncez au public. (*P*, I. i)

An excessive use of duet writing in *Atys* is highlighted with the use of the technical term in the parody. In the final act of the opera Quinault points to the parallels between the two sets of relationships by writing a whole scene as a double duet, for instance:

CYBÈLE et CELÆNUS

Venez vous livrer au supplice.

ATYS et SANGARIDE

Quoi! la terre et le ciel contre nous sont armés!
Souffrirez-vous qu'on nous punisse?

CYBÈLE et CELÆNUS

Oubliez-vous votre injustice?

ATYS et SANGARIDE

Ne vous souvient-il plus de nous avoir aimés?

CYBÈLE et CELÆNUS

Vous changez mon amour en haine légitime.[19]

Only two brief interventions interrupt this pattern, perhaps making the scene a rare miscalculation on Quinault's part. Piron does not attempt the same level of parallelism, but still cannot resist an allusion to the effect. In his version Célénus and Cybèle share only a single line, which perhaps weakens the potential comedy, but does make possible Cybèle's observation on the duetting of the other two characters, which would not be possible if she were constantly indulging in it herself:

ATIS

[...]

Je n'ai rien volé, sur mon âme.

CÉLÉNUS

Voyez un peu l'homme de bien!
Scélérat, tu me prends ma femme:
Appelles-tu donc cela rien?

ATIS et SANGARIDE

Bon, bon, ce n'étoit que pour rire.
Talaleri, talaleri, talalerire.

CÉLÉNUS

[...]

Une chose m'assassine,
C'est de le voir sans chapeau.

ATIS et SANGARIDE

Nous vous jurons ...

CYBÈLE *à Sangaride*

Paix, coquine!
Vous aimez trop le duo. (*A*, xvii)

This use of the technical terminology of theatre anticipates the similar effect we have observed in *La Métromanie*, although, while this is part of the stock in trade of writers of parody, it is much more unexpected in the world of *grande comédie* with its respect for *vraisemblance*.

I have suggested that in operatic parodies the emphasis is on mockery of the action more than the music. One reason was clearly the greater value placed on the text of an opera in France at this period than subsequently or in other traditions, but another is simply that it is much easier to send up the absurdities of an incoherent or foolish plot than to satirize a more abstract art form like music. Nevertheless, the mockery of the excessive use of duet writing we have just looked at, although deriving from Quinault's text, is already a specifically operatic effect; passages where characters share the same words, a common feature of sung works, are rare in spoken theatre. We have also seen examples of specific extracts from the music being parodied,[20] and, although the texts do not indicate what form this parody took, it seems reasonable to assume that one aspect of the send-up would have been mockery of the kind of voice required to project and sustain opera, in contrast with the more spontaneous singing we would expect from the singing actors most probably found at the Fairs and the Théâtre Italien. The complexity of operatic music also contrasted with the simplicity of the vaudevilles of *opéra-comique*,[21] and so the simple fact of substituting this type of music for the original score represented as much of a mockery of the original music as it did of the tragic plots: Piron has a particular fondness for vaudevilles with nonsense refrains, which underline the frivolity of the music as well as undermining any pretensions to seriousness in the subject matter.[22] Nevertheless, a particularly interesting commentary on the music is to be found in *Atis*.

The vaudevilles that were used for *opéra-comique* and satirical songs came from a wide range of sources, including opera. All that was important was that they were memorable and easy to sing. Once a tune had been adopted into the vaudeville repertoire, it became part of the common currency of the authors and actors using the technique and would have been performed in their usual manner, even if its source was operatic. Hence, it was perfectly possible to find tunes deriving from opera being used as part of the Fairs' stock in trade in works that parodied opera, and even alongside other operatic extracts that were being used parodically. This creates an interesting situation, for it is from Quinault and Lully's *Atys* that one of the most popular of all vaudeville tunes, 'Quand le péril est agréable', derives.[23] To include it in the parody would blur the division, normally satirically underlined by the Fairs, between operatic style and their own simplicity. But rather than take the easy way out by omitting it completely, Piron chooses to make a joke of his own. In the opera the air is sung by Sangaride to Atys in I. iii, a scene which is elided by Piron, whose parody begins with a dialogue between Atis and Sangaride that imitates I. vi of the original. Hence, we are joining the action after Sangaride has made the remarks contained in that air. Piron acknowledges this in the following way:

ATIS

Vous ne vous souvenez donc plus de ce que vous me disiez tantôt.

Air: *Quand le péril, &c.*

Quand le péril est agréable,...

(*Il change d'air.*)

Gnia pas d'mal à ça,
Gnia pas d'mal à ça. (*A*, i)

This is not usually one of those vaudevilles where any of the original words are preserved in the new version, so, by quoting the text as well as the tune, Piron is making the allusion to the opera quite clear. Since it is the most familiar part of the opera, we might expect the parody to deal with it, we might even look forward to hearing it; to leave it out might frustrate the audience, but not in a comic way. Here Piron creates comedy by a deliberate thwarting of expectations, beginning the air, and then cutting it off with a different vaudeville which, because of its dialect text, makes the most of the contrast. The sentence introducing it, indicating that it is something Sangaride said earlier, suggests that we have arrived in the action too late for its most familiar section, which, if we compare the sequence of Quinault's scenes with those of Piron, actually is true.

I have remarked that both operas parodied by Piron deal with transformation myths, but this requires some qualification in the case of *Philomele*. Roy prefaces his text with a disclaimer:

> La Fable de PHILOMELE est rapportée fort au long au sixiéme Livre des Metamorphoses; mais à proprement parler, on n'en a tiré que l'idée de l'intrigue, & les noms des principaux Personnages de la Piece. Il falloit adoucir des caracteres odieux, ôter des incidents qui auroient blessé la bienseance & la pureté du Theâtre, & en substituer de plus convenables. L'Histoire qui a donné lieu à la Fable, en a fourny quelques-uns, les autres sont purement d'imagination, & pour ainsi dire, hazardez: c'étoit presque le seul moyen de mettre PHILOMELE sur la Scene.[24]

It is true that the myth, as told by Ovid and others, is a singularly nasty one.[25] Procne takes revenge on her husband Tereus not only because he is in love with her sister

Philomela, but because he has raped her, then cut out her tongue and hidden her away to keep the crime secret. When she finds out, Procne not only kills their son, she cooks him and feeds him to his father, producing the boy's severed head when Tereus asks where he is. Clearly this action is of the type that was not permitted by the *bienséances*: even the murder of the son, the only detail Roy preserves, is strong stuff by French standards of this period, and, apart perhaps from retaining this murder in the parody to underline how shocking it is, rather than replacing it with a more anodyne event as parodies often do, Piron makes no apparent criticism of the decisions made by Roy over these violent events in his adaptation.[26] Roy's other omission, however, is more surprising, for the story ends with the transformation of the three main characters: as Tereus is on the point of killing the women, Philomela becomes a nightingale, Procne a swallow, and Tereus himself a hoopoe. Such a transformation would have been considered too unrealistic for inclusion in a spoken tragedy, but it is surprising that Roy chose to leave it out of his operatic version; with so few of the main features of the myth remaining, why claim to be adapting it at all? It is an omission Piron cannot tolerate, so he weaves one element of it back into his version by having a palm-reading spirit predict Philomèle's transformation. He even adds a further transformation of his own from nightingale to poppies:

LE GÉNIE *après lui avoir regardé la main*

[...]

Belle Princesse tu dois,
Changeant de nature,
Devenir hôte des bois,
Et tout charmer par ta voix.

PHILOMÉLE

Je serai oiseau! ah, j'irai nicher avec les moineaux!
La bonne aventure!
O gué,
La bonne aventure!
Et comment m'appellera-t-on?

LE GÉNIE

Rossignol.

PHILOMÉLE

Rossignol, oh le joli nom! Et, dites moi, cela durera t il?

LE GÉNIE

Une trentaine de siècles; après quoi, jaloux de la beauté de ton ramage:

[...]

Apollon, mal à propos,
Pour te faire injure,
Doit par un de ses suppôts,
Te rechanger en pavots;
La sotte aventure,
O gué,
La sotte aventure!

PHILOMÉLE

[...]

Ce changement me désespère.

LE GÉNIE

Qu'y faire?
C'est l'ordre du Destin.

PHILOMÉLE

Quoi, de joli réveil-matin,
Me faire un triste somnifère!
Ce changement me désespère.

LE GÉNIE

Qu'y faire?
C'est l'ordre du Destin. (*P*, III. vii)

Thus Piron rebukes Roy for omitting one of the most famous elements of the legend he has adapted, but also takes the opportunity to express his opinion about the adaptation, for the transformation of the nightingale into poppies by a servant of Apollo after about thirty centuries has nothing to do with any mythological tradition; Apollo appears here as divine representative of literature, his servant is Roy himself, and the soporific into which he has transformed Philomèle is his dire libretto.

Perhaps the most scathing expression of Piron's feelings about Roy's original is to be found in a remark that goes even further than those we have already examined in reminding us of the theatrical mechanisms behind the act of parody, for it makes reference to the parody itself in an address aimed directly at the audience: the allegorical character of La Jalousie comments: 'Du moins, Messieurs, si cette parodie-ci ne vous plaît pas, ne vous en prenez point à moi; je vous assure que je n'y ai point de part' (*P*, III. iii). Whatever has motivated this parody, it is not Piron's jealousy at Roy's achievement.

The juxtaposition of these last two examples also indicates the fluidity of chronological perspective common in parodies, moving back and forth between the pretence of being a self-contained telling of the story with its own chronological coherence, and the recognition that the work's true function is as an adaptation of another text; here Piron goes further by adding a reference to the fact that even the work being parodied is an adaptation of an existing myth. Hence, Philomèle, in her mythic chronology, will have to wait three thousand years for Roy to send everyone to sleep with his adaptation of her story, while La Jalousie can speak to the audience of her present role in Piron's parody.

Les Huit Mariannes is, as we have noted, a different kind of parody, and we must begin with some consideration of the circumstances surrounding the writing and performance of its principal subject, Voltaire's *Mariamne*, since these form the subject of the parody.[27] We begin before the first performance of Voltaire's tragedy, when in 1723 a *Mariamne* by an unknown author was given a reading at the Théâtre Français, but was turned down. Voltaire's *Mariamne* received its first performance at the Théâtre Français on 6 March 1724, and was regarded as such an important event that admission prices were doubled. Counter to expectations, the play was a failure, with the end being virtually drowned out by the reaction to calls of 'La reine boit' when Mariamne drank poison on stage.[28] Voltaire withdrew it, and this first version is now largely lost. He set to work on a revised version, but, in the meantime, we find Piron already making fun of its failure in the prologue to *Les Chimères*, first performed on 3 February 1725. On 15 February Nadal's *Mariamne* appeared at the Théâtre Français; it was generally agreed that it was no more successful than Voltaire's. It was also about this time that Tristan L'Hermite's *La Mariane* was reissued by a publisher hoping to cash in on the vogue for the subject.[29]

Shortly afterwards, on 1 March 1725, Fuzelier's *Les Quatre Mariamnes* was performed at the Foire Saint-Germain. Whether or not the idea was stolen from Piron, as he claimed, the play already makes use of the device used in *Les Huit Mariannes* of having each of the versions of the play represented by a character; in Fuzelier's play they are trying to gain admission to the Hôtel de la Comédie. At this stage, the second version of Voltaire's tragedy had not appeared, but enough was known about his intention to present a revised version for there to be allusions to it in the text.

That second version of Voltaire's work, retitled *Hérode et Mariamne* from the second performance, was first performed on 10 April 1725, and this time was a significant success. It had already received eight performances by the time Piron's parody was given by the Italians on 27 April.[30]

To the four Mariamnes represented in Fuzelier's play (the play by an unknown author read at the Théâtre Français, Voltaire's first version, Nadal's tragedy, and Tristan L'Hermite's reprinted play), Piron adds Fuzelier's four — a quartet of undistinguishable and jolly *foraines*. Hence, his title perhaps promises a little more than it delivers; but he also makes the most of the advantage he has over Fuzelier in being able to draw on Voltaire's second version; although not counted as an additional character in the eight Mariannes of the title, that version appears in two different manifestations and is treated at greater length than any of the others, including Voltaire's first version.

In contrast to his other parodies, it is not the content of these plays that particularly interests Piron here — although it is obviously an issue that crops up — but rather the coexistence of so many different versions of the same subject. As in Fuzelier's parody, the different versions become allegorical characters, but Piron's allegory is less straightforward, for he adds an additional level of transformation. The plays, instead of simply competing for entry into the Théâtre Français, become candidates for acceptance into the harem of a sultan, Le Public, who has as his chief eunuch Apollo. Apollo is often the representative of literature in drama of this period, so his role as guardian of the sultan's old wives — the heroines of the classics of the repertoire[31] — and as the person responsible for finding him new ones is logical, but his depiction as a eunuch is surely a commentary by Piron on the current state of literature similar to that found in *Arlequin-Deucalion*, where that other symbol of the writer's art, Pegasus, described in the *dramatis personae* as 'le moderne', has donkey's ears and turkey's wings (*AD*, II. iv).

Hence, the search for a good new play is dramatized as the search for a wife who is both young and beautiful, and Piron finds ingenious ways to allegorize other aspects of the story. The classics of the seventeenth century, therefore, are represented by their heroines being the sultan's well-loved but by now rather boring older wives, while recent works that have failed to please are unsuccessful recent recruits to the harem (*HM*, i).[32] The fact that the first of the tragedies of Mariamne, that by an unknown author, was never performed is represented by the character being seen not by Le Public, but by his vizier ('son essayeur' (*HM*, v), played by Polichinelle)[33] who keeps this prospective wife for himself. And while Le Public does see the characters representing Nadal's and both of Voltaire's versions himself, that representing the version of Tristan L'Hermite, revived only in print, is refused admission entirely (although she does appear later). The new plays all enter veiled, symbolizing the fact that their identity will be revealed only gradually, but then, when they unveil themselves, their grotesqueness is stressed by the traditional device of having them played by male archetypes of the *commedia dell'arte*. Hence the anonymous version is represented by Scaramouche, Voltaire's play by Arlequin (with the added grotesqueness of a Gascon accent for the first version), and Nadal's by Pantalon; Piron recognizes the classic status of Tristan L'Hermite's play by having it played by a woman, Fabia — an ugly old woman, it is true, who speaks archaic French, but a woman none the less. The four characters of Fuzelier's parody, who appear anachronistically after Voltaire's second version, are dressed in a way that underlines their non-tragic origin: 'Les Quatres Mariannes de la Foire, courte-vêtues, en corset & en cotillons rouges' (*HM*, xvi).

Nevertheless, it is the satire of Voltaire's work that most interests Piron, and so it is to the characters representing his tragedy that he devotes most time. The most obvious attribute of the representative of the first version is the antique goblet she carries. We have noted that the heroine's drinking of poison on stage and the reaction it produced was one of the downfalls of that first version, and Voltaire unsurprisingly suppressed it in his revision, making it the most salient feature setting the two versions apart. Piron seizes on the episode in the prologue to *Les Chimères*, where M. de La Brigue reminds M. de La Cabale that it was he who invented the famous quip (*Chim*, prologue, ii). The names suggest that Piron is conceding that, in this at least, the failure of Voltaire's play was not entirely justified. After all, a queen drinking poison on stage was not a novelty, being a feature of the dénouement of one of the classics of the repertoire, Corneille's *Rodogune*.

There is no mention of the heckling in the relevant scene of *Les Huit Mariannes*, but the fact that the drinking of the poison was so well known is shown in Piron's use of it as the central theme. It is coupled with another theme running through all the episodes in the parody devoted to Voltaire: his determination to have his play performed and retain it in the repertoire, something which Piron suggests shows unjustified confidence in his work. This Marianne uses moral blackmail to threaten the sultan, first saying she will leave if he refuses to love her, and then vowing to poison herself. The attitude of the public to Voltaire's play is demonstrated by the sultan's indifference to her threats — his eagerness, even, to see them carried out:

MARIANNE-ARLEQUIN

Munie heureusement d'un venimeux breuvage;
Marianne auroit tort de vouloir, un instant,
Survivre au déshonneur d'un affront si constant;
Voyons votre maintien. Me voilà prête a boire.

LE SULTAN

Et moi prêt à verser.

MARIANNE-ARLEQUIN

Non, je ne le puis croire;
Vous craignez mon trépas, Seigneur, vous m'éprouvez.
Répondez; m'aimez-vous? ou boirai-je?

LE SULTAN

Buvez.

MARIANNE-ARLEQUIN

Le terme est décisif; & la réponse est nette.
Buvons & mourons donc.

(*Elle boit.*)

LE SULTAN

[...]

Eh houppe, eh houplinette,
De pardieu!
Puisque nous sommes en si bon lieu.
Et que notre hôte est si courtois,
Buvez encore une fois.

MARIANNE-ARLEQUIN *tranquillement après avoir bu*

Autant seroit-ce, hélas! si c'étoit du poison.

LE SULTAN

Ce n'en étoit donc pas?

MARIANNE-ARLEQUIN

Quelque sotte! oh que non!
Je veux vivre; & bon gré mal gré, je veux te plaire,
Aime-moi. (*Sautant à la gorge du Sultan*)

LE SULTAN

Je ne puis.

MARIANNE-ARLEQUIN *pressant encore plus le Sultan*

Tu le dois.

LE SULTAN

Plus d'affaire. (*HM*, viii)

The loss of Voltaire's first version prevents us from knowing how close a parody this is of the original scene of the queen's suicide, but what is quite clear is that Piron comically contrasts her fate with Voltaire's determination for his play to survive in the comic turn of events that reveals even her suicide — in other words the withdrawal of the play — to be not an admission of defeat, but simply another sham to gain public support.

Voltaire's revised tragedy appears as a more refined version of the same character: Arlequin, but without the Gascon accent he had on his first appearance. His goblet has gone too, but instead he has acquired a cheaply bejewelled costume: 'un grand manteau de reine, tout couvert de clinquant' (*HM*, xiv), symbolizing the revisions Voltaire has made to his text, which are rejected as worthless by the sultan; Piron even includes a wicked allusion to the fact that, while prices were doubled for the first performance of the first version of the play, this was not repeated for the second version:

> Loin de rien voir en vous de nouveau qui m'enflamme,
> Votre prix a baissé de moitié. Quoi! Madame;
> Pour quelque aune d'étoffe, & de clinquant de plus,
> Pensez-vous que mes vœux vous en seront mieux dus?
> Non, non. (*HM*, xiv)

Even her repetition of her threat to poison herself fails to impress.

This scene is interrupted by the arrival of Fuzelier's four Mariannes and the subsequent return of all the others, including the previously unseen character representing Tristan L'Hermite's play, and finally Hérode, distraught at the death of his wife and yet, as in Voltaire's play, in his madness still seeking her alive, but unable to identify the real Marianne in any of those present. In other words, not a single one of these versions can be seen as a successful adaptation of the story.

The sultan's dismissal of all the Mariannes would seem to bring an end to the whole affair, but no, the determination of Voltaire's play to prevail is such that she reappears yet again, through the window this time (*HM*, xxvi).[34] In a particularly clever scene, Piron shows how time and familiarity can work a transformation in our appreciation of a work of art. For when the sultan, who has initially refused to look at her (in *Mariamne* IV. iv Mariamne refuses to look at Hérode), at last does so, he realizes what has been clear to us from her reappearance: that she no longer looks the same, for, as a symbol of the public's acceptance of the work, Arlequin has been replaced by Silvia as the character playing this second version of Voltaire's tragedy (*HM*, xxvi). And so the scene concludes with an apparent victory for Voltaire's play with Le Public saying: 'Je vous aime; aimez moi' (*HM*, xxvi).[35] This is an unusual conclusion for any parody, let alone a parody by Piron aimed at Voltaire, so it is no surprise that the victory is short-lived. The success of Voltaire's play at this second attempt could not be denied, but it is always possible to find a disobliging explanation for such a success, and that is precisely what Piron does. Marianne's new-found finery has been stolen, and, what is more, stolen from those of Le Public's wives who represent the classics of the repertoire:

> Sultane Élisabeth, Pauline, Iphigénie,
> Andromaque, que sais-je? Une foule infinie
> D'autres que vous aimez, souffrent ce coup-là. (*HM*, xxvii)

So how justified is Piron's accusation? It is true that there are similarities to all the plays enumerated here. Élisabeth is the central character of Thomas Corneille's *Le Comte d'Essex*,[36] whose vacillations over whether she should listen to her lover's enemies and have him beheaded for treason or give in to her love culminate in a scene in which he is executed off stage without her knowledge as she decides too late to save him, followed by the announcement of his death and her regrets. The similarity of the climax of Voltaire's play is undeniable and, since the off-stage execution of Mariamne is unique to the second version (in the first she drank poison), means that, in this case at least, Piron's decision to give the costume of stolen finery only to the character representing that second version of the play is certainly justified.

The similarity to Pauline, the principal female character of Pierre Corneille's *Polyeucte*, is clearest in Mariamne's insistence that her duty is to her husband, regardless of his deeds, and her rejection of the lover who tries to save her, although Piron has his character comically suggest that her behaviour has, in fact, been precisely the opposite to this (*HM*, xxvi).

In *Iphigénie* and *Andromaque* we again have prolonged vacillation over whether the victim should die, but in the latter we also have similarities in Hermione's angry reaction to the death of her beloved and Oreste's madness, although in *Hérode et Mariamne* the anger and the madness are both Hérode's. Spectators at Piron's parody would have had an additional feeling of familiarity during this scene, for Piron reinforces the sense of a debt to Racine by writing much of Marianne's role as a close parody of passages from the role of Hermione.[37] The accusation of the wholesale theft of specific lines, even whole passages, from other authors suggested by Piron's scene is not entirely borne out by Voltaire's text. Only two lines were lighted on by Voltaire's contemporaries as an example of borrowings,[38] and although Michael Freyne has identified a number of other reminiscences of classics of the repertoire,[39] the line picked on by Piron seems not to have been noted by any other critics of Voltaire. 'Je t'ai cherché moi-même au fond de tes provinces', from one of the very passages in *Andromaque* parodied by Piron, is echoed twice in Voltaire's text, first in: 'Qu'au fond de mon palais, on me vienne avertir' (II. iv), and then in: 'Venez, seigneur, venez au fond de mon palais' (IV. ii). It must be said that the resemblance is hardly striking in either case, but it is the closest match between *Hérode et Mariamne* and the lines from *Andromaque* that Piron puts in the mouth of the character who represents this play. Indeed, he increases the similarity by inverting the word order to bring the phrase closer to the first of Voltaire's echoes: 'Au fond de ton sérail, je t'ai cherché moi-même!'

In addition to these accusations in the parody of plagiarism from, or similarity to, other plays, Piron had already, in the prologue to *Les Chimères*, noted the resemblance between *Mariamne*[40] and Voltaire's own *Artémire*, which had failed when it was first produced in February 1720 (*Chim*, prologue, vi). This observation is entirely justified and has been remarked on by other critics;[41] nevertheless, despite the validity of the comparison, in *Les Huit Mariannes* Piron prefers to emphasize Voltaire's debt to the classics of the previous century, something that might be weakened by any concession that he is also imitating himself.

The treatment of the theme of identity is more subtle in Voltaire's tragedy than in Danchet's *Nitétis*, with its multiple recognition scenes. Here the audience is aware of Mariamne's true nature; the real subject is Hérode's perception of her: will he be led by those plotting against her to misinterpret her, or will he see her as she truly is? This question of Mariamne's identity is transformed into something more obviously symbolic by Piron, whose play represents not just a search for a new wife for Le Public's harem, but also a quest for the true Marianne. But, as each one reveals herself, the *commedia dell'arte* associations and, in some cases, male gender of the figure behind the veil make it clear that the impersonation is compromised, just as the inadequacies of the authors compromise the representation in the tragedies parodied by Piron. A truly tragic representation of such a figure is impossible in the current literary climate, and so the play contains no true Marianne. Even Voltaire's second version, which begins to please, reveals itself to be nothing more than a reworking of classics of the seventeenth century; she may have changed from Arlequin into a woman, but even that woman, Silvia, is still a *commedia* archetype in borrowed clothing, not the true Marianne. Hérode cannot identify the true Marianne among all those in play, and the reason becomes clear when the eunuch Apollo reports, in the final scene, that Pegasus has bolted. One symbol of literature has been castrated, the other has fled; such is Piron's comment on the state of contemporary literature, which is inadequate to the task of rivalling the classics of the repertoire. As the tragedy ends with Hérode's mad grief over the loss of Mariamne, the parody ends with Le Public's madness, brought on by the proliferation of false Mariannes (*HM.* xxviii).

These parodies clearly have both interest and entertainment value in their own right, but the inclusion of a subtext of literary criticism within the literary work, which is essential to the parodist's art, surely prepared the way for the much more subtle inclusion of a strand of reflection on the transformative functions of theatre that we find in his masterpiece *La Métromanie.*

Notes to Chapter 8

1. This means, of course, that the earlier date of 1722 suggested by Rigoley de Juvigny (see Verèb, *Alexis Piron, poète*, p. 636, n. 15) for the first performance of Piron's parody cannot be correct.
2. The spelling 'Mariamne' is that used by Voltaire and also in the first editions of Nadal's *Mariamne* and Fuzelier's *Les Quatre Mariamnes*; Piron's play appears as *Les Huit Mariannes* in its first edition by Rigoley de Juvigny and in Dufay's edition; the title of the first edition of Tristan L'Hermite's tragedy is *La Mariane.*
3. On the subject of *Atis*, see also Dominique Quéro, 'Alexis Piron parodiste, ou la "capitolade comique"', in *A rire et à pleurer: à travers six siècles de littérature en Bourgogne*, ed. by Yvette Quenot and Jacques Poirier ([Dijon: Centre Régional de Documentation Pédagogique de Bourgogne, 1996]), pp. 91–103.
4. See, for instance, Gérard Genette, *Palimpsestes: la littérature au second degré* (Paris: Éditions du Seuil, 1982), pp. 17–40; Margaret A Rose, *Parody: Ancient, Modern and Post-Modern* (Cambridge: Cambridge University Press, 1993), pp. 5–99; Daniel Sangsue, *La Parodie*, Contours littéraires (Paris: Hachette, 1994). More specifically on theatrical parody in eighteenth-century France, see Gustave Lanson, *Hommes et livres* (Paris: Lecène, Houdin, 1895), pp. 261–93; Valleria Belt Grannis, *Dramatic Parody in Eighteenth Century France* (New York: Publications of the Institute of French Studies, 1931); Rex, *The Attraction of the Contrary*, pp. 60–64, and, most interestingly, Philip Robinson, 'Reflexions on Early Eighteenth-Century French Theatrical Parody', in *Essays on French Comic Drama from the 1640s to the 1780s*, ed. by Derek Connon and George Evans, French Studies of the Eighteenth and Nineteenth Centuries, 7 (Berne: Peter Lang, 2000), pp. 139–52.
5. Probably in 1714. On the dating of this text and the issues surrounding its publication, see the comments of Frédéric Deloffre in Marivaux, *Œuvres de jeunesse* (Paris: Gallimard, 1990), pp. xvii–xviii, 1239–51.
6. Although making pertinent comment on this specialized usage, Daniel Sangsue appears to attribute it to Gustave Lanson in *Hommes et livres*, rather than to the eighteenth-century authors and public (*La Parodie*, p. 26).
7. Even its form is unusual: one of the characteristics of parodies in *opéra-comique* form that retell the story of the original is the way the mixture of prose and sung verse forms a mocking contrast with the alexandrines of classical tragedy or the noble *vers libres* of opera. *Les Huit Mariannes* mocks tragic style in a different way by the unexpected combination of parodic alexandrines with sung text.
8. Piron was not alone in writing parodies of this type. *Les Huit Mariannes* had been preceded by

Fuzelier's *Les Quatre Mariamnes*, which similarly personified the various plays in the persons of their heroines — although if Piron's claim in a note in his text that Fuzelier stole the idea from him is correct, then he takes at least some credit for the form of that play too (see *HM*, xv). Bidault de Montigny's parody of a later Voltaire tragedy, *Sémiramis*, features characters such as L'Exposition, Le Dénouement, Le Récit, and La Langueur and is what Walter Rex describes as 'a sort of metaphor for the experience of the play itself' (*The Attraction of the Contrary*, p. 62). Fuzelier even produced a dramatized discussion of the relationship between parody and other theatrical forms in *Parodie* (1723).

9. See Robinson, 'Reflexions on Early Eighteenth-Century French Theatrical Parody', pp. 143–46, for a possible explanation for this. Nevertheless, in this age of parody it was not only new works that were attacked: a classic like *Atys*, first performed in 1676, was parodied for the first time only in response to its sixth revival in 1709, but had attracted a further six parodies by 1738, and Roy's *Philomele* (1705), despite being much more deserving of the parodist's attention, was first parodied by Piron only on its second revival in 1723 (see the late David Trott's website, *Œuvres lyriques parodiées (1669–1752): liste de travail en cours* <http://www.chass.utoronto.ca/~trott/par-op.htm>).
10. It seems unlikely that Piron has an actual second parody in mind here, since no other was ever performed.
11. The version by Claude Florimond Boizard de Pontau was performed on 22 January 1726 at the Italians, and Piron's followed at the Foire Saint-Germain on 19 February. With *Les Huit Mariannes* Piron solved this problem by writing a parody of the earlier parody into his own parody.
12. The 'prince romain' is Romulus in *Pierrot Romulus; ou, le Ravisseur poli*, Lesage, Fuzelier, and D'Orneval's parody of La Motte's *Romulus*, and the 'prince portugais' is Dom Pedre in the same author's *Inès de Castro*, first performed in April 1723. In fact, Pierrot did not have his way: the highly successful parody *Agnès de Chaillot*, by Dominique Biancolelli and Legrand, was performed at the Foire Saint-Laurent in July of that same year not by Francisque's marionettes, but by the Italians.
13. The references to classics of the seventeenth century in *Les Huit Mariannes* have a different function, since they are intended not as satirical allusions to contemporary theatre but as illustrations of Voltaire's alleged plagiarism; yet even in those cases they were all standard repertoire pieces.
14. This casting suggests that the alternative title of *Arlequin-Atis* given by Pascale Verèb (see *Alexis Piron, poète*, p. 638) and found in other sources is erroneous. It seems most likely to be the result of confusion with the other parody mentioned in the prologue, by Boizard de Pontau, and Dominique's earlier version (1710), both of which were indeed called *Arlequin-Atys*.
15. This name is spelt Térée by Piron, but Terée by Roy.
16. Roy, *Philomele*, V. ii.
17. Roy, *Philomele*, III. vii.
18. Roy even has Terée use the word 'mégère' of her after he has discovered that she has murdered his son and burnt down his city, by which time it seems decidedly inadequate, even taking account of its classical origins (see *Philomele*, V. v).
19. Quinault, *Atys*, V. ii. The quotation follows the edition by Jacques Truchet and André Blanc in *Théâtre du XVIIe siècle*, 3 vols ([Paris]: Gallimard, 1975–92), III.
20. In addition to those we have noted, there is a direct quotation from Lully's score for *Atys* in *Atis*, XVI.
21. This contrast is made explicit in *Le Caprice* (XIII), where La Nature speaks out for the naturalness of the Fairs, which she prefers to the artifice of the Opéra.
22. For more of my views on the Fairs' promotion of musical simplicity in preference to the complexity of opera, see 'La Musique foraine: moyen d'expression ou message?', in *Les Théâtres de la Foire*, ed. by Françoise Rubellin (forthcoming).
23. See 'La Musique foraine' for details of the popularity of this vaudeville in the plays in Lesage and D'Orneval's *Théâtre de la Foire* in the first years of *opéra-comique*. Although my survey ends in 1718, preferences among the Fair authors had not changed significantly by the time of Piron's works in *opéra-comique* form.

24. Roy, *Philomele*, avertissement.
25. See *Metamorphoses*, VI.
26. Quinault's treatment of the myth of Attis is much more faithful to its model, but he too is forced by the *bienséances* to make a significant omission. One of the main aspects of the myth — indeed, perhaps its *raison d'être* — was to explain and inspire the self-castration of the priests of Cybele: in the myth, when the goddess drives him mad, Attis castrates himself and dies. Although Quinault remains as close to this as the conventions will allow, his version is inevitably watered down, the element of sexual deprivation being represented by Atys killing his beloved Sangaride, whom in his madness he takes for Cybèle, and then committing suicide in despair. Again, there is no implied criticism in the parody of this aspect of Quinault's adaptation and Piron makes no allusion to the events of the original tale (although Dominique Quéro draws attention to the appearance of the theme of castration in other contemporary parodies in 'Alexis Piron parodiste, ou la "capitolade comique"', pp. 91–93). However, we do see in this parody a good example of the tendency to play down violent events in the original: Atys's killing of Sangaride is replaced with a more banal act of domestic violence, as his parodic equivalent merely gives his beloved a beating (*A*, xviii–xx).
27. My source for most of the information relating to the genesis of Voltaire's play and the appearance of other plays on the subject is Michael Freyne's detailed introduction to his edition which forms volume IIIC (2004) of Voltaire, *Œuvres complètes*. See in particular pp. 28–34, 44–48, 50–52.
28. The comedy of this cry derives, of course, from the French traditions for Twelfth Night; the company calls out 'Le roi boit!' or 'La reine boit!' each time the person made king or queen for the evening drinks.
29. 'L'impression croyant profiter de la vogue qu'avoient les *Mariannes*, donna une nouvelle édition de la célèbre *Marianne* de Tristan l'Hermite', explains Piron in a note (*HM*, xiii). His chronology places the appearance of this edition after the performance of Nadal's tragedy, but it would appear that the edition in question is *Mariane, tragédie, par le sieur Tristan L'Hermite. Nouvelle édition, augmentée de la vie de l'auteur*, published by François Flahault, which is dated 1724.
30. There is not universal agreement on this date: see Verèb, *Alexis Piron, poète*, pp. 637–38.
31. Those mentioned at this stage are all from tragedies by Racine: 'Monime, Iphigénie, Athalie, Andromaque' (*HM*, i).
32. La Motte's *Romulus*, identified by its heroine Hersilie, *Inès de Castro*, Voltaire's *Artémire*, and the subject of Piron's earlier parody, Danchet's *Nitétis*.
33. We have noted that the appearance of Polichinelle as a live actor and not a puppet was relatively unusual at the Fairs, but in a work for the Italians he is a normal member of the cast.
34. She has first sent a message saying she is going to return at Le Public's request, a claim that he flatly denies. This is explained in a note to the text by Piron: 'M. de Voltaire fit faire un compliment au parterre, avant de représenter sa seconde *Marianne*, & dit qu'il la rendoit, par un juste respect pour l'empressement du public: on le désavoua tout haut' (*HM*, xxv). Michael Freyne points out that there is no extant record of this incident, nor any surviving text that could constitute the 'compliment' (Voltaire, *Œuvres complètes*, IIIC, 58, n. 137).
35. Nevertheless, Michael Freyne suggests that, rather than taking time to capture the public imagination, the revised version of the tragedy was a success from the outset (see Voltaire, *Œuvres complètes*, IIIC, 52).
36. There were also plays of this name by La Calprenède (premièred during the season of 1637–38 and first published in 1639) and Claude Boyer (1678), but it was Corneille's that had remained a popular repertoire piece, rivalling the popularity of Racine, and which would therefore have been the version best known to Piron's audience.
37. Compare *HM*, xxvi with *Andromaque*, IV. v.
38. See Michael Freyne's edition of *Mariamne* (Voltaire, *Œuvres complètes*, IIIC, 203, n. 9, 288, n. 5).
39. See Voltaire, *Œuvres complètes*, IIIC, passim.
40. In this case, the first version of the tragedy, since *Les Chimères* was performed before the appearance of the second.
41. See Freyne, Voltaire, *Œuvres complètes*, IIIC, 25–28.

CHAPTER 9

The *Opéras-Comiques*

L'Antre de Trophonius, *Tirésias*, *Le Mariage de Momus*, *L'Endriague*, *Le Claperman*, *Le Caprice*, *L'Âne d'or*, *Les Chimères*, *Le Fâcheux Veuvage*, *L'Enrôlement d'Arlequin*, *Crédit est mort*, *La Rose*, and *La Robe de dissension*

As we move from Piron's parodies in *opéra-comique* form, two of them written for the Italians, to the works actually designated *opéra-comique*, all destined for the Fairs, the true home of the genre, it may be useful to ask what constitutes an *opéra-comique*.[1] Most straightforwardly, it is a play written in a mixture of spoken dialogue and vaudevilles, in the original sense of that word: that is, pre-existing familiar tunes to which new words are set. Historically, it is the presence of sung text which is essential: when in 1714 Dominique's troupe negotiated with the Opéra to purchase permission for the actors to sing, it was this that allowed them to circumvent the monopolies that had previously attempted to keep them silent. The permission was for sung text, not spoken dialogue, and this is reflected in the earliest of the *opéras-comiques* written to be sung by the actors,[2] where the spoken dialogue was confined to odd words;[3] nevertheless, the amount of spoken dialogue rapidly increased as the writers increasingly tested the boundaries. That the music consists mainly of vaudevilles may have been an artistic decision (the use of familiar music had been successful in the *pièces à écriteaux*, where it had been indispensable to allow the audiences to sing along), or it may have been pragmatic, making life easier for actors and musicians in a rapidly changing repertoire. It seems reasonable to conclude that it was probably a combination of both; it was not required by the law, which would have allowed the use of original music. Original music often was included, particularly in the characteristic finales, in which the verses would all end with the same refrain ('vaudevilles' as they also confusingly became known because of their use at the end of *comédies en vaudevilles*, despite not being vaudevilles at all in the first sense of the word), but it was the use of vaudeville in the original sense which became a defining feature in the early days of *opéra-comique*.[4] This form had become established by the time Piron adopted it, and while in his first *opéra-comique*, *L'Antre de Trophonius* of 1722 (which includes, apart from its vaudeville finale, only three sung passages in its entire twelve scenes, the first not appearing until scene vi),[5] we might feel he was paying only lip-service to the form, he later shows significant skill in exploiting its various possibilities.

The use of vaudeville really is the only defining feature of the *opéra-comique*; other characteristics set it apart from the majority of comedies written for the Théâtre Français, but not, as we have seen in our study of *Les Enfants de la Joie*, from the repertoire of the Théâtre Italien (from which it originally derived) nor from the small number of other works, such as *Arlequin-Deucalion*, written for the Fairs in different forms. Nevertheless, these other features are worth reviewing, for they give an idea of the diversity of both the genre and Piron's contribution to it.

One of the most striking is the diversity of subject matter; while the comedy of the Théâtre Français tends to be concerned, in *grande comédie* at least, with the *vraisemblable*, and also to support its declared aims of 'plaire et instruire' by setting its action in France — and usually Paris — among the *haute bourgeoisie* and the minor aristocracy,[6] the Fairs are much more interested in topics removed from the everyday life of the spectators.

For instance, the publication of Galland's translation of *Les Mille et une nuits* between 1704 and 1717 had led to a taste for the exotic and the spectacular that was exploited in a number of Fair plays. Piron's contribution to the genre, *Le Fâcheux Veuvage* (1725), is not a direct adaptation from Galland, but shares its eastern setting and takes its central idea of a land where the surviving spouse is buried with the dead one from the fourth voyage of Sinbad, with Arlequin finding himself, like Sinbad, in the position of a foreigner who learns about this law only after he has married. Hence the east is not only foreign, it is also barbaric — a common stereotype, but then the Fairs are generally more interested in exploiting stereotypes than they are in overturning them.

Thus in another play with a foreign setting, *La Robe de dissension* (1726), set in Spain, it is the stereotypical jealousy of the Spaniards with regard to both their honour and their womenfolk that dominates the plot, while the Dutch setting of *Le Claperman* (1724) depicts a society concerned with bourgeois respectability, even if much sexual frustration seethes beneath the surface. Nevertheless, as in the plays of other Fair authors, there are plenty of French stereotypes in Piron's *opéras-comiques* too.

Another source of plots with this sense of otherness is classical literature and mythology. *L'Âne d'or* (1724), as its full title *L'Âne d'or d'Apulée* tells us, takes its plot directly from Apuleius's second-century prose narrative, and the subtitle of *Le Mariage de Momus* (1722), *La Gigantomachie*, indicates that it too has its roots in classical literature, although it was probably the more recent retellings by Hardy and Scarron that were Piron's immediate source, rather than the versions found in Homer, Hesiod, and Plato. *Tirésias* (1722) is based on an episode from Greek mythology best known from its retelling by Ovid,[7] and *L'Antre de Trophonius* is based on a legend recounted in Pausanias's *Description of Greece*, while *L'Endriague* (1723) draws on a text related to a different legendary tradition, the romance of *Amadis de Gaule*.

A third group consists of plots with an allegorical theme; although allegorical characters are most usually associated with the tradition of classical mythology,[8] their treatment is somewhat different in plays of this type. In *Le Caprice* (1724), *Les Chimères* (1725), and *Crédit est mort* (1726) the allegorical figures react with contemporary stereotypes to make a moral (or perhaps just cynical) point, but *La Rose* (1726)[9] is a much rarer thing in the theatre of the time: a true allegory, in which the whole action may be seen as a symbolic equivalent of something else. It clearly takes its inspiration from the *Roman de la rose*, but, whereas in that work the rose represents the beloved, in Piron's the content is more overtly erotic, with the rose belonging to the central character Rosette clearly symbolizing her virginity, and the action dramatizing the pubescent girl's efforts to rid herself of it as quickly as possible, while her mother rushes to get her married first. Despite Piron's protestations that 'le voile de l'allégorie étoit si heureusement tissu, qu'il n'y avoit pas le plus petit trou, par où l'on pût voir la nudité' (*R*, avertissement, p. 8), others thought differently, causing the play to be banned until 1744.

This leaves *L'Enrôlement d'Arlequin* (1726), Piron's only *opéra-comique* to be set in France, albeit in the provinces and not the more usual setting of Paris. Like the allegories, it has an element of the symbolic about it, for it dramatizes the entry of Arlequin into the theatre, but does so in a rather unusual way. Arlequin, as we know, is the Gallicization of Arlecchino, the archetype of the *commedia dell'arte* who originated in Bergamo, entered France with the old Italian theatre, and was adopted into the repertoire of the Fair companies when they filled the gap left by the banning of the old Italian troupe. Fair writers, including Piron, are usually more than happy to acknowledge the Italian origin of Arlequin and the other Italian archetypes they feature, whether by the inclusion of brief phrases in Italian or the occasional use of an Italian accent, usually for Scaramouche; Lesage, Fuzelier, and D'Orneval's *L'Ombre du Cocher Poète* (1722) even introduces the use of puppets in *opéra-comique* by dramatizing the arrival of a marionette troupe of Italian archetypes from Rome. But in *L'Enrôlement d'Arlequin* the character is given a quite different origin: he is part of a family of clearly French stereotypes in a French setting; one uncle, a surgeon, bears the name Massacre, another, a *procureur*, is Griffalerte, and the former argues that his nephew should be sent to study at Montpellier, while the other argues for Paris. Paris is also the stamping ground of Arlequin's cousin Ruzignac, a *chevalier d'industrie*. And the travelling theatrical troupe of which they all eventually become part is represented by actresses who, despite the potentially foreign sources of their names, Laurette and Timarette, pepper their conversation with quotations from the classics of French theatre. Hence, far from being of Bergamask origin, this Arlequin is a youth plucked from provincial France to enter directly into the French theatre. By denying Arlequin his Italian origin, this play underlines how the originally Italian characters have been fully assimilated into the French tradition.

This tendency to make plays relevant to the French audience despite their exoticism is another characteristic typical of *opéra-comique*. Hence, Arlequin is also a Frenchman, valet of the equally French Léandre, in both the eastern setting of *Le Fâcheux Veuvage* and the Spain of *La Robe de dissension*, which not only guarantees audience sympathy for the young lover and his servant, but also allows Piron to provide an ironic commentary on the bizarre behaviour of foreigners and show the superior Frenchman exploiting their beliefs and prejudices by using them against them. But Piron is not usually so protective of the vanity of his compatriots: he also frequently exploits another characteristic technique of the Fairs, peopling his exotic, mythical, and symbolic settings with figures drawn from contemporary

France, or, more properly, from a repertoire of conventional theatrical stereotypes of contemporary French figures. Such are the surgeon, *procureur*, soldier, *chevalier d'industrie*, and cuckolded pastry cook who are Arlequin's male relatives in *L'Enrôlement d'Arlequin*, and in other plays we will find financiers, poets, *petits-maîtres*, ageing roués and coquettes, and others, all with a particularly French outlook on life, whether the setting be ancient Greece or 'les Espaces imaginaires'.[10] In these cases, the aim is generally comic and satirical, representing the Fairs' contribution to the moral and didactic functions demanded of theatre at the period, although it must be said that the satire is so conventional that it is not always obvious what new message audiences were to learn from these stereotypical depictions.

L'Enrôlement d'Arlequin also illustrates another characteristic of *opéra-comique*, its obsession with theatre, although it does so in a slightly different way from the majority of *opéras-comiques*, for here it forms an integral part of the story and shows no concern to be topical. More usual in the Fairs is the dramatization of the relations between the various theatres, and the criticism of specific productions at the other theatres, whether by direct attack, parody, or other means. This is a particular feature of *Arlequin-Deucalion*, which we find in many of Piron's *opéras-comiques* too, whether it belongs or not. Hence, the prologue to *Tirésias*, based on a real event, dramatizes the arrival of Francisque's troupe in Paris after losing everything in a fire in Lyons; the prologue to *Les Chimères*, set in front of the Opéra-Comique, includes a pedlar trying to sell unsuccessful theatrical texts, characters called M. de La Brigue and M. de La Cabale being told by Le Public that he can do without their advice, and La Motte's Inès de Castro and Voltaire's Mariamne arguing about their relative merits; *L'Antre de Trophonius* includes, as well as an extended parody of a section of *Le Cid*, the flagrantly irrelevant episode in which Mercury, representing the *Mercure Galant*, satirizes contemporary theatre; the Greek gods of *Le Mariage de Momus* play games that satirize the different French theatrical troupes, which are then represented by the various spouses proposed for Momus; *L'Âne d'or* contains the performance of a ridiculous ballet. And there are numerous more passing references too.

Hence, Piron's *opéras-comiques* share enough common preoccupations and techniques with the productions of other authors for the Fairs to be entirely characteristic of the genre, the similarity going far beyond the simple use of vaudeville. Despite the reluctance to use vaudeville that we have noted in *L'Antre de Trophonius*, in the longer term Piron embraced not only this convention, but the others associated with *opéra-comique* too, making himself into an efficient provider of scripts for the Fair theatres with their specialized repertoire.

L'Enrôlement d'Arlequin is a play that represents the title character's search for an identity. Arlequin is, of course, a Protean figure, who preserves, along with his costume, certain essential character traits, but is transformed into a range of different characters and roles from play to play. It is a feature he shares with the other archetypes of the *commedia dell'arte*, but the fact that he became the dominant Italian figure of both the Fairs and the Italian theatre itself means that in his case the characteristic is the more striking. We have seen that in most of Piron's *opéras-comiques* his Italian origins have been elided to make him essentially French, even when, as in *Tirésias*, the setting is ancient Greece;[11] in *Le Claperman*, however, he is

Dutch (albeit in a play with virtually no sense of Dutch local colour), and we have seen him take on other roles in the plays for the Fairs and the Italians examined in the previous chapter. He is also a master of transformation within the plays, deliberately and fraudulently in *L'Antre de Trophonius*, where he becomes a priest of the oracle of the title, or in *Le Fâcheux Veuvage* and *La Robe de dissension*, in both of which he pretends to be a seer with special powers. More surprising transformations occur in *L'Endriague*, in which, despite the habitual cowardice of the archetype, he proves to be a more efficient dragon slayer than his master; *Les Chimères*, where he proves a reasonably effective replacement for the allegorical figure of La Vérité; and *Tirésias* and *L'Âne d'or*, in both of which he is the victim of physical transformation, in the former into a woman and in the latter into an ass.

Inventive as these transformations are, however, they are a conventional part of the Italian tradition that was taken over by the Fairs. More interesting is the way that, as well as transforming him into a Frenchman, *L'Enrôlement d'Arlequin* also uses him to provide a portrait of the adolescent finding his identity. His relationship with Laurette shows him to be awakening to sexual maturity, but perhaps more important is the concentration on the choice of a profession, for that is largely what defines the identity of the male figures surrounding him, his tutor, his cousin, and his various uncles, all of whom demonstrate the preoccupations, the prejudices, and the outlooks of the professions to which they belong. Arlequin is not an entirely blank canvas; he has the inherent characteristics of his archetype: a lack of intellectual ability (not to be confused with cunning, which he usually has in abundance), which prevents him from being a scholar, and both laziness and cowardice, which make him determined never to see active service as a soldier. While the characteristics we are born with count for something in our personal development, the male relatives with their various *déformations professionnelles* demonstrate the importance of the path we choose in life. Nevertheless, this play shows itself to be wholly committed to an eighteenth-century belief in the perfectibility of man. Whereas the seventeenth-century idea of *caractère* means that the central characters of Molière's *comédies de caractère* or of the *comédie de mœurs* which followed never really learn anything from their experiences to change their basic character, the eighteenth-century *comédie morale*, however unconvincingly, presents last-scene conversions that attempt to convince us that people can learn from their experiences and change. *L'Enrôlement d'Arlequin* too shows the possibility of an escape from the stereotypes into which society has forced us, for, as Laurette points out, these roles are not really our true selves: we are all acting:

> Eh mort-non de ma vie, tous les hommes ne sont-ils pas comédiens? [...] Quels rôles ne jouez-vous pas, si on en excepte celui d'honnête homme! Oui, Messieurs, vous êtes des comédiens comme nous, avec la seule différence, que vous en êtes de très-fâcheux; qu'on vous hait & qu'on nous aime; qu'on vous fuit & qu'on nous cherche; que vous traînez après vous le deuil & la tristesse, & que nous répandons partout le plaisir & la joie. (*EdA*, xiv)

Self-awareness brings the possibility of an escape from social stereotyping, and the family all duly become actors, allowing them to leave behind their former inflexible personalities, and liberating Arlequin to become the Protean figure beloved of the Fairs.

Piron is not always so optimistic about human nature; in *Les Chimères*, the baron infatuated with himself, the antique-collector infatuated with his possessions and the countess infatuated with her pets all show an inability to see themselves as others see them, despite being all too aware of the faults of others. Nevertheless, while we might usually expect a Fair play to keep up such a pattern, once established, for the rest of the action — with only perhaps a surprise at the dénouement — Piron takes a more positive view in his second act, where Arlequin's deputization for La Vérité has more success, and he shows an elderly coquette what she really is, sends a peasant couple who think their long-lost son must have made a success in Paris back to their village, and persuades a suicidal cuckold of the advantages of his condition. He even comes to terms with his own jealousies, and La Vérité herself convinces an actor from the French theatre that he is no more important than his colleague from the Fairs. 'Know thyself' seems to be the moral of this two-act *opéra-comique*, although Piron amusingly deflates any pretentiousness in this didactic message by calling into question the ability of the theatre to teach a moral lesson by his depiction of a young girl who has seen *Armide*[12] at the Opéra and entirely misunderstood its moral point.

One of Piron's most interesting themes, exploiting the Fairs' relatively liberal interpretation of the *bienséances*, is his exploration of sexual identity (although the responses to both *Tirésias*, where the actors were arrested after the first performance, and *La Rose*, which was banned, suggest that he was apt to go too far even for this medium). He had already approached the subject somewhat in passing in *Arlequin-Deucalion*, where we see the stereotypical indifference of the married man towards a wife desirable enough to appeal to the god Apollo, and the jealousy that this rival inspires. He followed this up in his next play, *L'Antre de Trophonius*, by including some of the usual confusions between lovers about whether their love is mutual. But it is his next play, *Tirésias*, which really launches a serious (although entirely comic) examination of the subject. At its heart is the inability of any of us to understand fully the experiences and feelings of others, something which is surely at its most acute in the way the two sexes perceive the sex act, since in that particular instance the differences between them are not only psychological, but physiological too. The age-old fascination of the subject is proved by the existence of a myth dealing with it, the argument between Zeus and Hera[13] over whether men or women gain more pleasure from sex, which can be resolved only by Tiresias, the one person to have been both male and female, who replies that women do. According to the version recounted by Ovid, Tiresias is transformed into a woman when he sees a pair of serpents copulating and strikes them; his retransformation is effected seven years later when the same incident is repeated. In this version of the tale, Hera, furious when Tiresias reveals her secret, blinds him, and Zeus, unable to undo her punishment, rewards him with second sight.

This provides the starting point for *Tirésias*. In adapting it to take account of both the time-frame required for a comedy — even at the Fairs, with their more liberal attitude to the unities, authors tended to keep the duration of the action short — and the need for a happy ending, Piron chooses to focus on the specific issue of the sexual experiences of men and women. Hence, Tirésias's much abbreviated transformation and the dispute between Jupiter and Junon, as they are in Piron's text, are the only elements retained from the myth. Gone are the serpents — Jupiter transforms Tirésias for refusing to let him take his place with his beloved Cariclée, and Junon transforms him (her?) back — and gone is the blinding: after what she has heard of the inferiority of the male sexual experience, Junon judges Tirésias's retransformation punishment enough for his indiscretion.

On the other hand, Piron also adds elements which illustrate the central thesis. Two aspects of male sexuality highlighted in the early stage of the play are its predatory nature and the search for novelty: Tirésias is besotted with his beloved Cariclée who has not yet capitulated to him, while it is not only Jupiter who is on the lookout for extra-marital sex — Tirésias's friend Mopse is thoroughly bored with his wife after only a fortnight of marriage (*T*, II. ii), leaving her in a state of heightened sexual frustration (*T*, I. v). Piron will return to this cliché concerning marital relations, most importantly in *Le Claperman*, but for the present it is most important to note that, despite his attitude to sex with his wife, Mopse wastes no time before indulging in extra-marital sex with the newly transformed Tirésie, as the female incarnation of Tirésias is known in the play; the text leaves us in no doubt about the extent of their relations, since Tirésie speaks of her fear of being pregnant:

MOPSE

Eh, bien donc, que craignez-vous?

TIRÉSIE

Turelure!
De rélargir ma ceinture.

MOPSE

Robin Turelure.

TIRÉSIE

Que dira-t-on de moi? N'avoir pu être vingt-quatre heures
honnête fille? Cela n'est arrivé qu'à moi. (*T*, II. ii)

To the transformation of Tirésias Piron adds a further complication, for Cariclée and her confidante Naïs, who set out to search for the missing Tirésias, disguise themselves as men as a means of protection on their journey.[14] This idea reappears not only in the subsequent *opéra-comique L'Endriague*, but also in the tragedy *Fernand Cortès*, but in neither is it exploited in such explicitly sexual terms as in *Tirésias*; Piron will return to such treatment only in *Le Claperman*, where the characters' transvestism has a quite different explanation.

Piron alludes to the influence of clothing on identity at the opening of the play: Mopse has bought an outfit for his wife that is intended to give a good impression of his social standing (*T*, I. i), but the issue of the impact of transvestism on gender is explored at greater length. On her very first appearance dressed as a man Cariclée expresses her nervousness, and Naïs comments: 'L'habit ne fait pas le sexe, comme vous voyez, Madame' (*T*, II. iii), but it is not quite so straightforward, for she subsequently finds herself allowing a flirtatious encounter with Tirésie (who has not recognized her and whom she fails to recognize as her previously male lover) not only to continue, but to become a tête-à-tête. Part of the comedy of this scene derives from an element of reversal in the stereotypical roles: while Cariclée remains timid, Tirésie, despite her transformation, has kept '[s]on cœur libertin'

(*T*, I. x), so it is the female Tirésie who plays the role of seducer and the apparent male Cariclée who resists; Tirésie even comments: 'Voici une scène à peu près comme celle que nous jouâmes ensemble hier au soir, Cariclée & moi' (*T*, II. vii).

If the sexual ambiguity in this scene nevertheless paradoxically serves to reinforce conventional stereotypes of the predatory male — albeit transformed into a woman — and the reluctant female, other aspects of the play introduce slightly more disturbing elements. Not only Tirésie but Mopse's wife Cléantis too finds the disguised women more attractive than they usually find men, even if they do explain it to themselves by suggesting that their greater attractiveness comes from the fact that they are from the town and not the country:

CLÉANTIS

Ma foi, l'on a beau dire, ces Monsieux-là de la ville, avons l'ar bian pu avenant, & bian d'eune autre dégaine que nos vilains marpaux de villageois.

TIRÉSIE

Je vous en réponds, cousine; & je le remarque aussi bien que vous. (*T*, II. v)

Moreover, Naïs, a rather bolder woman than Cariclée, has the personality to make more adventurous use of her disguise, and consequently we briefly see her involved in Sapphic caresses with Cléantis (*T*, III. i); and although Cléantis will express disapproval when she discovers the truth of Naïs's identity, Naïs herself — who, of course, has been aware of the situation all along — offers no excuses and seems quite unrepentant:

CLÉANTIS

Mais vous, qui m'en voulais conter, n'êtes-vous pas femme aussi, par hasard?

NAÏS

Tout comme toi, ma mie, pour le moins.

CLÉANTIS

Ne vl'à-t-il pas qui est bian, d'amusé comme ça lé jans. Autant seroit-ce, si je vous avois demandé l'impossible. Le bel honneur pour tous les deux! (*T*, III. xii)

It is not only the women whose sexual behaviour is less than straightforward. If, for instance, we feel that Mopse has entered surprisingly readily into a sexual encounter with a woman he knew to be a man only shortly before, our misgivings will be confirmed by the revelation that, even after the encounter, he is still not fully convinced that his partner actually is female:

TIRÉSIE

Ah! mon cher Mopse; bonjour!

MOPSE

Bonjour! belle Tirésie, pisque Tirésie y a.

TIRÉSIE

Viens-tu me dire encore que tu doutes du prodige? J'ai bien eu de la peine à te persuader; & tu ne te rends, comme je vois, qu'à de bonnes enseignes.

MOPSE

> Parguienne! acouté donc, on auroit de la doutance à moins. Eh, qui a jamais ouï parler de semblable affaire? Tenez, je m'imagine toujours, malgré tout ce que'ous savez, qu'il y a là queuque stratagème. (*T*, II. ii)

In addition, an appearance by Ganymède has so little dramatic function that it is clearly included simply to remind us of the breadth of Jupiter's sexual tastes, as is confirmed by the fact that the latter refers to him as 'petite garçonne' (*T*, III. v) and Junon reacts to him with jealous dislike.

Hence, the world of *Tirésias* is one in which, sexually speaking, nothing is quite as it seems. The married woman is sexually frustrated, since marriage represents an instant antidote to the male's predatory sexual nature, but only with regard to his wife, not as far as other women are concerned. Moreover, the complexities of identity are such that it is not always possible to identify with certainty who is male and who is female, although this is perhaps not as important as it might at first seem, since not all the characters show the same degree of concern about the gender of their sexual partners. We may also feel that, despite apparently devoting his entire play to an illustration of the answer to Junon's question about which gender experiences the highest degree of sexual pleasure, Piron has deliberately deprived us of a true solution, since the character that provides it, Tirésie, despite being a woman, has a sexual nature that is clearly influenced by her previous incarnation as a man. In any event, for most of the women in the play the issue remains academic; they are either, like Cléantis, saddled with an unresponsive but jealous husband, or, like Cariclée, as unmarried women, obliged to behave with modesty — indeed, in her case, this also seems to be her natural inclination. Women who do not observe the conventions, like Naïs and Tirésie, leave themselves open to the disapproval of others; Tirésie is even, as we have seen, shocked by her own behaviour.

These themes return in *Le Claperman*. This is set in Holland, although, the title apart, there is no attempt, not even in the names of the characters, to provide a convincing depiction of this location;[15] the names of the two married couples, Gautier and Garguille, clearly derive from that of the seventeenth-century French actor Gaultier-Garguille, while the others too either are French or belong to the *commedia dell'arte* tradition. We are shown a bourgeois society in which, behind a façade of respectability, the women are sexually frustrated by the lack of attention paid to them by their husbands. Hence, Mme Garguille, despite expressing prudish horror when her husband asks the servant girl whether the canary is male or female, is the first to bribe Arlequin to be sure to do his job next to her door once her husband has appointed him Claperman.

What then is a Claperman? Piron has taken the word from the Dutch 'Klepperman', literally a person equipped with a 'klepper' — a rattle. It is one of the standard Dutch words for a nightwatchman, and, as two of the other three I have traced — 'klapwaker', 'waker', and 'nachtwacht' — indicate, the rattle was related to his function of telling the time and acting as a human alarm clock, for he was a waker as well as a watcher. However, an additional detail supplied in Piron's job description, and clearly his own invention, is that the specific intention is to wake couples early so that the husbands can have sex with their wives. This is how M. Garguille explains it to Arlequin:

> Il te faut d'abord avoir un bon tambour; en battre, de toutes tes forces, par les rues, sur les deux ou trois heures du matin; & chanter ensuite à tue-tête, cette chanson-ci:
>
> [...]
>
> Maris, que l'on se réveille!
> Voici l'Aurore vermeille;
> De la part des magistrats,
> Ramonez-ci, ramonez-là, la la la,
> Les cheminées du haut en bas. (*Clap*, I. iii)

Clearly it would be a mistake to assume, as Arlequin seems to, that the song is to be taken literally. Initially his comments have a certain symbolic significance: 'Est-il rien en effet de plus dangereux qu'une cheminée mal ramonée? Le feu s'y met; & puis après: c'est le diable pour l'éteindre' (*Clap*, I. iv), but his subsequent remark that chimneys need sweeping only once or twice a year seems at this stage to suggest that we should not credit him with too much intelligence by assuming the double meaning to be deliberate on his part.

The response of the general population to Arlequin's new job is, as we would expect from our reading of *Tirésias*, enthusiasm from the women and anger from the men, although, again as we might expect, not because the men are not interested in sex at all, simply that they are not interested in doing it with their wives. So why would M. Garguille wish to create such a post when it would force him into having relations with the prudish Mme Garguille? Unsurprisingly, he has an ulterior motive: he gives the job to Arlequin as a reward for marrying their servant girl Olivette, but, since M. Garguille himself has designs on her, he is ensuring that Arlequin is out of the way doing his job at precisely the right time for him to be able to seduce her, as his comments when she complains that the wife of the Claperman is the only person who will not benefit from his job reveal: 'Tais-toi, innocente. Tu entends bien peu tes intérêts. Demande aux femmes des cavaliers du Guet' (*Clap*, I. iii). And while some of the men who object to Arlequin's activities seem merely to want a quiet life — 'Pour notre repos, nous avons besoin du sommeil de nos femmes' (*Clap*, I. iv) — others, like Mezzetin (*Clap*, I. vi), find that his racket interrupts their activities with other men's wives.

At the centre of this play are two ill-matched couples: Mme Garguille, whose prudishness suggests she is not interested in sex, but who nurses deep-seated frustration at the fact that M. Garguille is a philanderer, and Mme Gautier, who is adored but not sexually satisfied by her husband and so spends her time out socializing. As in *Tirésias*, the resolution is brought about by a descent into confusion created by sexual ambiguity. M. Garguille and Mme Gautier go to a fancy-dress ball, each dressed as a member of the opposite sex. They return to discover that Arlequin has woken their stay-at-home spouses, and, as they discuss what can be done about this, M. Gautier discovers what he supposes to be his wife, in fact M. Garguille in drag, talking to a man, in reality his wife. He furiously drags M. Garguille into his house. When Mme Garguille arrives looking for her husband, Mme Gautier, playing the predatory male just like Naïs in *Tirésias*, greets her with a chat-up line and takes her away too. When M. Garguille and Mme Gautier re-emerge each has a tale to tell: both have revealed their real identities before the situation got out of hand, but M. Garguille's mockery of M. Gautier leads Mme Gautier to defend her husband, while she provokes M. Garguille's jealousy by pointing out that, although her husband was under the impression that he was with his wife, Mme Garguille was perfectly happy to go off with a strange man and seemed 'plus fâchée qu'étonnée' (*Clap*, II. xvi) when the truth of that man's identity was revealed. Hence, the experiment in gender reversal has led to a greater understanding not only of their own feelings, but of their spouses' too. We find here a traditional and stereotypical view of gender difference in relation to sex, with hints of a male fantasy in the idea that women are much more interested in sex than they would have men believe (indeed, potentially more interested than men), a view related to the solution to the gods' puzzle in the Tiresias myth. The differentiation of the two couples indicates however that such stereotyping is an oversimplification. The underlying impulses that derive from a person's gender are less strong than individual identity, and so all men or all women are clearly not the same, despite their possession of certain gender-determined characteristics.

Given Piron's interest at this stage in his career in such issues of sexual identity and in the ambiguity created by role reversal, it is no surprise that the incident of 'la muse bretonne' should later have appealed to him so much, combining as it does issues closely related to this theme with the humiliation of his rival Voltaire.

Potentially the most interesting issue of identity in *Le Claperman*, however, surrounds the central character, Arlequin, the Claperman himself. We have seen how he accepts the office of Claperman without apparently realizing its sexual function, and still less the implications of this post with regard to the fidelity of his new wife. We appear to be confronted with an innocent, sexually and otherwise, who blunders through the action oblivious to the effect he is having on others, sometimes singing his song and banging his drum in front of the right doors, sometimes in front of the wrong, but always causing maximum inconvenience; sometimes being beaten up for his pains (*Clap*, II. iv), but also, as he points out, being bribed to do his job, and being bribed twice as much not to do it (*Clap*, I. x). Nevertheless, the arrival of the country girl Perrette looking for him in the second act shows that all is perhaps not quite as it seems. When she and Olivette finally meet, the truth is revealed:

ARLEQUIN *sans voir Perrette*

Oh çà, ma chère Olivette, nous nous marions dès qu'il sera jour.
Un petit baiser, en avancement d'hoirie.

PERRETTE

Tout doux, mon petit mari! Vous vous mariez dès qu'il sera jour?
Ah! je ne m'étonne plus! ...

OLIVETTE *à Arlequin*

Quelle est cette femme-là?

ARLEQUIN

Vous ne le croiriez pas: c'est la mienne.

OLIVETTE

La tienne! Comment, scélérat! tu en voulois avoir deux!

ARLEQUIN

Deux! parbleu, trente, s'il ne tenoit qu'à moi!

PERRETTE & OLIVETTE

Ah, voilà les chiens d'hommes! (*Clap*, II. xv)

So, no sexual innocent he. Arlequin is no different from other men; indeed, in being a potential bigamist, he may even be considered worse. But is his belief that he can marry more than one woman another example of foolish naivety, or is the whole affair a revelation that his stupidity has been an act and, like so many of Piron's Arlequins, he has been cleverly conning everyone? We are never given clarification, but it begins to seem possible that the double meanings in his original expressions of ignorance over the sexual function of the Claperman, which seemed to prove his naivety, were actually proof that, cleverest of all, he was laughing at everyone else as he went along with their schemes in which they thought him to be merely a passive victim.

An issue that arises clearly from these comedies of sexual identity is the mystery of the other, the impossibility of ever truly understanding someone else. Partial understanding may come from trying to put oneself in the position of the other, as the episodes of role reversal prove, but it is only ever partial: even Tirésias's transformation into Tirésie remains imperfect because the new female form does not entirely rid the character of all the gender traits of her previous male existence. Nevertheless, in the matter of trickery — always a popular theme in comedy, particularly in the lower comic forms from which *opéra-comique* derives — those characters who show enough intellectual flexibility to appreciate how others are likely to react will always be the most successful, while the most solipsistic will be the easiest dupes.

This is seen in another play which features gender stereotyping, but adds to it racial stereotyping too. *La Robe de dissension* is set in Spain, but the two central characters, Léandre and Arlequin, are French, and the latter's cunning, coupled with his understanding of national characteristics, allows him to exploit the weaknesses of others to resolve Léandre's romantic difficulties. For Léandre's Spanish beloved, Isabelle, has been betrothed by her brother, Dom Pèdre, to another Spaniard, Dom Fernand, and Dom Pèdre is himself to marry Dom Fernand's sister Elvire. But Spaniards are jealous, and jealousy makes them credulous, which is what Arlequin intends to exploit.

The plan is simple but preposterous, as so often in *opéra-comique*: Arlequin pretends to be a magician in possession of a magic robe which appears in its full colourful glory to any man whose wife is faithful or, if unmarried, whose sister is chaste, but is black when seen by a cuckolded husband or the brother of an unchaste sister. Of course, the robe is not magical and is always black, but predictably there are enough men who claim to see the colours to give some level of credibility to Arlequin's plan; a particularly successful comic scene occurs when Guzman, the valet of Dom Fernand, speaks aloud of the colours he sees and expresses in asides the emotions caused by the fact that he really sees only black (*RdD*, II. iii). These are men whose jealousy prevents them from making a rational assessment of the characters of their relatives, for all the women in the play have their honour intact.

Dom Fernand even misinterprets Elvire's motives when she tries to warn him before he sees the robe that it is likely to be a scam, seeing this already as evidence of her shame (*RdD*, I. ix). Comic convention tells us that such an absence of trust is reprehensible in a brother, and unforgivable in a lover, so when Dom Fernand both takes his own perception of the robe as black as an indication that his sister Elvire is unchaste, and the fact that Dom Pèdre too sees it as black as proof of the infidelity of his fiancée Isabelle, Dom Pèdre's sister, he becomes an unworthy partner, and we have no qualms about Léandre taking his place. He may have been duped, but this was possible only because of his lack of trust in the woman he loves, a fact which makes the audience to a comedy question the nature of his love.

Nevertheless, as with the sexual stereotyping in *Tirésias* and *Le Claperman*, Piron shows here too that personal individuality can transcend more general characteristics. For while one of the men who admits to seeing black, Dom Pèdre's valet Lazarille, is too stupid to be anything other than honest but believes in the proof of his wife's infidelity given to him by the robe, the other, Dom Pèdre himself, has a combination of emotional intelligence and common sense which leads him to conclude that the others must be mad to believe in such a thing. Piron is demonstrating that, despite the impossibility of entirely knowing other people, the way to prosper in interpersonal relationships is through trust, rather than a willingness to believe the worst of others, although he also suggests that such behaviour is not available to everyone.

Another lesson to be learnt from *La Robe de dissension* is to be found on the symbolic level, for in the quest to know others, we seize on any external signs available to help us. What the trick with the robe teaches is that we must be careful not to misinterpret the signs we are given or even base our judgement on inappropriate signs.

Another interesting view of both a character's failure to understand others and his gullibility is found in the comic villain of *Le Fâcheux Veuvage*, Aboulifar. He is a variation on the obstructive father of the *commedia dell'arte*, who stands in the way of his daughter's romantic ambitions because he has a spouse of his own choosing for her. However, it is not only the age difference between his daughter and his proposed match that makes this an extreme case — a difference that makes even the intended suitor feel the marriage is unreasonable, for he is sixty and Aboulifar's daughter fourteen — but also the fact that the custom in their country is to bury the surviving spouse alive with the first to die. It is his indifference to the fact that he is almost certainly condemning his daughter to a premature death that sets Aboulifar apart from the average father of comedy, and shows him to be deprived of both paternal affection and the ability to understand and sympathize with the feelings of others. While Dom Fernand's readiness in *La Robe de dissension* to believe the worst of others made him ideally susceptible to Arlequin's hoax, Aboulifar's complete indifference to the death of even his daughter apparently makes him impervious to the plan concocted by Léandre and Arlequin in *Le Fâcheux Veuvage*, which has Arlequin posing as a man who can raise the dead. While in *La Robe de dissension* the positive attribute of Dom Pèdre's trust allowed him to take the appropriate common-sense view of the miracle, here Aboulifar's indifference has the same effect, so that not even the promise of seeing his daughter, whom he believes dead, alive again can move him (*FV*, III. x). Indeed, even when his daughter is presented to him he remains impassive enough to reason (quite rightly, as it happens) that she must only have feigned death. Such rationalism in the face of a revelation that should provoke emotion might be forgivable in real life, but it is not in comedy, and such a lack of paternal feeling is forgivable in neither.

So it might appear that for once the tricksters have failed by choosing the wrong man to dupe. But they know human nature: the one issue that has concerned Aboulifar from the moment he receives the news that his daughter is dead is the effect it will have on his delicate wife, although we will suspect from the outset, given his attitude to his offspring, that the anxiety is not on his wife's behalf at all. Sure enough, when her death is announced (another trick), he is too concerned about his own safety to see through the plot, and undergoes a comic metamorphosis. The contrast between his lack of concern for others and his abject terror at the prospect of his own demise is beautifully handled, particularly in the way it makes him so susceptible to the plot that, not only does he now believe in Arlequin's ability to raise the dead, when the plotters admit that it was all a trick, he comically refuses to accept even this admission of what he was once convinced was the case, believing that it is the admission that is a cruel joke. Hence the stratagem succeeds, and, in an attempt to persuade Arlequin to raise his wife from the dead, he agrees to let him choose his daughter's spouse. In most comedies such an experience would bring about in the character a change of heart, but not here: as soon as he is convinced his wife is not dead and he is in no danger, and despite having given his word to the contrary, Aboulifar threatens his daughter once again; it is only the fact that the suitor refuses to marry her, coupled with the huge fortune Léandre has amassed from grave-robbing (!),[16] that persuades him otherwise and produces the happy ending. It may be impossible fully to understand others, but a failure even to try, Piron seems to be suggesting, makes a bad person — Piron may depict human perfectibility in many cases, but, as ever, he acknowledges the exceptions, those that are beyond redemption. On the other hand, a sensitivity to others may make one good, as in the case of Dom Pèdre, but it also ensures success as a con-artist.

The extremity of Aboulifar's reaction to his own pending doom also suggests a failure to know himself, clearly a contributory factor in his inability to sympathize with others. If one cannot anticipate one's own reactions in a given situation, how indeed can one understand how others are feeling? A failure to understand others may lead to actions which are reprehensible, a failure to understand oneself is more likely to be ridiculous. Another clear comic example of this is provided in this same play in the episode of the young widow Arlequin meets in the burial caves, who protests that she is happy to stay with her dead husband — until she discovers that escape is possible, at which point Arlequin can barely stop her for long enough to obtain an explanation for her change of mind. Nevertheless, there are also clues that, as with Aboulifar, this woman's lack of self-knowledge is accompanied by a failure to recognize the needs of others, for it appears that her dead husband's demise was caused by his doing too much housework. One of the lessons about human nature contained in Piron's plays is that we cannot always believe what people say about themselves; they may, of course, be lying, but it may simply be that they are wrong, that, like the widow and the characters in the first act of *Les Chimères*, they are not competent to understand their own personalities.

A clear link between *Le Fâcheux Veuvage* and *La Robe de dissension* is the use of trickery to make things seem other than they are. In the former, not only can we not trust that those who appear dead actually are, Arlequin also pretends to be other than he is in claiming to be an Indian sage who can raise the deceased; in the latter Arlequin similarly pretends to be a magician, and is armed with the robe, the 'faux prodige' of the work's subtitle.

We have found symbols like this of the treacherous link between appearance and reality in the later plays written for the Théâtre Français, and they abound too in the *opéras-comiques*. Given the importance of fantasy and mythology in these works, some of these transformed objects are actually real: Tirésie, the woman who was once Tirésias, the ass that is really Arlequin. In the works with more contemporary settings, however, Piron tends to reject magic; what appears to be something other than it really is will turn out to have a thoroughly mundane explanation, like the magic robe, which is not magic at all, or the unpleasant soft substance into which Arlequin falls face down in the dark in *Le Claperman* only to discover, to his delight, that his initial fears about what it might be are unfounded, for it is really cheese (*Clap*, II. vii).

We have seen the inability of characters to differentiate between falsehood and reality in relation to their own personalities in *Les Chimères*, while *Crédit est mort* illustrates the difficulty of telling the honest from the dishonest — yet more problems relating to the interpretation of personality. The latter centres on the problem of dishonesty in financial dealings, and, despite the presence of allegorical figures, very clearly deals with the subject in relation to contemporary France. If Crédit has died, it is because of the dishonesty of so many creditors, typified by the decision of La Mauvaise Foi to disguise herself as La Bonne Foi, for, as she says: 'Monsieur Crédit, vous m'avez toujours rebutée, vous m'avez toujours haïe' (*CEM*, iii). Trust is needed, Piron suggests, even in the sordid world of finance; without it, the only person who will prosper is the unpleasant moneylender Mme Gourgouran, who is herself so unscrupulous that she has no need of La Bonne Foi (*CEM*, xvii).

The theme of appearance and reality extends in the *opéras-comiques* even to the subject of religion. *L'Endriague* is generally characterized by its spirit of anarchy, with its ridiculous names (Caudaguliventer, Elfridérigelpot, Espadavantavellados), its giant animated dragon (the Endriague of the title), and the ludicrous jargon spoken by its hero:

> Jaçois que prou gorgiasement tu devises, si tel long propos commence-t-il à me molester par trop. Or me narre en brief l'émerveillable devis du gentil & courtois enchanteur, & comme aussi, sans détourbier aucun, tu sus de ce corps tien transpercer le Diable, en qui ma Mie a son tripeux manoir. (*E*, III. ii)

Yet we also find here a scene with almost Old Testament resonances, in which the voice of the island's presiding spirit denounces the inhabitants' worship of a false god:

LA VOIX

A genoux, écoute, & tremble.

ELFRIDÉRIGELPOT

Je tremble en effet. Eh bien! qui êtes-vous?

LA VOIX

Je ne suis pas moins que le génie Popocambéchatabalipa, dont ton père est le premier ministre, & qu'il offense par le culte sacrilège & cruel que les habitans de cette île & lui rendent à l'Endriague. Fuis, si tu ne veux avoir ta part de la terrible vengeance que je vais faire éclater ici!

ELFRIDÉRIGELPOT

Grand'merci. Faites ce que vous voudrez. Un homme averti, en vaut deux. Sauve qui peut. (*Voyant venir des jeunes filles, qui chantent & qui dansent*) Bon, bon; courage! Vive la joie! Vous allez voir beau jeu! Pour moi je m'enfuis. (*E*, I. x)

Of course, numerous aspects of the scene — the names, the cowardice of Elfridérigelpot, his Aboulifar-like disregard for the safety of others — prevent its becoming entirely serious, even sacrilegious, but the biblical echo is nonetheless present, as is the question it asks about the trustworthiness of religious belief.

The themes of religion and deception come together most clearly in Piron's first *opéra-comique*, *L'Antre de Trophonius*. The oracle of Trophonius was situated in a cave at Lebadaea in Boeotia; Piron gives us no more information than that the scene is set in a wood near to this cave. Nevertheless, neither place nor time are to be trusted in *opéra-comique*, and the indications here are that we are in the conventional contemporary France of the Fairs, peopled by the usual mixture of Gallicized Italian archetypes and stereotypical French figures (to say nothing of the gratuitous appearance of Mercure). The oracle was known proverbially for the fact that those who consulted it were said to suffer such a profound shock that it led to lifelong melancholia, hence it was said of a melancholic (or just plain miserable) person that he had received the oracle of Trophonius. Piron also alludes to the fact that the person who wished to consult the oracle descended into it to commune with his own destiny, although his priests provide the visions rather than just interpreting them as in the legend. Piron does not mention the myth of the oracle's creation, but obviously had it in mind: Trophonius and his brother Agamedes built a treasure chamber for King Hyprieus of Boeotia, but included a secret entrance allowing them to pillage his wealth. Hyprieus realized what was happening, but, not knowing the identity of the thieves, laid a trap for them. When Agamedes was caught in the trap, Trophonius cut off his head to prevent identification, and, for this crime, was swallowed up by the earth. The oracular cave was found on the site.

Robbery and trickery, as suggested by the legend, are present throughout this play. Arlequin steals money from his master Agrippain, although comic convention demands that we excuse him to an extent: Agrippain is a financier, and so stereotypically dishonest, and has also stolen Arlequin's beloved Marinette from him. The money is stolen from Arlequin and Scaramouche by two thieves; the priests of Trophonius readily admit to being the robbers, and invite the pair to become priests of Trophonius too. When Scaramouche points out that they do not have the gift for giving oracles, the priests reveal that the oracle is a con-trick. They appropriate the supplicant's offering, then respond to his question by filling the cave with relevant symbols of ill-omen, then burn soporific herbs, which cause the person to have dreams based on what he has seen. The priests make a living from the offerings and what they steal from passers-by. Hence, the basis of the whole oracular tradition of Trophonius's cave is a fraud, and a fraud based like the legend on theft. This first *opéra-comique*, and later *Le Fâcheux Veuvage* and *La Robe de dissension*, show that magic in the contemporary world is never what it seems; real magic exists only in myth or in allegory. And here, in contrast to *Tirésias* which shows that a change of clothing has only a partial effect on true personality, putting on a new costume is all that is required by the con-artist: 'L'habit ici fait le ministre' (*AdT*, v).

Thus, when Agrippain arrives to consult the oracle, it is Arlequin who decides what he is to experience; consequently, as in later plays we have examined, the dénouement brings the success of the lover's stratagem to win his beloved from his rival, and so invites us to forgive his trickery because it was in the name of love. There are, however, some potentially disturbing elements in the conclusion of this work, for Agrippain is led by his experience in the cave to legitimize not only Arlequin's marriage, but also his theft. Trickery has not only sorted out the romantic plot, it has also excused a crime which in the real world would be punishable by death, as Arlequin points out when he completes Marinette's comment: 'Me voilà revenue de mon pélerinage' with the remark: 'Et moi, du gibet' (*AdT*, xii). Furthermore, it would appear that Agrippain's generosity is not entirely the result of his experience in the cave; certainly the character we encounter after this experience seems to have a more mellow demeanour than before, but he is also better informed, and suggests that things could have been resolved at the outset simply by his being told the truth:

> L'Oracle m'en a dit plus que je ne lui en demandois. J'ignorois, par exemple, que vous vous aimiez l'un & l'autre [i.e. Arlequin and Marinette]; auquel cas j'ôtois plus à Arlequin qu'il ne me prenoit. Je m'exécute. Je lui pardonne ce qu'il a fait, & je vais lui rendre ce qu'il a perdu. Vous voyez d'où je sors; c'est vous dire assez que je vous rends l'un à l'autre, et que toute envie de rire est passée pour moi. (*AdT*, xii)

The combination of generosity and melancholy in this, his final speech, makes it difficult not to feel some sympathy for him. Consequently, the ending of this play is potentially more morally and emotionally ambiguous than is often the case in this type of comedy.

The issue of identity is a common feature of the *opéras-comiques*, where it is often enlivened by an element of fantasy not generally possible in the more serious world of Piron's later works for the Théâtre Français. They are entirely characteristic of the genre, and, alongside the archetypes drawn from the Italian theatre, also deal in similar stereotypes of contemporary French life to those found in the works of other authors for the Fairs. The conventional aspect of this theatre is clear — as well as the same character types, similar plot patterns recur from play to play too. And yet, despite its formulaic nature, whether in the hands of Piron or others, it has an energy and spontaneity and a level of invention which make it easy to understand its appeal. In one sense we can see these plays as a sort of workshop in which the ideas which would also dominate Piron's *grandes comédies* and his tragedies were worked out, but we must not allow that to cause us to neglect their own inherent appeal. For Piron and his contemporaries, work for the Théâtre Français may have been more highly regarded than plays written for the Fairs and the Italians, but for modern readers it may be in those 'minor' works that his wit and invention are more clearly perceptible. Neither are they without moral and psychological subtlety, for Piron is capable of using even these conventional characters to make key points about human nature and to show differences in the way individuals react which transcend stereotype. The *opéras-comiques* contain some of his best work for the theatre.

Notes to Chapter 9

1. Only those extant works that are entirely by Piron are dealt with here.
2. As opposed to the earlier *pièces à écriteaux*, in which the dialogue was sung by the audience.
3. See, for instance, Lesage's *Colombine Arlequin; ou, Arlequin Colombine*, or his *Parodie de l'opéra de Télémaque*.
4. *Opéra-comique* using *ariettes*, which began by using Italian music as the basis for French texts and then turned to original music, was a later development.
5. There is a single vaudeville in scene vi; scene vii contains a sung passage consisting of three vaudeville tunes in a row; scene x has a verse prophecy, probably not intended to be sung, but ends with another passage which, although having no *timbre* (the word or phrase indicating which vaudeville tune is to be used), is in a verse form that suggests it is intended to be sung. Piron, who was not always as meticulous at indicating his airs as the authors of *Le Théâtre de la Foire*, probably expected that the intended melody would be obvious.
6. Although, of course, more farcical comedy was also played, and we must not forget its tendency at this period to try to fight the challenge of the popularity of the Fairs by putting on plays which used similar material.
7. *Metamorphoses*, III.
8. Although, as we have seen, *Les Enfants de la Joie* also gives a certain allegorical significance to the archetypes from the Italian theatre.
9. Allegations of obscenity prevented the performance of this play in 1726, and it had to wait until 1744 for its première. It was, however, published in that same year, making it the only one of Piron's *opéras-comiques* to appear in print before the publication of Rigoley de Juvigny's edition of the complete works in 1776.
10. The setting of *Les Chimères*.
11. A note to the first scene tells us that he is 'une espèce de petit-maître' (*T*, I. i) and hence a typically French stereotype, although the words 'une espèce de' provide some acknowledgement of the non-French setting.
12. Lully's opera to a libretto by Quinault, first performed in 1686, but revived in November 1724, shortly before the performance of *Les Chimères* in February 1725.
13. Jupiter and Juno, in Ovid's Latinized version. The use of the Latin names in Piron's text does not, of course, constitute in itself an indication that Ovid was Piron's direct source, since it is entirely characteristic for French authors of the classical period, and even later, to prefer the Latin forms of the names of the gods even when dealing with Greek myths.
14. See on Piron's use of sexual role reversal in this play Nell, 'Trading Places: Dialogical Transvestites and Monological Gender Politics', passim.
15. Pascale Verèb identifies the source as a Dutch tale entitled *Le Passe-temps agréable*, but, unfortunately, gives only the French title and no further bibliographical information about either the text or the source of the attribution (see *Alexis Piron, poète*, pp. 104, 637); I have been unable to trace the original.

16. Since Léandre has indulged in this activity only to allow him to marry Balkis, the audience is clearly expected to forgive him — a particularly extreme example of the way we tend to excuse anything that is done in the name of love in comedy. Nevertheless, it is clear that Piron can permit himself this detail only because it is the exotic funeral practices of foreigners that are being defiled, and not standard French burial rites.

CONCLUSION

We have seen the great range of Piron's writing, and his ability to adapt to any form he adopts. Indeed, his very first play, *Arlequin-Deucalion*, represents a tour de force in a genre that his contemporaries writing for the Fairs were unwilling to attempt. Despite signs of initial reluctance in *L'Antre de Trophonius*, with its very small number of *couplets*, he also showed himself more than capable of challenging those authors on their own ground in the field of *opéra-comique*. When he came to write for the Théâtre Français, too, he showed himself capable of writing of the highest quality in both main genres: his tragedies may pose the same problems for modern readers as those of his contemporaries, but *Gustave Wasa* was one of the most successful works of the period in the form and *La Métromanie* followed its initial success with a place in that select group of eighteenth-century comedies which, even if they have disappeared from the stage, continue to be known and read. He even, with *Les Courses de Tempé*, showed himself capable of success in the more anodyne field of pastorale.

He also contributed to the debate about the nature of the theatre that went on throughout the century, and, while the remarks we find in his prefaces, most particularly on the role of love in tragedy, fall far short of the contributions made by writers like La Motte, Voltaire, Diderot, and Beaumarchais, the inclusion of elements of literary criticism within the plays themselves is much more innovative and individual. It first appears in the parodies or the parodic sections of the other works for the Fairs and the Italians, where it adds significantly to the comic impact, although at this stage it goes no further than what we find in parodies by other authors. It reappears at the opening of *Les Courses de Tempé*, where the first lines turn out to be not a characteristic example of the pastoral style, but a send-up of it. The technique reaches its peak, however, in *La Métromanie*, where the subjects of drama and dramatic adaptation form part of the very fabric of the argument of the play, the issue of adaptation in particular having strong links with other questions of identity within the action. The century would not produce another such accomplished consideration of dramatic theory within a play itself until that late and rarely performed work of Diderot *Est-il bon? Est-il méchant?*.

The way these plays adapt their sources, be they the parodies, those *opéras-comiques* that are based on other works, *La Métromanie*, or the tragedies, also gives us insight into both Piron's ideas of dramaturgy and the aspects of the originals that interest him. For despite the variety of technique and invention found in his treatment of the various genres, there is also a profound unity: the same questions about who we are and aspire to be occur from the beginning to the end of his career. Disguise and role reversal are long-standing staples of comedy, but in Piron's hands they often appear to be in the service of a deeper exploration of whether the assumption of an alternative identity can have any profound impact on who a character is, and, in certain cases, it is shown to lead to a deeper understanding of the individual's nature. And, much as Piron would like us to believe that the *Ode à Priape* was no more than a young man's folly, perhaps even there we find indications of lifelong preoccupations. For in the light of the inclusion of some, shall we call it, 'unconventional' sexual activity in that piece of hard-core pornography (or bawdy fun, depending on one's moral standpoint), it is no surprise to find that the exploration of gender and sexuality and its effect on the way people perceive us remained a lifelong preoccupation of his drama, from the censor-challenging explicitness of *Tirésias* to the much greater subtlety of *La Métromanie*.

Nevertheless, what makes Piron's work so very appealing is something much more difficult to pin down: a liveliness in the style, a quirkiness in his sense of humour, an almost anarchic desire to confront the establishment, to cock a snook at received values and to deflate pomposity which combine to give him one of the most individual voices of his age. Perhaps this is another reason why his tragedies have least to say to us today, for those are the works in which he aspires to join the very establishment he mocks elsewhere.

Which brings us to the final question — a question it is tempting to avoid, but which will hang in the air if ignored. Is there a future for any of Piron's works on the contemporary stage? In certain respects it is beside the point; if I set out to draw attention to Piron's stature as a playwright, I did not aim to rehabilitate him on the modern stage, and have stressed the pleasures to be gained from reading his work, which are significant pleasures indeed. But it is nevertheless a question that is present, whether tacitly or explicitly, at the end of any study of plays which are no longer performed.

It is clear that the tragedies have had their day, like all eighteenth-century French tragedies — it is difficult to imagine a theatrical revival ever occurring; there is certainly no sign of it at present. Of the best of the comedies for the Théâtre Français, *L'École des pères*, despite its obvious charms and the games it plays with the traditions of the genre, is probably still too conventional for modern audiences. *La Métromanie* is more of a puzzle: it would seem to have all sorts of characteristics that would appeal today and might also have appealed in the nineteenth and twentieth centuries, but the fact that it has disappeared completely from the stage despite never ceasing to be known on the page suggests that it has lost its appeal for actors and directors and that a revival is unlikely. The plays for the Italians and the Fairs often have the inbuilt problem of their topicality, which demands from their audience an acute awareness of what was going on in the theatre of the time. Clearly such an audience has not existed since the age in which they were written. Nevertheless, there are among these works some that are more general in content, and so do not pose this particular problem. Perhaps it is here that the twenty-first century may rediscover Piron on the stage. Pascale Verèb points out that, of all these plays, only *La Rose* was performed after the period in which it was written,[1] but, despite its cleverness and the slightly risqué elements that postponed its first performance, a pastoral allegory seems an unlikely candidate for a modern audience. My own preference would be for the more anarchic and bawdy works — *Tirésias*, *L'Endriague*, *Le Claperman*, *Le Fâcheux Veuvage*, or *La Robe de dissension* — which could perhaps work in lively and inventive productions. If any of them ever is put on, I will be one of the first in the queue for a ticket, but there is no sign of that queue forming quite yet.

Note to the Conclusion

1. *Alexis Piron, poète*, p. 497.

BIBLIOGRAPHY

AYMON, JEAN, and ABBÉ DESFONTAINES, *Mémoires pour servir à l'histoire de la Calotte* (Basle: chez les héritiers de Brandmyller, 1725)

BARTHÉLÉMY, MAURICE, 'Alexis Piron et l'opéra-comique', in *Grétry et l'Europe de l'opéra-comique*, ed. by Philippe Vendrix (Liège: Mardaga, 1992), pp. 191–200

BIDAULT DE MONTIGNY, JEAN-CHARLES-FRANÇOIS, *Sémiramis* (Amsterdam: Mortier, 1749)

BRAUN, THEODORE E. D., *Un ennemi de Voltaire: Le Franc de Pompignan, sa vie, ses œuvres, ses rapports avec Voltaire*, Bibliothèque de littérature et d'histoire, 14 (Paris: Minard, 1972)

CHAPONNIÈRE, PAUL, *Alexis Piron: sa vie et ses œuvres* (Geneva: Imprimerie du Journal de Genève, 1910)

CLARK, JANE, and DEREK CONNON, *'The Mirror of Human Life': Reflections on François Couperin's 'Pièces de Clavecin'* (Huntingdon: King's Music for Janiculum, 2002)

CONNON, DEREK, 'Alexis Piron's Ha-ha: Shifting Identities in *La Métromanie*', *Modern Language Review*, 101 (2006), 62–74

—— 'La Musique foraine: moyen d'expression ou message?', in *Les Théâtres de la Foire*, ed. by Françoise Rubellin (forthcoming)

—— 'Piron, Prévost and a Case of Plagiarism: *Gustave Wasa* and the *Mémoires et aventures d'un homme de qualité*', *British Journal for Eighteenth-Century Studies*, 27 (2004), 189–201

—— 'Piron's *Arlequin-Deucalion*: Fair Play or Anti-Fair Play?', in *Essays on French Comic Drama from the 1640s to the 1780s*, ed. by Derek Connon and George Evans, French Studies of the Eighteenth and Nineteenth Centuries, 7 (Berne: Peter Lang, 2000), pp. 127–38

—— 'The Servant as Master: Disguise, Role-Reversal and Social Comment in Three Plays of Marivaux', in *Studies in the 'Commedia dell'arte'*, ed. by David J. George and Christopher J. Gossip (Cardiff: University of Wales Press, 1993), pp. 121–37

—— and GEORGE EVANS (eds), *Anthologie de pièces du 'Théâtre de la Foire'* (Egham: Runnymede, 1996)

CURTIS, JUDITH, and DAVID TROTT (eds), *Histoire et recueil des Lazzis*, Studies on Voltaire and the Eighteenth Century, 338 (Oxford: Voltaire Foundation, 1996)

DESFONTAINES, PIERRE-FRANÇOIS GUYOT, and FRANÇOIS GRANET, *Vérités littéraires sur la tragédie d'Hérode et de Mariamne adressées à M. de Voltaire* (Paris: Musier, 1725)

DIDEROT, DENIS, *Œuvres complètes*, ed. by Herbert Dieckman and others, 33 vols (Paris: Hermann, 1975–)

EMELINA, JEAN, *Les Valets et les servantes dans le théâtre comique en France de 1610 à 1700* (Grenoble: PUG, 1975)

FORESTIER, GEORGES, *Le Théâtre dans le théâtre sur la scène française du XVIIe siècle* (Geneva: Droz, 1981)

FREUD, SIGMUND, *Abriß der Psychoanalyse*, in *Gesammelte Werke*, ed. by Anna Freud and others, 18 vols (London: Imago, 1940–68), XVII (1941), 63–138

FUZELIER, LOUIS, *Parodie, tragi-comédie*, in *Les Parodies du Nouveau Théâtre Italien*, new, rev. edn, 4 vols (Paris: Briasson, 1738), IV

—— *Les Quatre Mariamnes* (Paris: Flahaut, 1725)

GENETTE, GÉRARD, *Palimpsestes: la littérature au second degré* (Paris: Éditions du Seuil, 1982)

Gherardi, Evariste, *Le Théâtre italien; ou, le recueil général de toutes le comédies et scènes françaises jouées par les comédiens italiens du roi*, 6 vols (Paris: Briasson, 1741; repr. in facsimile, Geneva: Slatkine, 1969)

Gobin, Pierre, 'L'*Arlequin-Deucalion* de Piron: pertinence de l'impertinence', in *Transactions of the Fifth International Congress on the Enlightenment*, iii, Studies on Voltaire and the Eighteenth Century, 192 (Oxford: Voltaire Foundation, 1980), 1478–86

Goulbourne, Russell, 'The Eighteenth-Century "querelle des vers" and Jean Du Castre d'Auvigny's *La Tragédie en prose*', *Studies on Voltaire and the Eighteenth Century*, 2000.5 (Oxford: Voltaire Foundation, 2000), 371–410

Graffigny, Françoise de, *Correspondance de Madame de Graffigny*, ed. by Elaine Showalter and others, 15 vols (Oxford: Voltaire Foundation, 1985–)

Grannis, Valleria Belt, *Dramatic Parody in Eighteenth Century France* (New York: Publications of the Institute of French Studies, 1931)

Grimm, Friedrich Melchior, *Correspondance littéraire, philosophique, et critique*, ed. by Maurice Tourneux, 16 vols (Paris: Garnier, 1877–82)

Hall, H. Gaston, 'From Extravagant Poet to the Writer as Hero: Piron's *La Métromanie* and Pierre Cerou's *L'Amant auteur et valet*', *Studies on Voltaire and the Eighteenth Century*, 183 (Oxford: Voltaire Foundation, 1980), 117–32

Isherwood, Robert M., *Farce and Fantasy* (Oxford: Oxford University Press, 1986)

Justinus, Marcus Junianus, *Abrégé des histoires philippiques de Trogue Pompée et Prologues de Trogue Pompée*, ed. and trans. by Émile Chambry and Lucienne Thély-Chambry, 2 vols (Paris: Garnier, [1936])

—— *Epitome of the Philippic History of Pompeius Trogus*, trans. by John Selby Watson (London: Bohn, 1853)

La Motte, Antoine Houdar de, *Fables nouvelles* (Paris: Dupuis, 1719)

—— *Les Œuvres de théâtre de M. de La Motte* [...], *avec plusieurs discours sur la tragédie* (Paris: Dupuis, 1730)

Lancaster, Henry Carrington, *French Tragedy in the Time of Louis XV and Voltaire, 1715–1774*, 2 vols (Baltimore: Johns Hopkins Press, 1950)

—— *Sunset: A History of Parisian Drama in the Last Years of Louis XIV, 1701–1715* (Baltimore: Johns Hopkins Press, 1945)

Lanson, Gustave, *Hommes et livres* (Paris: Lecène, Oudin, 1895)

—— *Nivelle de La Chaussée et la comédie larmoyante* (Paris: Hachette, 1887)

Lesage, Alain-René, D'Orneval, [and Carolet], *Le Théâtre de la Foire; ou, l'opéra comique* (Paris: Étienne Ganeau, Pierre Gandouin, Prault fils, 1721–37; repr. in facsimile, Geneva: Slatkine, 1968)

López de Gómara, Francisco, *Histoire generalle des Indes Occidentales*, trans. by Martin Fumée, 5th edn (Paris: Michel Sonnius, 1584; repr. 1605)

Lurcel, Dominique (ed.), *Le Théâtre de la foire au XVIIIe siècle* ([Paris]: Union Générale d'Éditions, 1983)

Martin, Isabelle, *Le Théâtre de la foire: des tréteaux aux boulevards* (Oxford: Voltaire Foundation, 2002)

Nadal, Augustin, *Mariamne* (Paris: veuve de Pierre Ribou, 1725)

—— *Observations critiques sur la tragédie d'Hérode et Mariamne de M. de V**** (Paris: Ribou, 1725)

Nell, Sharon Diane, 'Trading Places: Dialogical Transvestites and Monological Gender Politics in Alexis Piron's *Tirésias* and *La Métromanie*', *European Studies Journal*, 17–18 (2000–01), 131–46

[Parfaict *frères*], *Histoire du théâtre français depuis son origine jusqu'à présent*, 15 vols (Paris: Le Mercier, 1745–49)

—— *Mémoires pour servir à l'histoire des spectacles de la foire, par un acteur forain*, 2 vols (Paris: Briasson, 1743)

Piron, Alexis, *Œuvres choisies de Piron*, ed. by Jules Troubat, introduction by Sainte-Beuve (Paris: Garnier, [1866])

—— *Œuvres complètes d'Alexis Piron*, ed. by Rigoley de Juvigny, 7 vols (Paris: Lambert, 1776)

—— *Œuvres complètes illustrées de Alexis Piron*, ed. Pierre Dufay, 10 vols (Paris: Guillot, 1928–31)

Plutarch, *Greek Lives: A Selection of Nine Greek Lives*, trans. by Robin Waterfield, introduction and notes by Philip A. Stadter (Oxford: Oxford University Press, 1998)

Quéro, Dominique, 'Alexis Piron parodiste, ou la "capitolade comique"', in *A rire et à pleurer: à travers six siècles de littérature en Bourgogne*, ed. by Yvette Quenot and Jacques Poirier ([Dijon: Centre Régional de Documentation Pédagogique de Bourgogne, 1996]), pp. 91–103

—— *Momus philosophe: recherches sur une figure littéraire du XVIIIe siècle* (Paris: Champion, 1995)

Quinault, Philippe, *Alceste; ou, le Triomphe d'Alcide* (Paris: René Baudry, 1674)

—— *Atys*, in *Théâtre du XVIIe siècle*, ed. by Jacques Truchet and André Blanc, III ([Paris]: Gallimard, 1992), 3–57

Rex, Walter, *The Attraction of the Contrary: Essays on the Literature of the French Enlightenment* (Cambridge: Cambridge University Press, 1987)

Roberts, Michael, *The Early Vasas: A History of Sweden, 1523–1611* (Cambridge: Cambridge University Press, 1968)

Robinson, Philip, 'Reflexions on Early Eighteenth-Century French Theatrical Parody', in *Essays on French Comic Drama from the 1640s to the 1780s*, ed. by Derek Connon and George Evans, French Studies of the Eighteenth and Nineteenth Centuries, 7 (Berne: Peter Lang, 2000), pp. 139–52

Rose, Margaret A., *Parody: Ancient, Modern and Post-Modern* (Cambridge: Cambridge University Press, 1993)

Rougemont, Martine de, *La Vie théâtrale en France au XVIIIe siècle* (Paris: Champion, 1988)

Roy, Pierre-Charles, *Philomele* (Paris: Jean-Baptiste-Christophe Ballard, 1734)

Russell, Barry, *Le Théâtre de la Foire à Paris: textes et documents* <http://foires.net/>

Sangsue, Daniel, *La Parodie*, Contours littéraires (Paris: Hachette, 1994)

Scott, Virginia, *The 'Commedia dell'Arte' in Paris, 1644–1697* (Charlottesville: University Press of Virginia, 1990)

Tristan L'Hermite, François, *La Mariane* (Paris: Augustin Courbé, 1637)

—— *Mariane, tragédie, par le sieur Tristan L'Hermite: nouvelle édition, augmentée de la vie de l'auteur* (Paris: Flahault, 1724)

Trott, David, *Œuvres lyriques parodiées (1669–1752): liste de travail en cours* <http://www.chass.utoronto.ca/~trott/par-op.htm>

—— *Théâtre du XVIIIe siècle: jeux, écritures, regards* (Montpellier: Espaces 34, 2000)

Truchet, Jacques (ed.), *Théâtre du XVIIIe siècle*, 2 vols ([Paris]: Gallimard, 1972–74)

——, Jacques Scherer, and André Blanc (eds), *Théâtre du XVIIe siècle*, 3 vols ([Paris]: Gallimard, 1975–92)

Venard, Michèle, *La Foire entre en scène* (Paris: Librairie Théâtrale, 1985)

Verèb, Pascale, 'Alexis Piron défenseur des modernes ou un épisode inédit de la Querelle des Anciens et des Modernes', *Revue d'Histoire Littéraire de la France*, 95 (1995), 282–93

—— *Alexis Piron, poète (1689–1773); ou, la difficile condition d'auteur sous Louis XV*, Studies on Voltaire and the Eighteenth Century, 349 (Oxford: Voltaire Foundation, 1997)

Vertot d'Aubœuf, René Aubert de, *Histoire des révolutions de Suède*, 2 vols (Paris: Ménard et Desenne, 1819)

Voltaire, *Œuvres complètes / Complete Works*, ed. by Theodore Bestermann and others, 135 vols (Oxford: Voltaire Foundation, 1968–)

—— *Œuvres complètes*, ed. by Louis Moland, 52 vols (Paris: Garnier, 1877–85)

WALLER, RICHARD, 'The Theatrical Writings of Jacques Autreau and the Problems of Experimentation', in *Essays on French Comic Drama from the 1640s to the 1780s*, ed. by Derek Connon and George Evans, French Studies of the Eighteenth and Nineteenth Centuries, 7 (Berne: Peter Lang, 2000), pp. 99–115

INDEX